FROM TALIBAN TO TALIBAN

Contextualising Nationhood in Afghanistan

FROM TALIBAN TO TALIBAN

Contextualising Nationhood in Afghanistan

Edited by

Niranjan Marjani

Shekhar B. Ashtikar

KW Publishers Pvt Ltd

New Delhi

ISBN 978-81-988857-7-7 Hardback

Published in India by Kalpana Shukla

KW Publishers Pvt Ltd
4676/21, First Floor, Ansari Road
Daryaganj, New Delhi 110 002
Phone : +91 11 43528107
Production : kw@kwpub.in
Marketing : sanjeev@kwpub.in
Website : www.kwpub.in

Printed and bound in India
Quiinkit Infotech Pvt. Ltd., Gurugram

To my mother,

Smt. Jyoti Marjani

– Niranjan

Contents

Foreword

For long, Afghanistan has been a land of myths and misery for India. Both the Ramayana and the Mahabharata mention mythical personages belonging to Afghanistan. Invaders and plunderers wreaking havoc on India also passed through Afghanistan. Bluntly put, it has historically been a cause of India's misfortunes because India was fabled for its riches, and Afghanistan's mountain passes provided a convenient staging post for attacks on it. The two countries were then geographically connected.

This link was snapped when the departing British whimsically divided India. Since 1947, the two countries have viewed each other nostalgically, barred by Pakistan from direct contact. Consequently, our knowledge of what constitutes the present day Afghanistan and what concerns its people suffers.

An unfortunate consequence of this inadequate knowledge is the dependence on third sources for information. This shortcoming has also affected our understanding of history where many of us have taken the easy option of going by the accounts penned by colonial historians.

I found this to my alarm as I set about writing *Where Borders Bleed* and then, *Durand's Curse*. It required a huge amount of research by me to form an independent and objective picture, but it was worth the effort. *Durand's Curse*, in particular, became a path- breaking exercise, where I uncovered the enormous deception by which British India's Foreign Secretary Mortimer Durand duped the Afghan Amir.

This so-called Durand Agreement was signed on November 12, 1893, in a language of which Amir Abdur Rahman had no knowledge! The details of how this deception took place shocked me even as I uncovered them and detailed the deed in *Durand's Curse*.

It is, therefore, important that scholars in India do their own research and give interpretation of events unaffected by what the British write, or have written, to protect and project their national interests. We owe it to our national interests and to our future generations to give an account faithful to the events.

Therefore the book, *From Taliban to Taliban: Contextualising Nationhood in Afghanistan,* is a useful step in this direction. Its editors, Niranjan Marjani and Dr Shekhar Ashtikar, are to be commended for it and for gathering together a wide range of scholars to contribute to this volume.

They concern themselves with multiple issues in these pages, but as is only to be expected from the task they have set out for themselves, the conditions in Afghanistan under the Taliban are largely shrouded in a fundamentalist *purdah.*

Still, many issues have been taken up, including some that have been accepted as facts over time. Thus, for instance, it is maintained that by drawing upon Pashtun cultural traditions, the Taliban sought to define Afghan nationhood in terms of Pashtun dominance. This, it is asserted, is evident in their imposition of Pashtunwali as a quasi-legal code in the areas under their control. Pashtunwali, it is further asserted, emphasises values, such as hospitality (*Melmastia*), honour (*Nang*), and revenge (*Badal*).

But is it really so? After all, how can hospitality and honour be reconciled with the marginalisation of non-Pashtun groups and the targeting of minorities like the Hazaras?

By privileging the Pashtun identity, the Taliban have exacerbated ethnic divisions. This raises serious concerns about the future of ethnic and sectarian relations in Afghanistan.

Besides, there are other issues adding to the complexities of Afghanistan. These issues have been left over from the injustices of history, the unjust Durand line being one of them.

Second, the 'Great Game' is often talked of in awe. This is unfortunate because it was essentially an adventure indulged in by ambitious young British officers and a contest between great powers at the cost of ordinary people. In this game, the Afghan people were mere pawns; their apprehensions were of no concern to the foreign powers.

Third, the Taliban's influence on the Afghan people and Afghanistan's nationhood is perhaps the most significant and contentious aspect of this country's recent history.

Finally, the scholars contributing to this book will surely be watching closely the interaction between the Taliban government and the rest of the world in the coming days, months, and years. As near neighbours with intimate historical links, the fate and the circumstances of the Afghan nation and its people will require the Indian government's attention and the academic interest of India's experts.

In this background, the book, *From Taliban to Taliban: Contextualising Nationhood in Afghanistan,* comes out at a time when the world, in general, and India, in particular, is curious and keen to know what is actually happening in Afghanistan.

Ambassador **Rajiv Dogra**
(Ambassador Rajiv Dogra is an eminent author and
a highly regarded commentator on foreign policy issues)

Preface

On August 15, 2021, the Taliban took over Afghanistan as the security forces of the United States and the NATO exited the country after 20 years. Afghanistan under the Taliban is mostly considered to present a dilemma for the external powers to engage. The Taliban rule is viewed from the governance perspective, which includes protection of human rights, women's rights, minorities' rights, and engagement with the external powers. However, it is equally important to study the Taliban's appeal across Afghanistan since the Taliban, in some form or other, seems to prevail over Afghanistan.

Afghanistan, owing to its strategically important location at the crossroads of South, Central, and West Asia, has always been of interest to regional and extra-regional powers. Afghanistan has also been instrumental in shaping the history of all of its surrounding regions. Multiple attempts by external powers to impose their governance system on the Afghans have not been successful. A primary reason for this has been the misinterpretation of Afghan society from the perspective of the Western concepts of nation-state. This book intends to look into an important but often lesser discussed phenomenon—the concept of nationhood in Afghanistan. This phenomenon includes whether the Afghans consider themselves as a nation, how the diverse ethnic groups of Afghanistan interact with each other, if they collectively constitute a nation, and how the Taliban fits into the socio-political landscape of Afghanistan.

The very concept of Afghanistan as a country can also, to a great extent, be attributed to the Western view of a nation. Afghanistan is a multi-ethnic and multi-lingual society, which has its own vision that is varied from the

Western interpretation. Comprising various groups like the Pashtuns, the Tajiks, the Uzbeks, the Hazaras, the Nuristanis, etc., Afghanistan has its own political and social dynamics that play out among these groups. In a simple and rather broad-based manner, it can be said that intra-Afghan politics is often dominated more by tribal loyalties than loyalty to a bigger and wider entity, such as a nation.

Some of the principal dynamics within Afghanistan are interaction among different ethnic groups, the fault lines created by advancement of Pashtun nationalism against the interests of minority groups like the Tajiks, the Uzbeks, the Hazaras etc., the South (Pashtun) versus North (minority groups) divide, the effectiveness of religion (Islam) as a binding force in the Afghan society, the status of women, and the challenges towards nation-building.

This book is an attempt on the part of the editors and all the contributors to study the concept of nationhood in Afghanistan and where and how the Taliban phenomenon fits in this concept.

Niranjan Marjani
Dr Shekhar B. Ashtikar

Acknowledgements

I dedicate this book to my mother, Smt. Jyoti Marjani. She is the one person who steadfastly supported me in the pursuit of my dreams. Although she is no more, she taught me the importance of discipline and dedication, which are necessary to achieve one's goals and dreams. For my part, I try my best to follow her teachings. I believe this book is the result of her blessings and best wishes that are always with me.

I express my sincerest thanks and gratitude to Ambassador Shri Rajiv Dogra-*ji*. He very kindly agreed to take time off his busy schedule and write a foreword for this book. His foreword is a huge encouragement for us in our research.

I thank all the contributors who have written a chapter for this book. Their hard work and meticulous research in writing their respective chapters have enriched this book.

My big thanks to Ms. Kalpana Shukla and the entire team of K.W. Publishers Pvt. Ltd. It was only because of Ms. Shukla's and her team's patience and cooperation during the journey of writing this book that it is being published.

Finally, I cannot thank my friend and co-editor, Dr Shekhar Ashtikar, enough. His constant support and cooperation have been most valuable during the publication process of this book.

I hope the readers find this book useful and a worthy addition to their reading list.

Niranjan Marjani

Acknowledgements

It has been a personally rewarding and intellectually stimulating experience to compile *From Taliban to Taliban: Contextualising Nationhood in Afghanistan* as an edited edition. This book is the culmination of teamwork, perceptive input, and thorough investigation of the intricate geopolitical situation in Afghanistan and the surrounding region. All the people who have helped and advised me during this journey have my sincere gratitude.

I want to start by sincerely thanking my parents, whose steadfast encouragement, values, and support have served as the cornerstone of my academic and professional endeavours. Their confidence in my skills and their unwavering encouragement have supported me along the way. I could not have completed this job without their blessings and direction. I also owe a debt of gratitude to my wife, whose understanding, patience, and unwavering support have been vital during this process. Her support and faith in my work have given me the fortitude to overcome the difficulties involved in assembling and revising this book. Her presence has inspired me and served as a reminder of the value of tenacity and commitment.

The primary editor of this book, Shri Niranjan Marjani Sir, deserves special recognition for his careful editing skills, perceptive criticism, and acute awareness of geopolitical issues, all of which have greatly enhanced this volume. His advice has been crucial in forming this work's depth and coherence and guaranteeing that it satisfies the highest academic requirements. I am incredibly appreciative of his time, work, and priceless contributions.

Without the contributions of renowned academics and researchers who have offered their thoughts, insights, and analyses on Afghanistan and its surrounding region, this book would not have been possible. I want to express my gratitude to each and every writer whose chapters have given this collection more depth and variety. Their knowledge has been crucial in ensuring that this book is a useful and thorough resource. I also want to thank my classmates, mentors, and co-workers who have participated in conversations, given constructive criticism, and offered assistance in different ways. The ideas and arguments put forth in this book have been improved thanks to their support and insightful criticism.

I also want to thank the publishing team for their assistance, as their expertise and commitment have been invaluable in making this book a reality. Their dedication to excellence and meticulousness has made sure that this work is presented to a larger audience in the best possible way.

Lastly, this book is devoted to everyone who wants to learn more about the complex dynamics of Afghanistan's nationhood and the country's geopolitical realities. It is my earnest hope that this publication will be a useful addition to the region's scholarly and policy debates.

Dr Shekhar B. Ashtikar

1 Routes and Roots

Unveiling the Layers of Afghan Nationalism

Saman Ayesha Kidwai

Introduction

On the one hand, nations can be broadly defined as 'territorial communities: they claim land as rightfully theirs. The homeland is sacred territory. It is imbued with meaning because it is the site of past events that define the group and where battles are fought, the dead are buried, and past generations flourished' (Garner, 2022).

Nationalism, on the other hand, is an ideology that espouses the superiority of a nation above the rest based on shared ethnic, religious, linguistic, cultural, or social values. Its modern-day interpretations are rooted in the 18th and 19th century British and French revolutions, the domino effects of which were visible in Latin America, Asia, and Africa by the 20th century.

Afghan nationalism, as per conventional understanding, refers to the cultural integration of all ethnic communities within Afghanistan to form a shared national identity of being Afghan. Scholars (Rasikh, 2010; Hyman, 2002) have argued that this brand of nationalism has its roots in the lead-up to forming a sovereign Afghan state and then following its independence from the British empire in 1919. This paper will use Pakhtun and Pashtun nationalism to denote the same subject.

However, inclusivity has often been eclipsed by the majoritarian tendencies practised by the Pakhtuns. They are the largest ethnic group, accounting for 40 per cent of the population. This has shaped its ties with ideological opponents and ethnic minorities and determined power relations and struggle over the last centuries.

Pakhtun Majoritarian Nationalism

The conflation and blurring of lines between the Afghan and Pakhtun identities have much to do with majoritarian nationalistic tendencies that have shaped the way nationalism has been perceived by outsiders and promoted from within by the dominant community.

Simply put, majoritarianism is a 'traditional political philosophy that asserts that a majority (sometimes categorized by religion, language, or social class, or some identifying factor) of the population is entitled to a certain degree of primacy in society and has the right to make decisions that affect the society…Taking on an ethnic dimension can render majoritarianism particularly pernicious, as it provides the justification for ethnic-majority groups to rule over minority groups without the need to ensure equal rights and protections…' (ECPS, n.d.).

This has mainly been the case under the Taliban rule, from 1996 to 2001 and from 2021 onwards, varying in intensity. On the one hand, Taliban 1.0, as its earlier manifestation is commonly dubbed, presented a more overtly polarising nationalistic character of the Afghan state, in which ethnic minorities, like the Uzbeks, Tajiks, and Hazaras, were brutally oppressed and persecuted in an intensifying manner.

Stories of religious processions being banned and places of worship targeted, diminishing opportunities, erosion of cultural symbols, and systematic killing being carried out became central to the Pakhtun Taliban leadership in the lead-up to 9/11. Pakhtunism and Afghan nationalism became entrenched deeper during their then five-year rule. However, it was the norm, not the exception.

Since Ahmad Shah Durrani swept into power in 1747 by establishing his Durrani empire, Pakhtuns have dominated Afghan society.

On the other hand, after retaking control of Kabul in August 2021, Taliban 2.0 has modified its interpretation of Afghan nationalism in a bid to gain international recognition. While Islam has remained as a unifying factor, specifically by promulgating its Hanafi-Deobandi interpretation, its leadership has sought to present a more inclusive Afghan identity that encompasses protection and respect for the very ethnic groups it had earlier systematically targeted for their heretical and un-Islamic views and customs.

Nonetheless, its interpretation of what it means to be an Afghan has consistently excluded the Salafi community from its fold. Some Salafi leaders, despite their insulation from violence or ISKP membership, have been systematically targeted, and reports about widespread human rights violations being committed against them have become more frequent. This is primarily due to Hanafi-Deobandi Taliban's continuing urban guerilla warfare against ISKP (a deadly Salafi jihadi terrorist group formed in 2014-2015), which abhors nationalism and ethnic identities since it believes they hinder its goal of creating a global Caliphate.

These opposing groups and ideological schools of thought—Hanafi-Deobandi and Salafi jihadi (Sayed, Van Ostaeyen & Winter, 2022) within Islam have been locked in a state of conflict since ISKP's inception over a decade ago, whose ideological leanings are considered deviant by the Taliban.

Besides the numerical supremacy of the Pakhtuns, another reason behind the lack of an inclusive pan-Afghan identity and domination of Pakhtun nationalism in Afghanistan could be attributed to the process of 'fusion and fission' in the political space as underlined by Louis B. Dupree:

'A charismatic leader arises in a tribal society and, by military power, intrigue, and judiciously arranged marriages, unites several tribes into a confederation, which spreads as far as its accumulated power permits, creating an empire, not a nation-state. With (sometimes before) the death of an emperor, fission occurs, and the great empire once again segments into a multiplicity of tribal kingdoms. Later, another charismatic leader arrives, and the process is repeated' (Dupree, 1973).

It has also been pointed out that Islam was used as a unifying factor to mobilise Afghans against the foreign or un-Islamic forces that invaded or were homegrown—British invaders during the 19th and 20th centuries, Soviet forces during the 20th century, Hamid Karzai and Ashraf Ghani's elected governments (deemed puppet regimes of the international coalition led by the United States), and the armed forces associated with the North Atlantic Treaty Organization (NATO) (Raqib, 2011).

Simply put, a designated enemy has always been at the centre of mobilising Afghans and rallying behind a unified banner of pan-Afghan identity, however fragmented, protracted, or temporary it might have been.

Fusing Afghan and Pakhtun Nationalism

Interestingly, the term 'Afghan' was used to reflect the demographic composition formed by the Pathan or Pakhtun community living in the pre-colonial Indian subcontinent and was later used to reflect the generalised identity of all those who resided in Afghanistan after the initiation of the modernisation period. The minority tribal communities in Afghanistan—Hazaras, Uzbeks, Baloch, and Tajiks—were clubbed with the Pathan community who had settled in Afghanistan, thereby erasing their unique identifying characteristics (Nishat, Shelley, Karimi & El-Badawy, 2022). The constant reiteration of what it means to be an Afghan and, to that extent, what represented Afghan nationalism became conflated with the Pakhtun identity over a period of time.

Notably, the Tajiks quickly assumed leadership positions by aiding the Americans following the Soviet invasion in 1979 and then in the immediate aftermath of the US invasion in 2001. This greatly unnerved the Pakhtun tribes, who rallied behind the Taliban in fear of the capture of absolute power by the Tajiks, and this is believed to have partially contributed to the rise of the Taliban to power during its initial ascension to power (Ayoob, 2019). Therefore, fearing the natural order based on the premise of the Pakhtuns wielding absolute power being threatened, the Pakhtuns in Afghanistan have quickly moved to eliminate potential opposition.

The hostility against the Tajiks could also be attributed to the fact that the community, under the leadership of Ahmad Shah Massoud, was closely aligned with President George W. Bush's policy objectives to overthrow the Taliban in 2001 and constituted a powerful force as part of the Northern Alliance, the anti-Taliban front. A similar anti-Pakhtun anti-Taliban front is being led by his son, Ahmad Massoud, after August 2021. Moreover, during the Afghan civil war, the ethnic confrontation between Afghan Millat (a Pakhtun nationalist organisation) and Seetam-a-Milli (a Tajik and anti-Pakhtun organisation formed to counter King Abdul Rahman's campaign against ethnic minorities in Afghanistan) inflamed the tensions (Wahlang, 2021) in the majority-minority tussle for power and influence.

Scholars have argued that there was a sweeping wave amongst the Pakhtun elites that advocated for a decisive crackdown on Uzbek and Tajik aspirations to seize power for themselves and restore the dignified return of the Pakhtuns as the country's rightful rulers under the Afghan Taliban. It has been reportedly claimed that Zahir Shah, the exiled king of Afghanistan, expressed his gratitude to the Taliban forces for restoring the country in the hands of the Pakhtun community (Saikal, 2010; Ahmed, 2014; Shahrani, 2013).

Notably, the unveiling of the layered definitions of Afghan nationalism reveals that the dominant narrative, spearheaded by the Pakhtuns, emerged in response to the power vacuum that was created after the deadly civil war that was waged between the various Islamist Mujahideen factions, like Gulbuddin Hekmatyar's Hezb-i-Islami and Burhanuddin Rabbani's Jamiat-i-Islami, after the Soviet withdrawal in 1989. These violent non-state actors that unified under the shared banner of Islam to defeat the communist forces and liberate their country, as the above-mentioned precedent dictates, severed ties to launch themselves to the seat of power soon after.

This development created the perfect opportunity for the Taliban, who had been trained in the hardliner Deobandi mosques in Pakistan, to step in to fill the sudden vacuum created by the dearth of unified leadership, lawlessness, and a shared pan-Afghan ideological vision.

It has been argued that these mosques served as the breeding ground for the combined interpretation of hardliner Islam and Pakhtun nationalism exhibited and espoused by the Taliban leaders (Ayoob, 2019).

As rightly noted by experts:

> 'Over time, the Taliban has developed ties to both an extreme form of the Deobandi movement and a hegemonic expression of Pashtun nationalism. This combination has helped to define the group's dogma and ideological characteristics while compromising its capacity to authentically represent the country's diverse ethnic and religious composition. The Taliban's strategy over the past 20 years—whether as militant opponent to the government of Afghanistan or as de-facto rulers—has been to forge alliances and enforce

> loyalties among local and regional ethnic groups, and non-state actors based on these two essential ideologies' (Nishat, Shelley, Karimi, and El-Badawy, 2022).

The period leading up to the Taliban's subjugation of the Afghan territory and the following five years under the first phase of the Taliban leadership from 1996 to 2001 saw the crumbling of a pan-Afghan and multi-ethnic Afghan resistance movement in favour of Pakhtun extremists who used their interpretation of Sharia to enact swift justice and repressive rule while promoting Pakhtun supremacy across centres of power in Afghanistan.

They sought to reverse the perceived indignity caused to the Pakhtun tribe, culture, and Pashto language that lost its dominance after years of instability and chaos caused by the end of monarchy, the Soviet invasion, and years of civil war, which saw the Tajik community establishing influence over centres of power in Afghanistan.

Despite Mullah Omar's claims to consolidate a unified Afghan state with the view of establishing a pure Islamic state governed by Sharia, an inclusive Afghan agenda never featured in the edicts issued.

Instead, as has been rightly noted, 'The Taliban's strategy was innovative and ruthlessly effective. Unlike the Soviets, they focused their initial efforts on bottom-up efforts in rural Afghanistan, especially the Pashtun south. They approached tribal leaders and militia commanders, as well as their rank-and-file supporters ... they offered to restore Pashtun control of Kabul, which was run by the Tajik Rabbani (former President of Afghanistan who led the country from 1992 to 1996 until the Taliban takeover and reportedly was later assassinated by a Taliban suicide bomber in 2011) ... it was a strategy accomplished on a very personal level: Taliban leaders who spoke the local dialect travelled to the Pashtun villages and district centers...' (Jones, 2009).

The resentment and marginalisation experienced by the Pakhtun community in Afghanistan were reignited in the years leading up to August 2021 and could have contributed to the blitzkrieg of support for the Taliban instead of the Afghan armed forces.

It has been explained that besides the Presidential office, notable positions, including Vice-President, Director of Military Intelligence, and Chief of Army Staff, were occupied by members of the Tajik community. Moreover, despite being a minority, its clan members held 70 per cent of the Afghan National Army. The sentiment (and accompanying resentment) that was stirred up as a result of this among the majority community was that 'They (Tajiks) get the dollars, and we (Pakhtuns) get the bullets' (Chua, 2023).

Therefore, it could be argued in this instance that the Tajiks could have been perceived as collaborators who colluded with the occupying force (American-led international coalition) to unseat the Pakhtuns from positions of power from 2001 onwards and required punitive justice to be meted out once the Pakhtuns regained control.

The above- mentioned sentiment was likely evident among hardliner and secular Pakhtuns, in whom a key principle is ingrained from infancy—'To resist foreign domination is part of what it is to do Pashto' (Lieven, 2012). Therefore, it would have been unsurprising if the Tajiks had been condemned as traitors and retribution against them deemed justifiable, as it would have been against foreign forces.

The Taliban, during its years as an extremist insurgent movement, portrayed itself as the Mujahideen or an Islamist fighter waging a holy war against the invading colonial forces, seeking to unite all Afghans under the banner of Islam (it was a strategic tactic considering Afghanistan is a predominantly Muslim country). However, there was clear evidence of a narrow ethno-nationalist interpretation of Islam that favoured Sunni Pakhtuns above the rest of the population.

Furthermore, instead of applying the guidelines laid down as per Sharia to all Afghans without any convolution, the Taliban leaders combined the tenets of Pashtunwali—the code of conduct regulating the dominant community's traditions and way of life—with their rigid interpretation of Islam (Lincoln, 2024).

Taliban officials, even after resuming control two decades after they were pushed out of power, especially those associated with the Kandahar faction, have allegedly pushed for the fusion of the Pakhtun belief system and the Islamist edicts issued to the public, creating a balancing act in their eyes (*HinduPost*, 2023).

Even in the lead-up to August 2021, the Taliban officials and foot soldiers used the grievance narrative to underline how the then elected governments were complicit in denying the majority community their sanctioned leadership roles while drawing overlapping themes between the minimalist state advocated by Pakhtun customs and the Taliban's system of governance to reinforce the support (Shivamurthy, 2023).

However, this has only served to widen the divide between the majority community and the numerous ethnic minorities who have a visible presence in the country. This includes groups such as the Tajiks (27 per cent), Hazaras (9 per cent), Uzbeks (9 per cent), Aimak (4 per cent), Turks (3 per cent), and Baloch (2 per cent) (Kumar and Malhotra, 2024), who have been deprived of representation in the government institutions or other positions of influence. The resultant asymmetric competition, between majoritarian nationalist tendencies practised by the Taliban despite their claims of promoting inclusive governance (*Business Standard*, 2021) and resistance carried out by minority communities like the Hazaras and the Tajiks, still brewing on Afghan soil has prevented the emergence of an inclusive pan-Afghan nationalism.

Furthermore, one finds that the legitimacy sought by the Taliban remains elusive due to the latter's narrow interpretation (in actuality) of Afghan identity and interests and the continued marginalisation of ethnic minorities. At the same time, not all non-Pakhtuns seem to be driven by the hardliner demand for recapturing the Pakhtun-dominated territories in Pakistan as part of the Greater Pakhtunistan project, and the weakness of the state elites and the machinery that existed in the 1950s in mobilising the wider population (Lieven, 2021) has held to this day. Unsurprisingly, opposition movements to the Taliban rule based on ethnic lines have emerged among the ethnic minorities, predominantly the Tajiks.

The Durand Question: Context and Implications for Bilateral Ties with Pakistan

One must consider that any state's brand of nationalism and sense of being is closely interlinked with the territorial question. To be classified as a nation-state, one of the key requirements a state must fulfil is possessing a defined territorial space. Once a territorial space is identified for a community of nation to live in, it is considered their prerogative to reside and govern over said territorial space. At the core of Afghan-Pakhtun nationalism is the ardent belief that some of the Pakhtun-majority areas under Pakistani control must be returned to be governed under Afghan suzerainty to reverse the indignity and shame experienced by the Afghans.

What becomes challenging in the Afghan context is that the Khyber Pakhtunkhwa (KP) Province, erstwhile Federally Administered Tribal Areas (FATA, now integrated into KP), and a portion of Balochistan—areas which are currently under Pakistani control and falling beyond the contested Durand Line—are considered to rightfully belong to Afghans.

At the same time, despite Pakistan's Islamist military leader Zia-ul-Haq's support being instrumental in ensuring the Taliban's advent to power, the latter formally laid claim to the Pakhtun-dominated territories lying in modern-day Pakistan in 1998 and expressed the illegitimacy of the Durand Line as part of the Greater Pashtunistan project (Hyman, 2002; Tanner, 2002).

As rightly noted, 'A nation exists when a significant number of people in a community consider themselves to form a nation, or behave as if they formed one' and that 'national communities are constituted by belief: nations exist when their members recognise one another as compatriots and believe that they share characteristics of the relevant kind.'

Therefore, no Afghan government has ratified or legitimised the drawing up of the Durand Line through an agreement signed in 1873 between Mortimer Durand and Amir Abdur Rahman, signing over portions of Afghan territory to British control (Bedi, 2022). Nor has the British handover of Pakhtun-dominated areas in modern-day Pakistan been accepted as part of the Greater Pakhtunistan movement, which seeks to unify the lost territories under the Afghan fold.

Moreover, 'in the Pashtun nationalist narratives in Afghanistan, Pakistan is an unnatural state, a British project, and the Punjab regiment, that uses Islam to ward off its public attention from its occupation of the Pashtun lands' (Taj, 2022).

At the same time, a significant portion of the Pakhtuns (in modern-day Pakistan), who still identify themselves as Afghans, fondly recall a Pakhtun saying, 'you cannot separate water with sticks' (Chua, 2023), to denote how people on both sides of the disputed border consider themselves to be part of a shared clan divided by an artificial boundary and who consider the Durand Line as a fluid border despite Pakistan's fencing attempts.

One key reason Afghanistan has rejected the legitimacy of the Durand Line is that according to it, the agreement that demarcated the British-occupied territories from the rest of Afghanistan had ceased to exist after the British withdrew from the subcontinent, transferring the ownership of Pakhtun-dominated territories to Pakistan in 1947 (CIA, 1961).

The incomplete Afghan nationalist project has resulted in a sense of pervasive ontological insecurity among the populace on both sides of the border. Broadly speaking, Afghans, and to be more specific, Pakhtuns on either end of the Durand Line, due to the contentious history of partition that separated families and ethnic kins, 'expect the state (Afghan) to snatch the Pashtun areas beyond the Durand Line that are now in Pakistan and incorporate them into Afghanistan' (Taj, 2022).

The vehement opposition to the Durand Line could be stated as the primary driver behind Afghanistan's decision to vote against Pakistan's admission as a member state to the United Nations in 1947.

American intelligence officials, by July 1961, had avowedly stated that Afghanistan harboured an annexation agenda, i.e., to incorporate Pakhtun tribal lands into the modern-day Afghanistan and weaken its neighbouring country of Pakistan.

One of the declassified reports released by the Central Intelligence Agency (CIA) highlighted the key area within the Greater Pakhtunistan debate and discourse concerning the legitimacy of the disputed border between Pakistan and Afghanistan:

'Friction over the Pushtunistan issue has occurred along several sectors of the Durand Line, both demarcated and undemarcated, on one or both sides of the Line. Over the years, the chief area of concern has been the Mohmand tribal area, where the Durand Line divides the Mohmand clan owing allegiance to Afghanistan from those owing allegiance to Pakistan (before 1947 to British rule). Prior to 1947, Britain had offered to rectify the Line in this area in a manner that she felt was favorable to Afghanistan. At the time, Afghanistan rejected the offer and since then has had no interest in redefining and demarcating a Line that it longer recognises as a boundary' (CIA, 1961).

While one could debate the legitimacy of the claims propounded by the CIA in the above-mentioned report, including Afghanistan's ambition to reclaim the territories it considers to be under its suzerainty, one has to account for the geopolitical context in which this assessment was made. During that period, Pakistan was a member of two military alliances led by the United States—the Central Treaty Organization and Southeast Asia Treaty Organization—while Afghanistan did not occupy primacy in the American foreign policy establishment.

Furthermore, the erstwhile Soviet Union was increasingly expanding its influence in Afghanistan through its association with the People's Democratic Party of Afghanistan, bringing Kabul closer to it vis-à-vis the United States of America. By September 1961, Pakistan and Afghanistan's diplomatic ties had plummeted abysmally due to the Bajaur Campaign, originating in a border dispute over the Durand Line. Furthermore, Afghanistan, after closing its borders with Pakistan, had directed the Americans to carry out trade and economic assistance via routes controlled by the Soviets as Pakistan was accused of relying on American aircraft to bomb Afghan territory.

Even the more moderate and secular (non-Islamist) forces within the Pakhtun nationalist movement in Pakistan have been given little ground to reason with the hardliner faction and prevent further disruption on the border and regional instability. Their attempts in the early 2000s to rename the erstwhile FATA as Pakhtunkhwa (Land of the Pashtuns) were thwarted by the Punjabi-dominated military establishment (Arnoldy, 2009) while they have often been at the receiving end of targeted attacks, including during the Global War on Terror. In the post-9/11 era, several defenceless civilians were killed in drone attacks in the Pakhtun-dominated tribal areas in which Pakistan's state establishment was complicit. This was done at the American government's urging.

The Ideological ISKP-Taliban Conflict

The ISKP's ideological opposition, inspired by Salafi-jihadi ideology, to nationalistic tendencies has been one of the fundamental tenets of its turf war with the Taliban, even before the latter regained control over the country. The Khorasan wilayat seeks to incorporate parts of Pakistan and Afghanistan within its fold, undermining the Taliban's Pakhtun nationalist objectives and its claims of having established control over vast swathes across Afghanistan. Within the first year of the Taliban 2.0's rule, the ISKP staged a deadly campaign that lasted at least seven months, carrying out approximately 136 operations. Over 70 per cent (Sayed, Von Ostayen & Winter, 2022) of these targeted attacks were directed against Taliban officials who were denounced for their nationalist project that contradicts the ISKP's global Islamist agenda.

Furthermore, by discrediting the Taliban as heretics and not being extreme enough to achieve the global jihadi ambition of establishing a caliphate spanning the world, the ISKP has capitalised on the festering anger and resentment felt by the ethnic minorities due to the Taliban's majoritarian nationalist tendencies, with the Tajiks making up more than half of the affiliate's recruits (MacFarquhar & Schmitt, 2024). In one of the attacks this year in March, ISKP suicide bombers targeted the City Centre Bank in Kandahar, resulting in the death of at least 20 people and injuring approximately 50 others (*BBC News*, 2024).

Notably, Kandahar is the ideological anchor of the Taliban and where Mullah Akhundzada, the current Taliban Emir, resides.

In addition, while the ISKP's targeted attacks were initially largely constrained to the Nangarhar province and areas in and surrounding Kabul, it was in 2022 that the ISIS affiliate branched out to stage attacks in Pakistan's Khyber Pakhtunkhwa province. That year alone, at least 22 per cent (Jadoon, Mines, and Sayed, 2023) of its total attacks occurred in Pakistan's restive province, which later surged to 55 per cent in the first half of 2023 alone. Notably, in one of its deadliest attacks in the province, the ISKP attacked Jamiat Ulema-e-Islam's (a pro-Taliban party) political rally in 2023, killing more than 50 people and wounding over 200 (Baloch and Ellis-Peterson, 2023).

These events seek to highlight how the ISKP wants to undermine the Taliban's influence within Afghanistan and beyond by carrying out deadly attacks against those sympathetic to its cause, especially in areas considered integral to the Greater Pakhtunistan project. Moreover, Nangarhar borders the erstwhile FATA, another key strategic area deemed integral to Pakhtun nationalist aspirations. Therefore, the presence of the ISKP and occurrence of targeted attacks in such areas is also part of the ISKP's attempt to denigrate and disintegrate the nationalist ambitions of the Pakhtun Taliban.

At the same time, as reports about Salafi preachers' tortured bodies appearing in drains or mosques and seminaries being constantly raided (Siddiqui, 2021) have been doing the rounds in Afghanistan, a parallel increase in recruitment in the Khyber Pakhtunkhwa province has been visible, an area which has historically (Jadoon, Mines, and Sayed, 2023) been a key hub. It has also contributed to a broadening recruitment pool with Afghanistan's Salafi community, possibly even the quietest Salafi community (although there are no verified reports yet of such events occurring, it is a trend that could take form in the foreseeable future), a demographic which traditionally refrains from participating in public life or violence.

Conclusion

The numerical strength of the Pakhtuns has allowed them to consolidate their hold over state institutions, including the governance structures (as monarchs, elected leaders, or extremist theological movements like the Taliban), despite lagging behind groups like the Tajiks with superior educational qualifications and literacy levels.

Furthermore, the domineering attitude cultivated among and by the Pakhtuns in Afghanistan has resulted in a pan-Afghan nationalism being conflated with Pakhtun nationalism. This helps us understand the inter-ethnic conflicts, the majority vs. minority nationalism, and the ideological conflict between the ISKP and Afghan Taliban plaguing Afghanistan, each in its own capacity since the establishment of the modern Afghan state in the 1770s.

In addition, by using Islamic justifications to legitimise their claim to leadership, the Taliban leaders have effectively pushed back against any probability of an inclusive Afghan nationalism emerging.

Finally, the border dispute has caused an immense strain on Afghanistan-Pakistan bilateral ties, including under the leadership of Islamabad's former clients—the Afghan Taliban. Decades of bloodshed, hostility, border skirmishes, and diplomatic condemnation have set the tone for their tenuous relationship.

References

Arnoldy, B. (October 8, 2009). "Pakistan's Pashtuns, looking for statehood, may look to Taliban". The Christian Science Monitor. https://www.csmonitor.com/World/Asia-South-Central/2009/1008/p08s04-wosc.html

Ayoob, M. (January 10, 2019). "The Taliban and the Changing Nature of Pashtun Nationalism". *The National Interest*. https://nationalinterest.org/feature/taliban-and-changing-nature-pashtun-nationalism-41182

Baloch, S. M. & Ellis-Petersen, H. (July 31, 2023). "Islamic State says it carried out Pakistan suicide bombing that killed 54". *The Guardian*. https://www.theguardian.com/world/2023/jul/31/islamic-state-pakistan-suicide-bombing-taliban

BBC News (March 21, 2024). "Afghanistan: IS claims responsibility for suicide bomb at Kandahar bank". https://www.bbc.com/news/world-asia-68625242

Bedi, R. (January 11, 2022). "Pakistan-Afghanistan Ties Come Under Strain After Taliban Opposes Border Fencing". *The Wire*. https://thewire.in/south-asia/pakistan-afghanistan-ties-come-under-strain-after-taliban-opposes-border-fencing

Business Standard (November 25, 2021). "Taliban believe current govt in Afghanistan is inclusive: Spokesperson". https://www.business-standard.com/article/international/taliban-believe-current-govt-in-afghanistan-is-inclusive-spokesperson-121112500098_1.html

Central Intelligence Agency (CIA) (1961). "Geographic Support Project: The Durand Line". https://www.cia.gov/readingroom/docs/CIA-RDP08C01297R000100140005-3.pdf

Chua, A. (2023). "Political Tribes: Group Instinct and the Fate of Nations". Army University Press. https://www.armyupress.army.mil/Journals/Military-Review/English-Edition-Archives/January-February-2023/Chua/

Dar, A. M. (2022). "Revisiting key debates in the study of nationalism". *Humanities and Social Sciences Communications*, *9*(1). https://doi.org/10.1057/s41599-022-01432-w

Dupree, L. B. (1973). *Afghanistan*. Princeton University Press.

European Center for Populism Studies (n.d.). "Majoritarianism". Retrieved June 26, 2024, from https://www.populismstudies.org/Vocabulary/majoritarianism/

Garner, R.P. (2022). "Nationalism". *Oxford Research Encyclopedia of Politics*. https://doi.org/10.1093/acrefore/9780190228637.013.2039

Hindu Post (May 3, 2023). "How fusion of Deobandi ideology and Pashtun Nationalism is driving Taliban 2.0". https://hindupost.in/terrorism/how-fusion-of-deobandi-ideology-and-pashtun-nationalism-is-driving-taliban-2-0/

Hyman, A. (2002). "Nationalism in Afghanistan". *International Journal of Middle East Studies*, *34*(2), pp. 299–315. https://www.jstor.org/stable/3879829

Jadoon, A., Mines, A., & Sayed, A. (2023). "The Enduring Duel: Islamic State Khorasan's Survival under Afghanistan's New Rulers". *CTC Sentinel*, *16*(8), pp. 8–15. https://ctc.westpoint.edu/the-enduring-duel-islamic-state-khorasans-survival-under-afghanistans-new-rulers/

Jones, S. G. (2010). *In the Graveyard of Empires: America's War in Afghanistan*. W. W. Norton & Company.

Kumar, A. & Malhotra, A. (April 17, 2024). "Factoring Ethnicity in Taliban's Quest for Legitimacy". *Georgetown Journal of International Affairs*. https://gjia.georgetown.edu/2024/04/17/factoring-ethnicity-in-talibans-quest-for-legitimacy-an-anthropological-rewiring-of-the-power-structure/

Lieven, A. (2012). *Pakistan: A Hard Country*. Penguin Books Ltd.

Lieven, A. (2021). "An Afghan Tragedy: The Pashtuns, the Taliban and the State". *Survival, 63*(3), pp. 7–36. https://doi.org/10.1080/00396338.2021.1930403

Lincoln, D. (2024). "Pashtunistan, Islamism, and Order: A Critical Analysis of the Multifaceted Identity, Discursive Strategies, and Origins of the Taliban in Afghanistan". http://dx.doi.org/10.13140/RG.2.2.30582.37440

MacFarquhar, N. & Schmitt, E. (April 18, 2024). "An ISIS Terror Group Draws Half Its Recruits From Tiny Tajikistan". *The New York Times*. https://www.nytimes.com/2024/04/18/world/europe/tajikistan-isis-k-terrorism.html

Nishat, Z., Shelley, J., Karimi, S., & El-Badawy, E. (September 22, 2022). "Why Do People in Afghanistan Object to Taliban Rule?" Tony Blair Institute for Global Change. https://www.institute.global/insights/geopolitics-and-security/why-do-people-afghanistan-object-taliban-rule

Raqib, M. A. (2011). "Resistance by Other Means: The Taliban, Foreign Occupation, and Afghan National Identity". Northeastern University. https://repository.library.northeastern.edu/files/neu:1521/fulltext.pdf

Rasikh, J. (2014). "Nationalism in Afghanistan - A Descriptive Analysis". JMU Scholarly Commons; "Middle Eastern Communities and Migrations". Student Research Paper Series. https://commons.lib.jmu.edu/mecmsrps/3

Sayed, A., Van Ostaeyen, P., & Winter, C. (January 25, 2022). "Making Sense of the Islamic State's War on the Afghan Taliban". Hudson Institute. https://www.hudson.org/node/44711

Shivamurthy, A. G. (August 11, 2023). "Mobilising to a Victorious Insurgency: Locating Identity, Grievance, and Greed in the Taliban's Strategy". Observer Research Foundation. https://www.orfonline.org/research/mobilising-to-a-victorious-insurgency-locating-identity-grievance-and-greed-in-the-taliban-s-strategy

Siddique, A. (October 22, 2021). "Taliban Wages Deadly Crackdown On Afghan Salafists As War With IS-K Intensifies". RFE/RL. https://www.rferl.org/a/taliban-crackdown-salafis-islamic-state-khorasan/31524687.html

Taj, F. (2022). "Clash of Identities". *Policy Perspectives, 19*(2), pp. 1-20. https://doi.org/10.13169/polipers.19.2.ra1

Tanner, S. (2009). *Afghanistan: A Military History from Alexander the Great to the War against the Taliban*. Da Capo Press.

Wahlang, J. (November 10, 2021). "Tajikistan's Confrontational Stand vis-à-vis Taliban". Manohar Parrikar Institute for Defence Studies and Analyses. https://www.idsa.in/idsacomments/tajikistan-confrontational-stand-taliban-jwahlang-101121

2 Afghanistan's Nationhood Shaped by the Taliban

Shirish Waghmare

Introduction

The concept of nationhood is a central theme in political science, sociology, and history, embodying the collective identity of a people who share common cultural, historical, and linguistic traits. Nationhood is more than just a political construct; it is a sense of belonging, a shared consciousness that binds people together within a specific territorial entity (Smith, 1991). In the case of Afghanistan, the notion of nationhood is particularly complex and multifaceted, shaped by a myriad of factors, including its diverse ethnic composition, tribal culture, historical experiences, and external influences (Saikal, 2006). This chapter seeks to explore Afghanistan's concept of nationhood through a theoretical lens, focusing on the impact of the Taliban on the nation's identity.

In Afghanistan, nationhood, a concept that encompasses the collective identity, governance, culture, and sovereignty of a people, has been profoundly shaped by the country's tumultuous history (Rubin, 2002). Afghanistan's nationhood has evolved through centuries of conflict, foreign interventions, and internal strife, with the Taliban emerging as a critical force in defining the nation's identity in the late 20th and early 21st centuries (Barfield, 2010). This chapter delves into the concept of nationhood, with a particular focus on Afghanistan, examining how the Taliban's rise, fall, and resurgence have impacted the nation's governance, social fabric, and geopolitical significance. It also explores how the Taliban's vision contrasts with other competing ideologies within the country.

Afghanistan presents a unique and challenging case study in the analysis of nationhood. The country is a mosaic of diverse ethnic groups—Pashtuns, Tajiks, Hazaras, Uzbeks, and others—each with its own distinct language, culture, and historical narrative. Despite these differences, the various ethnic groups have coexisted within the geographical boundaries of Afghanistan, though their sense of nationhood has often been fragmented and contested. The Taliban's rise to power and their subsequent impact on Afghanistan's national identity add another layer of complexity to the nationhood debate.

To analyse Afghanistan's nationhood, this chapter draws on the theoretical frameworks provided by various prominent scholars. The scholars offer different perspectives on nationhood, nationalism, and the factors that contribute to the formation of national identity. By applying these theories to the Afghan context, we can gain a deeper understanding of the challenges and tensions that define the concept of nationhood in Afghanistan.

Anthony D. Smith's ethno-symbolism is particularly relevant to the study of nationhood in Afghanistan. In his seminal work, *National Identity* and *The Ethnic Origins of Nations*, Smith argues that nationhood is deeply rooted in ethnic identity and cultural heritage (Smith, 1991). He emphasises the importance of myths, symbols, and traditions in the formation of national identity, suggesting that nations are not merely political entities but also cultural communities with a shared historical consciousness. Applying Smith's framework to Afghanistan, we can see how the country's diverse ethnic groups have developed distinct identities based on their own cultural symbols and historical experiences. The Pashtuns, who form the largest ethnic group in Afghanistan, have traditionally dominated the country's political landscape, with their tribal code, Pashtunwali, serving as a key element of their identity (Rubin, 2002). This ethno-cultural dominance has, at times, led to tensions with other ethnic groups, complicating the process of nation-building in Afghanistan (Barfield, 2010).

Theoretical Perspectives on Nationhood: Anthony D. Smith's Ethno-Symbolism and its Application to Afghanistan

In exploring the concept of nationhood in Afghanistan, Anthony D. Smith's ethno-symbolism provides a highly relevant theoretical framework.

Smith's theory, which places significant emphasis on the role of ethnic identity, myths, and symbols in nation-building, fits well in the context of Afghanistan due to the country's deep-rooted tribal and ethnic divisions. By focusing on identity and ethnicity as core elements of nationhood, Smith's theory offers insights into how the concept of Afghan nationhood has evolved, particularly under the influence of the Taliban and their vision for the nation. This chapter will primarily focus on Smith's ethno-symbolism to trace the impact of the Taliban on Afghanistan's national identity, while acknowledging aspects of other theories that may offer some relevance to the discussion.

Anthony D. Smith's Theory of Nationhood

Anthony D. Smith, one of the most influential scholars on nationalism, argues that nationhood is deeply rooted in the pre-existing ethnic identities of a people. In his works, such as *National Identity* and *The Ethnic Origins of Nations*, Smith posits that nations are not solely political entities constructed in modern times but are cultural communities that draw upon ethnic ties, myths, symbols, and shared historical consciousness (Smith, 1991). Smith's theory of ethno-symbolism emphasises the importance of collective memory and the role of long-standing traditions, which, according to him, shape the national identity of a group. These elements provide the basis for a cohesive national identity that transcends modern state boundaries and political structures (Smith, 1986).

Smith's definition of nationhood is particularly applicable to Afghanistan because it recognises the centrality of ethnicity in the construction of national identity. Afghanistan is a highly diverse country with a mosaic of ethnic groups—Pashtuns, Tajiks, Hazaras, Uzbeks, and others—each with their own cultural traditions, languages, and historical narratives (Barfield, 2010). These distinct ethnic identities, which have coexisted for centuries, form the foundation of Afghan society. According to Smith's framework, these pre-existing ethnic groups, with their unique symbols and cultural heritage, would play a significant role in shaping Afghanistan's sense of nationhood. This theory allows us to explore how the diverse ethnic composition of Afghanistan has impacted the development of its national identity, especially under the influence of the Taliban.

Application of Smith's Theory to Afghanistan

Afghanistan presents a compelling case study in the application of Smith's ethno-symbolism because the country's national identity has historically been fragmented along ethnic lines. The Pashtuns, the largest ethnic group in Afghanistan, have traditionally dominated the political landscape, with their tribal code, *Pashtunwali*, serving as a central pillar of their identity (Rubin, 2002). The rise of the Taliban, who are predominantly Pashtun, further solidified the ethnic dimension of nationhood in Afghanistan. The Taliban, during their rule from 1996 to 2001 and their resurgence after 2001, advanced a vision of Afghan nationhood that was closely aligned with Pashtun majoritarianism. This alignment between the Taliban and Pashtun identity created tensions with other ethnic groups, such as the Tajiks, Hazaras, and Uzbeks, who felt marginalised under the Taliban's rule.

Smith's theory helps to explain the role of ethnicity in the Taliban's vision of nationhood. By drawing upon Pashtun cultural traditions, the Taliban sought to define Afghan nationhood in terms of Pashtun dominance, which was evident in their imposition of *Pashtunwali* as a quasi-legal code in the areas under their control (Saikal, 2006). This emphasis on ethnic identity as the basis for national identity aligns with Smith's idea that nationhood is rooted in long-standing cultural symbols and traditions. For the Taliban, the Pashtun tribal code became a symbol of Afghan nationhood, reinforcing their ethno-cultural dominance over other groups.

Smith's theory also offers insights into why the Taliban's vision of nationhood has been so contested. Afghanistan's other ethnic groups have their own distinct cultural symbols, historical narratives, and identities that do not necessarily align with the Pashtun-centric vision promoted by the Taliban. For example, the Hazaras, a Shia Muslim ethnic group, have historically been marginalised and persecuted under Pashtun rule, and their identity is shaped by a sense of historical victimisation (Marsden, 2002). The Tajiks, another significant ethnic group, have their own rich cultural heritage that is closely linked to Persian language and literature, which contrasts with the Pashtun-centric narratives advanced by the Taliban (Roy, 1990). By privileging Pashtun identity, the Taliban exacerbated ethnic divisions, making it difficult to construct a unified national identity in line with Smith's vision of a culturally cohesive nation.

Pashtun Majoritarianism and its Impact on Nationhood

Pashtun majoritarianism, as advanced by the Taliban, has had a profound impact on the concept of nationhood in Afghanistan. The Taliban's reliance on Pashtun identity as the cornerstone of their vision for Afghanistan alienated many of the country's minority ethnic groups, creating deep social and political divisions (Barfield, 2010). The exclusion of non-Pashtun groups from key positions of power and the Taliban's efforts to impose their cultural values on the rest of the country undermined the possibility of building a more inclusive national identity (Giustozzi, 2010).

Smith's ethno-symbolism provides a useful lens for understanding the consequences of this ethnic dominance. According to Smith, nationhood requires a shared sense of identity based on common cultural symbols and historical experiences (Smith, 1991). In Afghanistan, however, the Taliban's promotion of Pashtun culture as the defining element of Afghan nationhood disrupted this shared identity, leading to a fragmented and contested sense of nationhood. The exclusion of other ethnic groups from the Taliban's vision of Afghanistan suggests that the process of nation-building in the country has been incomplete and fraught with conflict.

Alternative Theoretical Perspectives

While Anthony D. Smith's ethno-symbolism offers the most relevant framework for understanding nationhood in Afghanistan, other theories of nationalism can also provide some useful insights. For example, Benedict Anderson's concept of the "imagined community" emphasises the role of print capitalism and modern state structures in the formation of national identity (Anderson, 1983). While this theory is less applicable to Afghanistan's tribal and ethnic dynamics, it offers a useful contrast by highlighting the role of modern state institutions in shaping national identity. Similarly, Ernest Gellner's theory of nationalism, which emphasises the role of industrialisation and modernity in the construction of nations, can shed light on the challenges Afghanistan faces in building a unified national identity in the absence of strong state institutions (Gellner, 1983). However, these alternative frameworks are less relevant to the Afghan context, where ethnicity and tribalism play a much more central role in shaping national identity.

The Rise of the Taliban

The Taliban emerged in the mid-1990s as a response to the anarchy that followed the Soviet withdrawal and the subsequent civil war. Composed primarily of Pashtun fighters from southern Afghanistan, many of whom had been educated in religious schools (madrasas) in Pakistan, the Taliban sought to impose a strict interpretation of Sharia law as a means of restoring order (Crews & Tarzi, 2008). Their rapid rise to power was fuelled by widespread war-weariness and disillusionment with the corrupt and factionalised Mujahideen leaders who had failed to stabilise the country.

The Taliban's vision of Afghanistan was one rooted in a return to what they perceived as an authentic Islamic society. This vision was not just religious but also deeply political, as it sought to redefine Afghan nationhood in opposition to both the secular nationalism of previous regimes and the ethnic and tribal divisions that had long plagued the country (Rashid, 2010). By 1996, the Taliban had captured Kabul and declared themselves the rulers of Afghanistan, a position they would hold until the U.S.-led invasion in 2001.

Defining Nationhood, Afghanistan's Nationhood, and the Taliban's Nationhood

Nationhood

Nationhood is a foundational concept in political science and sociology, denoting the collective identity of a group of people who share common characteristics, such as culture, history, language, and often, political governance (Kedourie, 1994). It reflects a sense of belonging and unity among individuals who identify as part of a nation. Nationhood is intricately linked to the idea of the nation-state, which is a political entity defined by its sovereignty over a specific territory and population. This sovereignty allows the nation-state to establish and enforce laws, conduct diplomacy, and represent its people on the global stage.

Nationhood encompasses both objective and subjective elements. Objectively, it involves the structural components of a nation-state, including its borders, government institutions, and legal systems (Carr, 1945). Subjectively, it involves the psychological and cultural aspects of national identity, such as shared values, symbols, and narratives, which foster a sense of community and collective purpose. The concept of nationhood often involves balancing these elements to create a cohesive and functional political entity that can sustain stability and development.

Afghanistan's Nationhood

Afghanistan's nationhood is deeply shaped by its rich tapestry of ethnic diversity and tribal affiliations. The country is home to a complex mosaic of ethnic groups, including the Pashtuns, Tajiks, Hazaras, Uzbeks, and others, each contributing to the nation's multifaceted identity. Historically, Afghanistan's strategic location as a buffer state between major empires, such as the British and Russian empires, has influenced its national identity and political landscape.

The nationhood of Afghanistan is characterised by a combination of tribal loyalties and a shared sense of resistance against external domination. The country's tribal structure has played a crucial role in its political organisation and social dynamics. Additionally, Islam has served as a unifying force, providing a common cultural and religious framework that binds the diverse ethnic groups together. However, Afghanistan's nationhood is also marked by internal divisions and regional conflicts, which have often hindered efforts to achieve a cohesive national identity.

Afghanistan's history of conflict and foreign intervention has further complicated its nationhood. The various attempts at nation-building and modernisation have often clashed with traditional tribal structures and cultural practices. As a result, Afghanistan's national identity remains a complex and evolving concept, shaped by both its historical experiences and ongoing challenges.

The Taliban's Nationhood

The Taliban's nationhood represents a more ideologically rigid and exclusionary vision of Afghan identity. The Taliban's concept of nationhood is grounded in their interpretation of Deobandi Sunni Islam, combined with Pashtunwali, the traditional code of the Pashtun people (Rashid, 2010). This vision emphasises a strict adherence to Sharia law and seeks to establish a homogeneous Islamic state.

Under Taliban rule, nationhood is characterised by a narrow, puritanical interpretation of Islam that often marginalises ethnic and religious minorities, as well as women. The Taliban's approach to governance is focused on creating a unified Islamic identity, which often conflicts with the diverse and pluralistic nature of Afghan society. Their vision of nationhood involves the rejection of Western influences and secularism, aiming to replace these with a theocratic system based on their interpretation of religious principles.

The Taliban's nationhood is exclusionary in nature, as it tends to overlook the cultural and ethnic diversity of Afghanistan. This exclusionary approach has led to significant tensions and conflicts with other ethnic and religious groups within the country. The imposition of a uniform religious identity has further complicated efforts to achieve a cohesive national identity that accommodates Afghanistan's diverse population.

Overall, the Taliban's vision of nationhood highlights the challenges of reconciling ideological aspirations with the realities of a multi-ethnic and multi-religious society. The contrast between the Taliban's rigid interpretation and the diverse realities of Afghan society underscores the complexities involved in defining and achieving a unified sense of nationhood in Afghanistan.

Tribal Culture of Afghanistan and Its Influence on Nationhood

Afghanistan's tribal culture is a foundational element of the country's social and political fabric, deeply influencing its sense of nationhood. The country is home to a diverse mosaic of ethnic groups, with the Pashtuns, Tajiks, Hazaras, Uzbeks, and others forming the core of its population. Among these, the Pashtuns are the largest ethnic group, and their tribal code, known as Pashtunwali, has significantly shaped Afghan society.

Pashtunwali is an unwritten code of conduct that governs the social, political, and cultural life of the Pashtuns. It emphasises values such as hospitality (*Melmastia*), honour (*Nang*), and revenge (*Badal*). These principles are not only central to Pashtun identity but also play a crucial role in the broader Afghan society, influencing how communities interact with one another and with the state. The emphasis on tribal loyalty and autonomy has often conflicted with efforts to build a centralised national identity, leading to a fragmented sense of nationhood.

The tribal structure in Afghanistan is hierarchical, with tribal elders and leaders wielding considerable power over their communities. This decentralised power structure has historically posed challenges to state-building efforts, as allegiance to the tribe often supersedes loyalty to the central government. Consequently, Afghanistan's nationhood has been characterised by a delicate balance between tribal autonomy and the authority of the state (Dorronsoro, 2005).

During the rise of the Taliban in the 1990s, tribal culture played a pivotal role. The Taliban, primarily composed of Pashtuns, leveraged Pashtunwali to gain support and legitimacy among Pashtun tribes. Their enforcement of a strict interpretation of Islamic law was, in some ways, aligned with traditional Pashtun values, which facilitated their acceptance in Pashtun-dominated areas. However, the Taliban's attempt to impose a uniform theocratic state clashed with the diverse tribal customs of other ethnic groups, leading to resistance and further fracturing of the nation's unity (Crews & Tarzi, 2008).

The influence of tribal culture on Afghan nationhood is also evident in the country's ongoing conflicts and governance challenges. Tribal leaders often serve as intermediaries between the central government and local communities, negotiating the terms of governance and security. This dynamic has contributed to the persistence of local power structures that sometimes operate independently or in opposition to the central authority.

Moreover, tribal culture has played a role in Afghanistan's resistance to foreign influence. The deeply ingrained sense of honour and autonomy within tribal communities has fuelled a long history of resistance against foreign invaders, from the British in the 19th century to the Soviets in the 20th century, and more recently, the United States (Carr, 1945). This resistance is often framed not just as a defence of the nation but as a defence of tribal identity and autonomy.

The Impact of the Taliban on Afghanistan's Nationhood

The Taliban's influence on Afghanistan's nationhood is perhaps the most significant and contentious aspect of the country's recent history. The rise of the Taliban in the 1990s marked a significant turning point in Afghanistan's national identity. The Taliban, a fundamentalist Islamic movement primarily composed of Pashtuns, sought to impose a strict interpretation of Sharia law across Afghanistan. Their vision of an Islamic Emirate was at odds with the diverse cultural and ethnic identities that make up the Afghan nation (Nojumi, 2002).

The Taliban's rule from 1996 to 2001, and their return to power in 2021, has had profound implications for Afghanistan's concept of nationhood. The imposition of a theocratic state has often clashed with the traditional tribal structures and the more secular, nationalistic aspirations of other ethnic groups. The Taliban's emphasis on a singular religious identity has, in many ways, undermined the pluralistic nature of Afghan society.

Moreover, the Taliban's rule has been characterised by a rejection of many aspects of modernity, including the nation-state model itself. In this sense, the Taliban's impact on Afghanistan's nationhood can be seen as both a continuation of and a departure from the historical patterns of governance in the country.

The Taliban's theocratic governance, which sought to homogenise Afghanistan under a singular Islamic identity, posed a direct challenge to the pluralistic nature of Afghan society. The imposition of a strict religious code, which included the suppression of women's rights, the banning of cultural practices deemed un-Islamic, and the persecution of religious and ethnic minorities, created deep divisions within the country. The Taliban's attempt to redefine Afghanistan's nationhood through a religious lens often led to resistance from those who saw their identity, whether ethnic, tribal, or cultural, being marginalised or erased.

The Taliban's impact on Afghanistan's nationhood can also be seen in their relationship with traditional tribal structures. Afghanistan's tribal culture, particularly among the Pashtuns, has historically been characterised by a degree of autonomy and resistance to centralised authority (Gannon, 2005). The Taliban's efforts to impose their rule over these tribes often led to conflicts, as tribal leaders resisted what they saw as an encroachment on their traditional rights and autonomy (Coll, 2004). This tension between the Taliban's theocratic vision and the tribal structures that have long been a cornerstone of Afghan society underscores the difficulties of establishing a unified national identity in such a diverse and decentralised country.

Moreover, the Taliban's rise to power has also had significant implications for Afghanistan's relationship with the international community. The group's strict interpretation of Islam and their harbouring of international terrorist organisations like Al-Qaeda led to their initial ousting by the U.S.-led coalition in 2001 (Dorronsoro, 2005). However, their resilience and eventual return to power in 2021 demonstrate the enduring appeal of their vision of nationhood to certain segments of Afghan society, particularly in rural areas where tribal and religious identities remain strong. This persistence of the Taliban's influence highlights the deep divisions within Afghanistan and the challenges of building a nation that can accommodate its diverse population (Hayes, 1926).

The Future of Afghan Nationhood

The future of Afghan nationhood is intrinsically linked to how the country addresses its deep-seated divisions and embraces its complex diversity. The ongoing conflict and external interventions have left Afghanistan in a state of flux, with significant implications for its national identity and unity. The Taliban's resurgence has accentuated the challenges of nationhood by imposing a rigid framework that often clashes with the pluralistic and multi-ethnic fabric of Afghan society.

For Afghanistan to move forward, it must engage in a thorough and inclusive process of nation-building that genuinely reflects its diverse identities. This involves more than merely accommodating different ethnic, tribal, and cultural groups; it requires actively integrating these groups into the political and social framework of the nation. This inclusive approach would help to foster a sense of belonging and shared purpose among Afghanistan's varied populations, thus strengthening national cohesion.

The role of governance is crucial in this context. The establishment of a political system that genuinely respects and incorporates the country's ethnic and tribal diversity is essential. This means moving beyond centralised, top-down governance models and instead adopting a more decentralised approach that empowers local communities and leaders. Such a system would allow for greater representation and address the unique needs of various groups, thus promoting stability and reducing the potential for conflict.

Furthermore, the protection and promotion of fundamental rights, including those of women and minorities, will be critical in shaping the future of Afghan nationhood. The Taliban's approach to these issues has drawn significant international criticism, and it remains to be seen how the group will address these concerns moving forward. Ensuring that all citizens have equal rights and opportunities, regardless of their gender, ethnicity, or religious beliefs, is not only a matter of justice but also a cornerstone of a stable and cohesive nation.

External actors, including international organisations and foreign governments, also have a role to play, but their involvement must be carefully calibrated. Support for Afghanistan should prioritise bolstering internal processes and fostering local ownership of the nation-building efforts rather than imposing external models or solutions. This support could take various forms, such as providing technical assistance, facilitating dialogue between different Afghan groups, and supporting economic development initiatives that benefit all segments of society.

Ultimately, the future of Afghan nationhood will hinge on the country's ability to balance its rich cultural heritage with the demands of a modern state. By embracing its diversity and fostering inclusive governance, Afghanistan has the potential to build a more unified and resilient nation that can navigate the complexities of its past and present while paving the way for a more stable and prosperous future.

Conclusion

Afghanistan's nationhood, as shaped by the Taliban, is a complex and multifaceted reality. The Taliban's rise, rule, and resurgence have left indelible marks on the country's identity, governance, and societal structures. Their vision of an Islamic state has clashed with other notions of Afghan nationhood, creating a contested and often, violent, political landscape. As Afghanistan continues to navigate its future under Taliban rule, the legacy of the past decades will undoubtedly continue to shape its path forward. The story of Afghanistan's nationhood, influenced so profoundly by the Taliban, is one of a nation in constant negotiation with itself, striving to reconcile its diverse identities with the forces of history and ideology.

The Taliban's impact on Afghanistan's governance has been transformative, shifting the nation from attempts at modernisation and democratic governance to a theocratic state with limited tolerance for diversity and dissent. The changes they have brought, particularly in the realm of women's rights, education, and cultural expression, have left an indelible mark on the social fabric of the country.

This development has profound implications not only for Afghanistan but also for the broader South Asian region and the global Muslim community.

In conclusion, the enduring influence of the Taliban on Afghanistan's nationhood highlights the complexities of nation-building in a country marked by deep ethnic, religious, and tribal divisions. It underscores the challenges of reconciling competing visions of identity and governance in a land that has long been a crossroads of empires, ideologies, and cultures. As Afghanistan continues to grapple with its identity and future, the legacy of the Taliban will remain a central, and often, contentious, part of its story.

Afghanistan's journey toward defining its nationhood is far from over. The theoretical perspectives explored in this chapter provide valuable insights into the complexities of Afghan nationhood, highlighting the challenges of building a cohesive national identity in a country marked by deep-seated divisions and external interventions. The Taliban's impact on Afghanistan's national identity, the role of foreign powers, and the enduring influence of tribal and ethnic loyalties all underscore the challenges of nation-building in Afghanistan. As the country moves forward, the question of nationhood will remain central to its future, shaping its path toward peace, stability, and self-determination.

References

Barfield, T. (2010). *Afghanistan: A Cultural and Political History*. Princeton University Press.

Carr, E. H. (1945). *Nationalism and After*. Macmillan.

Coll, S. (2004). *Ghost Wars: The Secret History of the CIA, Afghanistan, and Bin Laden, from the Soviet Invasion to September 10, 2001*. Penguin.

Crews, R. D. & Tarzi, A. (Eds.). (2008). *The Taliban and the crisis of Afghanistan*. Harvard University Press.

Dorronsoro, G. (2005). *Revolution Unending: Afghanistan, 1979 to the Present*. Columbia University Press.

Gannon, K. (2005). *I is for Infidel: From Holy War to Holy Terror in Afghanistan*. Public Affairs.

Gellner, E. (1983). *Nations and Nationalism*. Cornell University Press.

Hayes, C. J. H. (1926). *Essays on Nationalism*. Macmillan.

Kedourie, E. (1993). *Nationalism*. Blackwell.

Marsden, P. (2002). *The Taliban: War and Religion in Afghanistan*. Bloomsbury Academic.

Nojumi, N. (2002). *The Rise of the Taliban in Afghanistan: Mass Mobilization, Civil War, and the Future of the Region*. Palgrave Macmillan.

Rashid, A. (2010). *Taliban: Militant Islam, Oil and Fundamentalism in Central Asia*. Yale University Press.

Roy, O. (1990). *Islam and Resistance in Afghanistan*. Cambridge University Press.

Rubin, B. R. (2002). *The Fragmentation of Afghanistan: State Formation and Collapse in the International System*. Yale University Press.

Saikal, A. (2006). *Modern Afghanistan: A History of Struggle and Survival*. I.B. Tauris.

Smith, A. D. (1986). *The Ethnic Origins of Nations*. Blackwell.

Smith, A. D. (1991). *National Identity*. University of Nevada Press.

3 Doctrine in the Mountains
Unravelling the Taliban's Ideology Tapestry

Vaasu Sharma

Introduction

The rise of the Taliban to power in Afghanistan on two occasions has failed to eradicate the prevailing misunderstandings regarding their ideological foundations. The complex nature of this ideology requires a thorough understanding, with conflicting views attributing its origins to Islamic principles or Pashtun cultural traditions. Thus, a detailed assessment of the Taliban's governing strategies and actions is necessary to uncover the factual underpinnings of their ideological structure. This analysis is necessary not only for understanding the operational methods of the Taliban but also for dispelling potentially harmful misconceptions about Islam and Pashtun culture that have emerged from surface-level connections.

The doctrine of the Taliban has evolved significantly over the past two decades. Formerly characterised by a 'traditionalist' interpretation of Islam, highlighting a specific version of Islam prevalent in southern Pashtun communities, the movement now, in its insurgency phase, shows resemblances to prominent political Islam ideologies in the Arab region. This transition does not suggest a decrease in conservatism or authoritarianism within the Taliban ranks but rather demonstrates modifications in the targets of their suppression and the narrative surrounding their objectives. The discourse and ideological doctrines espoused by the Taliban have been vital in supporting the movement's capacity to sustain heightened levels of violence, despite significant transformations in the political scenario over time. This rhetoric has wielded influence across multiple levels, from the individual to institutional and societal domains.

This chapter will examine the Taliban's ideology from Mujahideen resistance to the Soviet occupation to its current role in Afghan politics. The chapter begins by discussing Afghanistan's socio-political dynamics before and during the Soviet invasion, which led to the rise of the Taliban. It will trace the movement's transformation from a traditionalist organisation to a political force that aspires to impose its Islam on Afghanistan. This chapter will also examine the Taliban's nationhood and connection with the world community, particularly in light of its rejection of Western principles and the nation-state. The Taliban's appeal across Afghanistan's numerous ethnic groups will be examined to determine how it has gained support. The chapter will also critically evaluate the Taliban's impact on human rights, particularly women's and religious and ethnic minority rights. This chapter concludes by exploring the difficulties external powers face in dealing with Afghanistan under the Taliban. The chapter seeks to examine the Taliban's ideology and its effects on Afghanistan and the world.

Historical Roots of the Taliban Movement and its Ideology

The Taliban surfaced in the early 1990s, originating from Afghan Mujahideen, or Islamic guerrilla fighters, who had resisted the Soviet occupation of Afghanistan (1979–89) with covert support from the CIA and the Inter-Services Intelligence Directorate (ISI) of Pakistan. The group was subsequently bolstered by young Pashtun tribesmen who had received education in Pakistani madrasas, or religious schools; the term 'Taliban' translates to 'students' in Pashto. The education imparted aimed to promote the Deobandi version of militant Islamism that eventually resulted in the formation of the group. The Pashtuns are the primary ethnic group in Afghanistan, particularly in the southern and eastern regions, and are also a significant ethnic community in the northern and western parts of Pakistan (Maizland, 2023).

The movement achieved notable public approval during the initial post-Soviet context by committing to promote stability and the rule of law after four years of fratricidal warfare (1992–96) involving competing Mujahideen factions. In November 1994, the Taliban marked their arrival in Kandahar (Rashid, 2014) with the intent of restoring order in the crime-stricken southern metropolis, and by September 1996, they had effectively captured the capital, Kabul, from President Burhanuddin Rabbani, an ethnic Tajik whom they considered both anti-Pashtun and corrupt. In that same year, the Taliban designated Afghanistan as an Islamic emirate, with Mullah Mohammed Omar, a religious authority and veteran of the anti-Soviet resistance, taking on the title of Amir Al-Mu'minin, or 'commander of the faithful' (Maizland, 2023). Prior to its demise in 2001, the regime controlled about 90 per cent of the national landscape.

The Taliban's first move was to institute a strict interpretation of Quranic instruction and jurisprudence. In practice, this meant often merciless policies on the treatment of women, political opponents of any type, and religious minorities. The legal foundation of the regime was mainly constituted from the pre-Islamic tribal code of the Pashtun people, further enriched by interpretations of Sharia that reflected the austere Wahhabi doctrines propagated by the Saudi-affiliated madrasas. The governance framework showed a pronounced apathy towards social services and fundamental state roles, while concurrently, the Ministry for the Promotion of Virtue and Prevention of Vice mandated that women wear the full-body burqa, or chadri (Pal, 2021); restricted musical expression and visual media; and imprisoned men whose facial hair did not meet the required length.

Taliban's Interpretation of Islam

The political milieu within which the Taliban arose constituted a pivotal factor in their ideological development. The Taliban arose within the context of the civil strife in Afghanistan, following the collapse of the Soviet-backed Afghan government in 1992 and the failure of the Mujahideen factions to achieve a consensus on a new political structure. Despite this, given that the Mujahideen included Muslim Afghans who had fought against the Soviet incursion, the Taliban felt compelled to derive religious justifications to rationalise their conflict with these groups. The credibility of the group's struggle with other Islamist factions was indeed unstable when judged by the established tenets of Islam and the cultural expectations of Afghan society.

To rationalise their aggressive campaign, the Taliban embraced a fresh ideological framework rooted in Jihadist Salafism. This Salafi ideology, advanced by organisations like Al-Qaeda under the leadership of Osama bin Laden, categorised Muslims into two groups: 'good Muslims' and 'bad Muslims'. This division permitted the 'good Muslims' to engage in warfare against the 'bad Muslims'. It served as the ideological basis for the Taliban's justification of their conflict with other Muslim factions in Afghanistan and aligned their ideology with transnational Salafi Jihadist groups like Al-Qaeda.

Therefore, in theory, the Taliban can be described as a fusion of Pakistani Deobandism and militant Salafism, rooted in a 'Takfiri' approach within Salafi Islam that categorises Muslims into 'true Muslims' and 'apostates'. This has subsequently become the fundamental ideology of the Taliban movement, establishing a strategic alignment with other groups, such as the Islamic State in Iraq and Syria (ISIS), with little theological disparities between them. The primary distinction between them is political, specifically about matters of leadership and tactics.

As previously articulated, the Taliban originated from the foundational principles of Deobandism, assimilating a considerable segment of their theological doctrines via instruction in Deobandi educational institutions. Given that an inordinate emphasis and predisposition towards political engagement constitutes the essence of these doctrines, the theological framework of the Taliban may be typologically classified as a variant of "political theology". Within the political theology articulated by the Taliban, the notion of 'politics' is perceived as the paramount goal, whereas the 'theological teachings' serve as the instruments utilised to realise this goal, regardless of the Taliban's declaration that their ambition for political dominance is primarily focused on upholding religious tenets and enacting 'God's law' (Zaeef, 1930, pp. 36-37).

As an astute analyst of Afghan political dynamics articulates, the Taliban were characterised as 'neither radical Islamists influenced by Ikhwan (the Muslim Brotherhood established in Egypt in 1928), nor mystical Sufis, nor traditionalists. The Taliban embodied solely their own identity and acknowledged no interpretation of Islam apart from their own.'

Javed Ahmad Ghamidi, a renowned Pakistani theologian, delineated four fundamental factors contributing to religious extremism that inform the ideologies of groups like the Taliban. The first principle asserts that polytheism and apostasy warrant capital punishment, a conviction that fuels the Taliban's violent acts, including attacks on Hazara Shias and the destruction of non-Islamic artefacts. This intolerance is consistent with extremist organisations such as Lashkar-e-Jhangvi and Sipah-i-Sahaba, which further bolster the Taliban's rigid doctrines. The second principle claims that non-Muslim governments lack legitimacy and that Muslim rulers who ally with them must be deposed, thereby rationalising the Taliban's targeted actions against leaders like President Burhanuddin Rabbani and Dr. Muhammad Najibullah for their failure to implement a genuine theocracy (Khan, 2024).

The third cause posited by Ghamidi is the advocacy for a unified Islamic caliphate, undermining the legitimacy of distinct Muslim states, as the Taliban aims to supplant Afghan nationalism with pan-Islamic allegiance. This ideology is reminiscent of the perspectives held by Muslim Brotherhood theorists such as Sayyid Qutb. The final cause involves the repudiation of the modern nation-state, perceived as a harmful Western imposition, which extremist factions, including the Taliban, aspire to abolish in favour of a rigorous application of Sharia. This perspective, underpinned by Wahhabism and Deobandism, fuels the Taliban's purported divine mandate to impose their interpretation of Islamic governance (Khan, 2024).

The Taliban's Relationship with the Afghan Nation and Nationhood

The Taliban articulates a multifaceted and frequently conflicting understanding of nationhood. This understanding is profoundly interwoven with both religious fundamentalism and ethnonationalism, culminating in a distinctive ideological framework that has propelled the Taliban's revival and preserved its impact. The concept of nationhood advocated by the Taliban goes beyond a simple political construct; it represents a fusion of religious and ethnic narratives that serve to legitimise its power and actions.

For a thorough understanding of Afghan nationhood, it is vital to analyse the doctrine of Pashtun nationalism. Pashtun nationalism functions as a political and cultural force striving to advance the interests and identity of the Pashtun demographic, predominantly inhabiting the regions of Afghanistan and Pakistan. This notable form of nationalism brings to light the shared language, culture, and historical narratives of the Pashtun ethnic group, often seeking enhanced autonomy or recognition within the expansive national frameworks of Afghanistan and Pakistan.

The interplay between the Taliban and Pashtun nationalism is characterised by its intricate and diverse nature. On one hand, the Taliban has been described as a group that embodies the key aspects of Pashtun ethnonationalism, especially considering its mainly Pashtun leadership and community backing. The group has been highlighted for its incorporation of Pashtun customs and narratives to frame its ideological structure and operational methods (Kamel, 2015), which some researchers assert places the Taliban as a modern manifestation of Pashtun nationalism (Kaplan, 2009).

On the other hand, although the Taliban assimilates certain features of Pashtun culture, it typically refrains from overt ethnic dialogue and occasionally confronts conventional Pashtun cultural customs that diverge from its radical religious principles (Gopal, 2016). This reflects a selective interaction with Pashtun nationalism, as the Taliban harnesses ethnic identity as a means for mobilisation and legitimisation, instead of treating it as a central ideological bond. Additionally, a substantial body of academic discourse argues against the portrayal of the Taliban as merely a Pashtun nationalist group. Critics argue that the movement includes individuals of non-Pashtun descent and serves broader strategic objectives, including those of Pakistan, which may aim to undermine Pashtun nationalism rather than promote it (Kamel, 2015). This highlights the Taliban's pragmatic strategy, where Pashtun nationalism is one of multiple narratives employed to achieve its objectives.

The identity of the Taliban is not confined to Pashtun nationalism; instead, it manifests as a nuanced combination of religious fundamentalism and ethnic identity. In some measure, this complexity is determined by regional dynamics, requiring the Taliban to handle its engagements with Pakistan and other regional participants expertly. The Taliban's adeptness in leveraging Pashtun identity in alignment with broader strategic pursuits showcases this multifaceted connection (Hyman, 2002).

Furthermore, the pursuits and frameworks of the group often resonate with the foreign policy aspirations of regional entities, such as Pakistan. Islamabad tactically utilises radical Islamism to offset Pashtun nationalism (Saikal, 2010). Fundamental to this argument is the longstanding reliance of the Taliban and Hekmatyar's Hezb-e Islami on the Inter-Services Intelligence (ISI) of Pakistan along with religious institutions. The argument suggests that Pakistan supports these factions to undermine and diminish the irredentist ambitions of the Pashtun community that contest the legitimacy of the Durand Line boundary between the two nations (Ibrahimi, 2023).

The Taliban's Appeal to Diverse Ethnic Groups

Afghanistan constitutes a multiethnic society, encompassing more than 30 distinct ethnic groups. Notwithstanding their geographical dispersion, numerous ethnic groups, including the Tajiks, Pashtuns, Uzbeks, Hazaras, and Turkmen, maintain profound cross-border connections with adjacent nations. A salient characteristic among Afghan ethnicities is their propensity to assert dominance over one another. These hegemonic inclinations manifest in their ethnic narratives, which aspire to unify their ethnic counterparts across borders, exemplified by the Pashtun ambition for a consolidated Loy Pakhtunistan (Great Pakhtunistan), the Tajiks' conception of Khorasan-e-Bozorg (Greater Khorasan) and Anjuman Tajikan Jahan (the World Council of Tajiks), as well as the Pan-Turkist aspirations of the Uzbek community. The Taliban do not deviate from this trend. Largely composed of Pashtuns, the Taliban persist as a formidable entity within Afghanistan. Nevertheless, their power distribution, predominantly Pashtun-centric, facilitates the emergence of ethnic fault lines (Ali, 2024).

In the 1990s, the Taliban sought alliances with non-Pashtun entities. Fighters were mobilised nationally, while local militias were integrated to manage specific regions post-disarmament under Taliban agreements. These militias comprised the Hazaras, Uzbeks, and Tajiks. Their political affiliations were diverse, encompassing former members from parties, such as Hizb-i Islami, Jamiat-i Islami, and Junbesh-i Milli, and Shiite factions like Hizb-i Wahdat and Harakat-i Islami (Giustozzi, 2010).

The Taliban in the past faced considerable challenges in their attempts to recruit northern Tajiks and Uzbeks. This situation is not primarily attributable to the notion that these ethnic groups possess a greater inclination towards liberalism compared to the Pashtuns, as there is a considerable reservoir of deeply conservative sentiments within the Tajik and Uzbek populations. Rather, this challenge stems from the profoundly negative experiences associated with Taliban governance in these regions, during which the Taliban "armies" perpetrated various abuses against numerous northern Tajik and Uzbek communities (Giustozzi, 2010).

At present, ethnic power dynamics are observable. To mitigate ethnic dissent, the Taliban prioritised the enlistment of non-Pashtun individuals in northern regions. This strategy significantly facilitated the Taliban's northern conquest in August 2021, eliminating the necessity for deploying Pashtuns from southern areas. Initially, local leaders were appointed as governors and district heads. However, subsequently, various Taliban administrators of Uzbek, Tajik, and Hazara descent were supplanted by Kandahari Pashtuns, occasionally inciting local disputes.

There also exists an increasing ethnic rivalry within the Taliban, notably among factions such as the Haqqani Network and other regional commanders (Siddique, 2022). Non-Pashtun Taliban members are aware of the prevailing Pashtun dominance, leading to ethnic tensions within the Taliban ranks. In March 2022, Salahuddin Ayubi, a prominent Uzbek commander, was demoted from his military role. In October 2022, he declared his refusal to participate until the Taliban implemented measures for an inclusive governance structure and educational access for women and halted land seizures (Ali, 2024).

Ethnic power dynamics and policy disagreements weaken Taliban unity. Their focus on Pashtun identity escalates ethnic tensions, both internally and externally. Regional stakeholders advocate for an inclusive governance structure reflecting Afghanistan's diverse ethnic groups. The Taliban's ongoing ethnic discrimination fosters an environment ripe for civil war, threatening Afghanistan with renewed conflict and worsening an already fragile situation.

The Taliban's Impact on Human Rights

In the preceding two decades, Afghanistan has achieved significant progress in the domain of human rights, supported by vigorous efforts to uphold freedom of expression, establish democratic structures, promote gender equality, improve access to education and healthcare, and foster a more inclusive societal framework. Afghanistan has been acknowledged as a commendable regional standard exemplified by a robust media framework and a spirited exchange of ideas.

The re-emergence of the Taliban in Afghanistan, paired with the following disintegration of the previously recognised republic on August 15, 2021, has caused a notable setback in the developments obtained in the field of human rights and the foundations of a free society.

In the late 1990s, during their prior governance, the Taliban regime implemented a highly restrictive interpretation of Sharia law, significantly diminishing both individual and collective liberties (Maizland, 2023). Women and girls experienced abhorrent treatment, which included the denial of access to education, employment opportunities, healthcare services, and freedom of movement. Public executions, amputations, and floggings effectively suppressed dissent and restricted freedom of expression.

The Taliban initially promised a more lenient governance style compared to their earlier dominion from 1996 to 2001; however, they progressively revived their uncompromising interpretation of Islamic law, often referred to as Sharia. The current administration consistently curtails freedom of expression, constraining independent media entities and employing intimidation tactics against individuals who exhibit dissenting viewpoints (Ramizi, 2023). Such repressive measures, encompassing incarceration and even threats of lethal violence, obstruct the democratic process and hinder the essential exchange of ideas.

The position of the Taliban regarding female education and women's rights raises significant concerns. UNESCO indicates that around 1.2 million Afghan girls have been barred from secondary education and higher learning. The International Labour Organization notes a 25 per cent decline in female employment in Afghanistan since the Taliban's resurgence (Ramizi, 2023).

In addition to prohibiting girls and women from obtaining education beyond sixth grade, most forms of employment, and many public venues, the Taliban have harassed or beaten women at checkpoints for not wearing a hijab, or Islamic headscarf, according to Volker Turk, chief of UN Human Rights Council (*PBS News*, 2023).The Taliban have forced women to return home following shopping trips without a male guardian. According to the report, women and girls have less opportunities for legal representation and access to justice since female lawyers and judges are barred from working or practising the law (*PBS News*, 2023).

The Taliban's interpretation of political parties, civil society, and human rights is fundamentally flawed. They assert that these notions are of Western origin and inherently incompatible with Islamic principles and Afghan cultural norms. Following their resurgence, they have prohibited female participation in non-governmental organisations (NGOs), curtailed their operational scope, and disbanded the division tasked with the registration of civil society entities and political parties within the Ministry of Justice. This has culminated in the dissolution of over 5,000 civil society organisations and 84 political parties. Presently, only approximately 5,791 NGOs that are registered with the Ministry of Economy are permitted to function for humanitarian and educational objectives. Nonetheless, owing to fiscal constraints and physical intimidation, 95 per cent of these organisations have been compelled to cease operations or to engage solely in online activities from international locations (Ramizi, 2023).

Challenges and Dilemmas of External Powers

The ascendancy of the Taliban in Afghanistan has posed a considerable obstacle for external actors, especially those that have endeavoured to advocate for Western principles and exert influence within the region. The group's repudiation of Western standards and its prioritisation of Sharia law as the cornerstone for governance significantly hinder diplomatic interactions and the dynamics of international relations.

The Taliban has traditionally conceptualised democracy as a "Western construct" that fundamentally contradicts the tenets of Islamic doctrine. This inflexible ideological stance not only estranges prospective allies but also exacerbates any endeavours aimed at fostering constructive discourse with external powers aspiring to exert influence over Afghanistan's political milieu.

The Taliban's disregard for fundamental rights pertaining to Afghan women and girls, together with the enforcement of rigid social regulations after their re-ascendancy to power in August 2021, has adversely affected its diplomatic interactions with global entities, thereby limiting Afghanistan's socio-economic and political growth.

Regional and Western stakeholders are unable to attain a consensus regarding the most suitable strategy for engagement with the Taliban. Even after the total withdrawal of all foreign military forces from Afghanistan,

Western nations still grapple with a cultural conflict. The United States, in partnership with its allies, advocates for the Taliban to remove their limitations on women's rights; nonetheless, the Taliban remains firm in rejecting what they interpret as an imposition of a feminist ideology.

Governments globally have urged the Taliban to establish an inclusive administration. During pre-August 2021 peace negotiations in Doha, the Taliban proposed power-sharing with rival Afghan factions to conclude hostilities. However, following their military success, they asserted the prerogative to exclude non-Taliban politicians from governmental roles. Taliban officials argue that "inclusivity" is merely an ambiguous concept, potentially ranging from broader governance participation (which they may consider, at least for men) to the inclusion of figures from the ousted government (which they reject).

Thus, Afghanistan persists in a state of deadlock, lacking a feasible trajectory for the government to extricate itself from its pariah designation, alleviate sanctions, and obtain representation within the United Nations. The Taliban steadfastly reject any compromises that would compromise their stature among core constituents and, in their perspective, tarnish their ethical principles. Conversely, Western officials contend that endorsing diplomats from a regime that so overtly discriminates against women would be antithetical to their own values and politically detrimental.

The policies of regional nations towards the Taliban exhibit significant variability; however, there exists a consensus regarding the necessity of maintaining communication with the regime, albeit their engagement has thus far been minimal. Kabul, along with its neighbouring partners, is making efforts to establish a modus vivendi on shared issues, including enhancing trade, addressing water resource disputes, and curbing transnational militancy. This undertaking is fraught with challenges; nevertheless, it is deemed invaluable, and Western capitals ought not to obstruct this process.

Even as Western diplomats withdrew from engagements with the Taliban, regional actors pursued increased interactions with Kabul. Despite the criticism surrounding the Taliban's treatment of women, especially in education, regional officials tend to overlook these concerns. Concurrently, they believe that sustained dialogue with Kabul is more effective than isolation for safeguarding national interests and influencing Taliban conduct.

The connections formed between Kabul and regional capitals seem to provide the Taliban with significant prospects for diplomatic relations in the forthcoming years.

The level of regional collaboration has not aligned with what Afghanistan's neighbours anticipated. Some advocated for a comprehensive agreement that would associate diplomatic recognition with the Taliban's commitment to inclusive governance, particularly emphasising support for Afghan politicians they had previously endorsed. The Taliban dismissed efforts to include former adversaries in governance. Consequently, regional actors have largely resorted to selective engagement with Kabul, tackling issues individually. This strategy, more out of necessity than intent, coincides with the Taliban's preference for transactional relations that minimise perceived foreign interference in Afghan matters.

For its part, China is advocating for the extradition of Uyghur militants from the Taliban, who favour their relocation away from the border. Central Asian states share similar security dilemmas and responses. Pakistan, a longstanding supporter of the Taliban, urges action against the Tehreek-e-Taliban Pakistan (TTP), a militant group engaged in conflict with Islamabad since 2007. Despite Taliban assertions, the TTP operates in Afghanistan, and TTP-related violence in Pakistan has surged since mid-2021, resulting in a significant increase in fatalities compared to the preceding two years (Bahiss & Smith, 2023).

The ongoing presence of the Islamic State Khorasan Province in Afghanistan poses a significant concern for residents and Western nations. Taliban forces have effectively targeted ISKP leaders, often with foreign intelligence support. However, the Taliban has not fully eradicated the group, raising fears among neighbouring countries about potential threats emanating from Afghanistan. Trust issues hinder effective information-sharing between the Taliban and regional or international security agencies (Bahiss & Smith, 2023).

Three years after the Taliban's assumption of authority, it is pertinent to heed the perspectives of neighbouring nations that currently allocate significantly greater attention to dialogues with Kabul's newly established governance than Western diplomatic entities and who stand to incur the most detriment should the nation deteriorate. They assert that the global community must prevent Afghanistan from devolving into a failed state, contending that international seclusion will merely exacerbate the challenges in engaging with the Taliban. Advancing and endorsing regional collaboration does not equate to relinquishing aspirations for negotiations between the Taliban and the international community regarding attaining formal recognition.

Conclusion

The comprehension of the Taliban's ideological framework and its resultant effects on governance is imperative for both the prospective trajectory of Afghanistan and the dynamics of international relations within the region. As the Taliban 2.0 has now completed three years in power, the forthcoming challenge lies in reconciling its ideological principles with the exigencies of contemporary governance and the multifaceted requirements of Afghan society. The future trajectory remains ambiguous; however, the cultivation of dialogue and the advocacy for human rights will be pivotal in constructing a stable and inclusive Afghanistan. The global community must persist in its vigilance and engagement, meticulously balancing humanitarian concerns with steadfast commitments to human rights and governance principles.

References

Ali, U. (July 16, 2024). "Afghanistan's ethnic faultlines under Taliban rule". Centre for Strategic and Contemporary Research. https://cscr.pk/explore/themes/politics-governance/afghanistans-ethnic-faultlines-under-taliban-rule/

Bahiss, I. & Smith, G. (August 11, 2023). "The World Has No Choice But to Work With the Taliban: How to Help Afghanistan Without Normalizing Relations". *Foreign Affairs*. https://www.foreignaffairs.com/afghanistan/world-has-no-choice-work-taliban

Giustozzi, A. (2010). "The Taliban Beyond the Pashtuns (Afghanistan Paper #5)". Centre for International Governance Innovation. https://www.cigionline.org/publications/taliban-beyond-pashtuns/

Gopal, A. (2016). "The Combined and Uneven Development of Afghan Nationalism". *Studies in Ethnicity and Nationalism*, *16*(3), pp. 478–492. https://doi.org/10.1111/sena.12206

Hyman, A. (2002). "Nationalism in Afghanistan". *International journal of Middle East studies*, *34*(2), pp. 299-315.

Ibrahimi, N. (2023). "A Violent Nexus: Ethnonationalism, Religious Fundamentalism, and the Taliban". *The Review of Faith & International Affairs*, *21*(3), pp. 22–37. https://doi.org/10.1080/15570274.2023.2235809

Kamel, K. (2015). "Understanding Taliban Resurgence: Ethno Symbolism and Revolutionary Mobilization". *Studies in Ethnicity and Nationalism, 15*(1), pp. 66–82. https://doi.org/10.1111/sena.12128

Kaplan, R. D. (2009). "The revenge of geography". *Foreign Policy*, (172), pp. 96-105.

Khan, N. (February 15, 2024). "Sifting Facts from Fiction: The Underpinnings of the Taliban's 'Islamic Emirate'". *The SAIS Review of International Affairs*. https://saisreview.sais.jhu.edu/sifting-facts-from-fiction-the-underpinnings-of-the-talibans-islamic-emirate/#_ftnref15

Maizland, L. (January 19, 2023). "The Taliban in Afghanistan". Council on Foreign Relations. https://www.cfr.org/backgrounder/taliban-afghanistan#chapter-title-0-6

Pal, A. (September 17, 2021). "Taliban replaces women's ministry with ministry of virtue and vice". *Reuters*. https://www.reuters.com/world/asia-pacific/taliban-replaces-womens-ministry-with-ministry-virtue-vice-2021-09-17/

PBS News (September 12, 2023). "The Taliban have waged a systematic assault on freedom in Afghanistan, says UN human rights chief". https://www.pbs.org/newshour/politics/the-taliban-have-waged-a-systematic-assault-on-freedom-in-afghanistan-says-un-human-rights-chief

Ramizy, M. K. (July 10, 2023). "Human Rights Situation Under Taliban Regime". Friedrich Naumann Foundation. https://www.freiheit.org/south-asia/human-rights-situation-under-taliban-regime

Rashid, A. (June 5, 2014). "Pakistan: Worse Than We Knew". *The New York Review of Books*. https://www.nybooks.com/articles/2014/06/05/pakistan-worse-than-we-knew/

Saikal, A. (2010). "Afghanistan and Pakistan: The Question of Pashtun Nationalism?" *Journal of Muslim Minority Affairs, 30*(1), pp. 5-17.

Siddique, A. (June 2, 2022). "'Unprecedented Differences': Rifts Within The Taliban Come Out In The Open". *RadioFreeEurope/RadioLiberty*. https://www.rferl.org/a/taliban-rifts-exposed-afghanistan/31880018.html

Zaeef, M. A. S. (1930). *Taliban From Kandahar to Mazar: Vol. First*. Aksos.

4 Nationhood in Afghanistan through the Lens of the Great Game and the Graveyard of Empires

Shekhar B. Ashtikar

Introduction

Afghanistan is a landlocked nation in South and Central Asia that borders China to the northeast, Turkmenistan, Uzbekistan, and Tajikistan to the north, Pakistan to the east and south, and Iran to the west. Its terrain is characterised by rough mountains, dry deserts, and rich valleys, and it covers an area of about 652,230 square kilometres (251,830 square miles). Much of the central and northeastern regions are dominated by the Hindu Kush mountain range, which has the 7,492-metre (24,580-foot) high peak, Noshaq. Afghanistan's political disarray and poor internal connectedness have historically been impacted by this topography (Barfield, 2010). Extreme seasonal changes, including hot summers and freezing winters, are a feature of the country's continental climate, particularly in mountainous areas. In an otherwise arid climate, the Amu Darya, Helmand, Kabul, and Hari Rud Rivers are essential water sources that support human settlement and cultivation (Dupree, 1973). Afghanistan has always been a hub for trade, conquest, and cultural exchange due to its advantageous location at the intersection of South Asia, Central Asia, and the Middle East. According to archaeological findings, humans have lived on the planet for at least 50,000 years, with the first agricultural towns appearing around 3000 BCE. One of the first urban societies in history, the Indus Valley Civilisation, included the area. Afghanistan was part of a wide Persian imperial network under the Achaemenid empire (c. 550–330 BCE), with cities like Bactra (Balkh) acting as administrative and cultural centres (Frye, 1992). The Greco-Bactrian kingdom, which blended Hellenistic and indigenous cultural aspects, was formed as a result of Greek influence brought by Alexander the Great in 330 BCE. The colossal Buddhas of Bamiyan, which remained in place for centuries before being destroyed in 2001, are proof that the later Kushan empire (1st–3rd century CE) promoted trade along the Silk Road and contributed significantly to the development of Buddhism (Hansen, 2017). Afghanistan gradually converted to Islam as a result of the Islamic conquests in the seventh century CE, initially under the Umayyads and then under the Abbasids. It developed into a disputed area during the Middle Ages between transcontinental and regional forces, such as the Mongols, Samanids, Ghaznavids, and Ghurids. With its capital at Ghazni, the Ghaznavid empire (977–1186 CE) was a pinnacle of Persianised Islamic rule and encouraged the spread of Islam throughout the Indian subcontinent (Bosworth, 1977). Genghis Khan's Mongol raids in the 13th century decimated the area, destroying cities and interfering with trade. Nonetheless, cities like Herat developed into hubs of Persianate culture and scholarship throughout the Timurid dynasty (14th–15th century CE) (Soucek, 2000). Up until the advent of the Hotak dynasty (1709–1738) and subsequently the Durrani empire (1747–1823), which is frequently considered the origin of the modern Afghan state, Afghanistan was disputed by the Safavids, Mughals, and Uzbeks in the early modern era. The empire's founder, Ahmad Shah Durrani, united different Pashtun clans and expanded his dominion into what are now India, Pakistan, and Iran. Afghanistan's current political landscape was shaped after his death by both internal strife and external forces, especially those from the British empire and Tsarist Russia. The Great Game, the geopolitical contest between Russia and Britain for dominance in Central Asia, centred on Afghanistan throughout the 19th century (Hopkirk, 1992). Afghanistan fought against British interference during the Anglo-Afghan Wars (1839–1842, 1878–1880, and 1919). Afghanistan gained complete independence from British rule following the Third Anglo-Afghan War (1919), and King Amanullah Khan instituted modernising measures. But the 20th century was marred by foreign interventions, coups, and political instability. A decade-long battle, civil unrest, and the establishment of the Taliban government in the 1990s were all brought on by the Soviet invasion in 1979. Afghanistan's current geopolitical and societal issues are still shaped by the U.S.-led intervention in 2001 and the decades of struggle that followed (Rubin, 1995). Over the course of millennia, Afghanistan's distinct terrain and history have significantly influenced its political and cultural character.

The nation is a centre for trade, conquest, and cultural exchange, frequently acting as a meeting place for civilisations due to its strategic location at the intersection of South Asia, Central Asia, and the Middle East. In the past, its hilly landscape—which is dominated by the Hindu Kush—has served as a barrier and a route for invasions and migrations. Afghanistan's political fragmentation has been greatly exacerbated by its rocky terrain, which makes central control difficult and permits local tribal and ethnic groups to retain a high level of autonomy (Barfield, 2010). Afghanistan's early history is strongly linked to its participation in a number of empires and trade routes, such as the Silk Road, which linked the Mediterranean, China, India, and Persia. Ancient cities like Balkh, known as the "mother of cities", were important hubs for education and culture. Sites like the Buddhas of Bamiyan, which were colossal symbols of Buddhist influence until the Taliban destroyed them in 2001, demonstrate Afghanistan's historical ties to Buddhism (Hansen, 2017). Islam increasingly supplanted previous Buddhist and Zoroastrian traditions, bringing about significant cultural and theological changes in the 7th century CE. Several Islamic dynasties, such as the Samanids, Ghaznavids, and Ghurids, fought in the area and spread their power throughout the Indian subcontinent (Frye, 1992). Afghanistan played a significant role in the spread of Persianate culture during the Middle Ages. Great intellectuals like Al-Biruni and Ferdowsi were produced in Afghanistan, which developed into a hub of Persian-Islamic civilisation under the administration of Mahmud of Ghazni (998–1030 CE). The area was later destroyed by the Mongol invasions in the 13th century CE, but it was restored during the Timurid empire in the 14th and 15th centuries CE, with Herat becoming a significant centre of culture and thought (Soucek, 2000). Afghanistan's position as a buffer between strong neighbouring states was reflected in the early modern era, when it was disputed by the Mughal, Safavid, and Uzbek empires. Under Ahmad Shah Durrani, a Pashtun commander who united different Afghan tribes and extended his rule into modern-day Iran, Pakistan, and India, the Durrani empire (1747–1823) was established, marking the beginning of modern Afghanistan. However, his successors found it difficult to stay in power, which resulted in both foreign interventions and internal disintegration. The Great Game, a geopolitical conflict between the British empire and Tsarist Russia over control of Central Asia, cantered on Afghanistan by the 19th century.

The establishment of Afghan nationhood is a complex and multifaceted endeavour. Afghanistan's ethnic diversity, tribal allegiances, and history of foreign intervention have resulted in a fragmented political and social framework, rendering the notion of a cohesive Afghan nation-state elusive. This paper conducts a historical analysis of these imperial rivalries and their repercussions, exploring how foreign intervention and internal dynamics have influenced Afghanistan's national identity.

The Great Game and its Impact on Afghan Nationhood

The Great Game was a geopolitical conflict between the British empire and the Russian empire in the 19th and early 20th centuries, concentrating principally on Afghanistan and Central Asia. Britain, fearing Russian encroachment into its prized colony of India, intended to keep Afghanistan as a buffer state, whilst Russia sought to expand its influence southward. This competition resulted in a number of diplomatic moves, intelligence operations, and military confrontations, including the Anglo-Afghan Wars. The Great Game reshaped Afghanistan's political landscape, cementing its status as a battleground for world powers. Though it officially ended with the Anglo-Russian Convention of 1907, the struggle for regional control lasted into the 20th and 21st centuries.

British Involvement and the First Anglo-Afghan War (1839-1842)

Protecting India, their most valuable colony, against possible Russian expansion was the strategic reason for the British involvement in Afghanistan throughout the 19th century. Russia and Britain fought for control of Central Asia in this geopolitical conflict, which was later dubbed the 'Great Game', with Afghanistan acting as a vital buffer state (Hopkirk, 1992). During the

First Anglo-Afghan War (1839–1842), the British were directly concerned that Afghanistan, ruled by Dost Mohammad Khan, may turn to Russia and endanger British sovereignty over India (Dalrymple, 2013). The British invasion of Afghanistan in 1838 was ostensibly intended to reinstate the exiled Afghan ruler, Shah Shuja Durrani. The British Governor-General of India, Lord Auckland, planned the military operation because he thought it would benefit Britain to replace Dost Mohammad with Shah Shuja, who was more amenable (Tanner, 2009). Armed with both Indian and British soldiers, the British formed the Army of the Indus and proceeded through the Bolan Pass and Sindh. They entered Kabul in 1839 and installed Shah Shuja as a puppet monarch after successfully capturing Ghazni and Kandahar (Dalrymple, 2013). However, the Afghan populace, who saw Shah Shuja as a foreign-imposed leader and remained faithful to Dost Mohammad, made it difficult for the British to win their allegiance despite their early military victories (Noelle, 1997).Widespread unrest followed over the next two years from growing hatred against British occupation. Due to their strong sense of independence and tribal identity, the Afghans were extremely hostile to British taxes and involvement (Dalrymple, 2013). By 1841, a widespread uprising was the result of anti-British feeling. The British garrison was forced into a defensive position in November 1841 due to an uprising in Kabul, which marked a turning point. Dost Mohammad's son, Afghan chieftain Akbar Khan, assassinated British diplomat Sir William Macnaghten amid rising unrest (Hopkirk, 1992). As a result of the rapidly worsening circumstances, the legendary withdrawal from Kabul occurred in January 1842. During this difficult winter retreat, one of the biggest military catastrophes in British history occurred. According to Tanner (2009), only one European, Dr William Brydon, reportedly made it to Jalalabad out of the about 16,000 fleeing soldiers and camp followers; the others were either murdered or arrested. In revenge, the British conducted a punitive expedition in 1842, briefly retaking Kabul and demolishing portions of the city before leaving it completely (Dalrymple, 2013). Following the assassination of Shah Shuja, Dost Mohammad regained power. The war represented a humiliating failure for British imperial aims and highlighted the challenge of imposing foreign rule on Afghanistan (Hopkirk, 1992). The First Anglo-Afghan War was an important influence on Afghan nationhood. Even though Afghanistan had historically been a tribally divided society, the war strengthened the sense of patriotism against outside intervention. Afghanistan's long-standing tribal and ethnic divisions were brought to light by the battle, but it also strengthened the country's sense of identity through resistance to outside influences (Noelle, 1997).

The final restoration of Dost Muhammad cemented the Barakzai dynasty's dominance and influenced the contemporary political system in Afghanistan. A motif that would recur throughout Afghanistan's history, including subsequent wars against the British, Soviets, and Americans, was the war's establishment of Afghan tenacity in the face of international powers (Tanner, 2009). The conflict taught the British a sobering lesson about the dangers of going to war in Afghanistan. It made clear the shortcomings of their military plan and the risks associated with underestimating Afghan resistance. British policy toward Afghanistan consequently changed from direct occupation to indirect influence (Hopkirk, 1992). However, the First Anglo-Afghan War did not signal the end of British involvement in the region; Afghanistan's geopolitical trajectory was still shaped by later conflicts, especially the Second Anglo-Afghan War (1878–1880) (Dalrymple, 2013).

Second Anglo-Afghan War (1878-1880)

A crucial struggle between the British empire and Afghanistan, the Second Anglo-Afghan War (1878-1880), profoundly influenced the political climate of the area and shaped Afghan national identity. British concerns about Russian expansion in Central Asia, which endangered British rule over India, were the root cause of the war. Afghanistan became a strategically important buffer state during the 'Great Game' between Russia and Britain. Britain invaded Afghanistan in 1878 because Afghan Emir Sher Ali Khan declined to accept a British diplomatic mission while hosting a Russian one, citing a security danger (Kakar, 1979). In November 1878, the British began a military operation that quickly occupied key Afghan regions by moving through the Khyber Pass, Kandahar, and Quetta. Yakub Khan signed the Treaty of Gandamak (May 1879), which gave Britain authority over Afghanistan's foreign policy and gave up important frontier territories like the Kurram, Pishin, and Sibi districts, after Sher Ali Khan retreated to Mazar-i-Sharif and passed away in early 1879 (Dalrymple, 2013). Afghan resistance, however, meant that British dominance was short-lived. Following the death of British envoy Sir Louis Cavagnari in Kabul in September 1879, Britain responded by reoccupying the city. Widespread Afghan uprisings followed, which culminated in a national conflict commanded by Yakub's half-brother, Ayub Khan. Ayub Khan's victory over the British at the Battle of Maiwand in July 1880 demonstrated the tenacity of the Afghan military (Robson, 2007). However, at the Battle of Kandahar (September 1880), British forces, under General Frederick Roberts, mounted a counteroffensive and defeated Ayub Khan, bringing the war to a close. Afghanistan's national identity was significantly impacted by the conflict. Even though the British left Afghanistan in 1881, their meddling strengthened Afghan nationalism by bringing disparate ethnic groups together to fight a common foe. The conflict strengthened Afghanistan's position as an independent country, despite British influence outside, and showed its opposition to foreign domination. The establishment of the modern Afghan state began with the coronation of Abdur Rahman Khan as Emir (1880-1901). Through centralisation, the repression of tribal uprisings, and the Durand Line Agreement (1893) with British India—later a source of territorial disputes—Abdur Rahman established control in Afghanistan (Gregorian, 1969). Afghanistan's current national identity was shaped by resistance and self-determination during the Second Anglo-Afghan War, which solidified the notion of Afghanistan as an autonomous nation apart from both the Russian empire and British India.

Afghanistan as a Graveyard of Empires

Afghanistan has long been known as the 'Graveyard of Empires', a phrase that emphasises the country's past as a battlefield where powerful nations have fought before ultimately failing. Afghanistan's complex socio-political processes, harsh terrain, and fierce tribal opposition have all contributed to its reputation as a country that has historically resisted Western dominance. From the armies of Alexander the Great in the fourth century BCE to the American, British, and Soviet operations in the 19th, 20th, and 21st centuries, empires have had a difficult time bringing Afghanistan under control. While Afghanistan's dispersed tribal civilisation has resisted centralised rule, making long-term occupation extremely difficult, the country's rugged mountains and deep valleys have naturally favoured local guerrilla fighters. Major nations' failure in Afghanistan has strengthened its reputation as an insurmountable nation, solidifying its status as a country that defies subjugation in world history (Barfield, 2010). Afghanistan's ability to withstand imperial domination in the face of military loss was demonstrated during the Second Anglo-Afghan War (1878-1880). Despite their superior weaponry and early successes, the British encountered fierce opposition from Afghan tribes. The British eventually withdrew because their control was still shaky even after they appointed Abdur Rahman Khan as Emir. The Soviet invasion (1979-1989) took a similar course a century later. Mujahideen forces fiercely opposed the Soviet Union's attempt to instal a communist regime in Afghanistan, using both domestic support and outside aid from Pakistan and the United States. Soviet resources and morale were depleted by the war, which ultimately led to the USSR's demise (Grau & Gress, 2002). This further solidified Afghanistan's position as the 'Graveyard of Empires'. The U.S. and NATO engagement (2001-2021), which was initiated to destroy terrorist networks and overthrow the Taliban, similarly ended in departure after 20 years. No matter how sophisticated, foreign military operations have failed to establish long-term peace in Afghanistan, as evidenced by the Taliban's 2021 comeback to power (Giustozzi, 2018). Afghan nationhood is a complicated idea that has been created by centuries of defiance against outside authority rather than by a single ethnic or political identity. The Pashtuns, Tajiks, Hazaras, Uzbeks, and other ethnic groups make up the diversified people of Afghanistan, each having their own unique language and cultural traditions. Afghanistan's historical identity has been based on a balance between national sovereignty and tribal autonomy, in contrast to the contemporary nation-state model that is centred on centralised governance. During the rule of Abdur Rahman Khan (1880–1901), who aimed to consolidate power, put down uprisings, and establish a single, cohesive authority over the nation, contemporary Afghan nationhood began to take shape. Although his policies established Afghanistan's territorial integrity, the idea of a single Afghan identity remained elusive since tribal and regional affiliations continued to hold sway (Gregorian, 1969). Afghanistan's fight for independence persisted throughout the 20th century in spite of both internal and external obstacles. Afghanistan's sovereignty was strengthened after the Third Anglo-Afghan War in 1919 and the signing of the Treaty of

Rawalpindi, which gave the country complete independence from British rule. However, different rulers adopted diverse strategies for nation-building since there was a lack of effective central governance. King Amanullah Khan (1919-1929) made an effort at modernisation, but reactionary groups opposed his changes, which ultimately led to his collapse. Ethnic divides and political instability remained despite the efforts of later rulers, such as Zahir Shah (1933-1973), to unite Afghanistan through gradual modernisation (Poullada, 1973). Afghan nationhood was put to the ultimate test in the 20th and 21st centuries as foreign interventions and succeeding administrations sought to influence the political system of the nation. In the 1980s the Soviet-backed government in Afghanistan tried to enforce socialist reforms that threatened the traditional social order. Tribal elders and religious leaders, who held deep influence over local communities, strongly resisted these changes, leading to widespread rebellion and undermining national cohesion by deepening divisions between the government and the people.

The Taliban's attempt to enforce a rigid religious identity during its 1996–2001 administration alienated non-Pashtun tribes and widened rifts. The U.S.-backed government (2001–2021) made an effort at democratic reforms but found it difficult to reconcile rural conservatism with urban modernism. Each resistance movement strengthened the nation's longstanding defiance of foreign control, and the concept of Afghan sovereignty remained fundamental to national identity in spite of these obstacles (Giustozzi, 2008).

Afghanistan's national identity has also been significantly shaped by its geopolitical location. Despite being a crossroads of civilisations, Afghanistan has retained its unique character based on freedom and self-determination while also being impacted by Persian, Indian, Turkic, and Arab cultures. Many Afghans do not acknowledge the Durand Line Agreement (1893), which divided Afghanistan from British India (now Pakistan). They consider it a colonial imposition that split Pashtun groups. As a result, the agreement is still controversial. Afghanistan's relations with its neighbours are still impacted by this unresolved border conflict, which also fuels the country's continued instability (Barfield, 2010). Afghans continue to place a high value on the country's independence and invincibility despite its past difficulties. The phrase 'Graveyard of Empires' refers to more than just a historical designation; it also captures Afghanistan's unwavering devotion to sovereignty and its steadfast opposition to outside interference. The common experience of opposing foreign rule has served as a unifying factor and shaped Afghanistan's national consciousness throughout generations, despite the fact that internal conflicts and outside forces have frequently threatened Afghan nationhood. Regardless of outside efforts to influence its future, Afghanistan will remain a major actor in regional and international affairs because of its continued tribal autonomy, cultural variety, and geopolitical importance.

US-NATO Intervention from 2001 to 2021

The 2001-2021 US and NATO intervention in Afghanistan had a significant impact on the political climate and national identity of the country. The intervention, which was started in reaction to the September 11 attacks, sought to destroy Al-Qaeda and stop Afghanistan from becoming a safe haven for terrorists. Even if there have been some initial military victories, the long-term effects for Afghan nationhood are intricate and varied. NATO made its first operational commitment outside of Europe in August 2003 when it took over command of the International Security Assistance Force (ISAF). In order to facilitate rebuilding and the formation of democratic governance, the ISAF's aim was to help establish security throughout Afghanistan. Notwithstanding these initiatives, the insurgency turned out to be more resilient than expected, resulting in protracted hostilities and instability. The US invested almost $2 trillion over the course of the two-decade engagement, with additional funding coming from NATO partners. Notwithstanding these expenditures, the Taliban's quick and mainly uncontested restoration to power in 2021 was made possible by NATO's abrupt withdrawal, casting doubt on the success of outside nation-building initiatives. Afghan nationhood has been significantly impacted by the extended foreign presence and the Taliban's ultimate return. Attempts to create a centralised democratic state during the intervention period frequently ran afoul of Afghanistan's intricate social structure, which is marked by strong regional and tribal relations. A reassessment of national identity, sovereignty, and the role of outside forces in determining Afghanistan's destiny has resulted from the sudden pull-out and the Taliban's comeback. Although Afghanistan's political and social systems saw substantial changes as a result of the US and NATO operation, its effects on Afghan nationhood are still being examined and discussed.

Disintegration of Afghan National Identity

The nationhood of Afghanistan has been significantly divided due to international interventions and domestic resistance, resulting in a complex interaction of external influence and internal processes that has persistently redefined its national identity. Afghanistan's historical ethnic diversity, comprising the Pashtuns, Tajiks, Hazaras, and Uzbeks, has cultivated a vibrant cultural landscape while simultaneously presenting obstacles to centralised authority. Foreign interventions have frequently intensified these internal divisions, hindering attempts to establish a unified national identity. The Soviet invasion in 1979 serves as a significant illustration. The ensuing decade-long occupation not only exacerbated internal dissent but also increased ethnic and sectarian divisions. The Mujahideen factions, initially unified against a common adversary, subsequently turned on one another following the withdrawal, resulting in a devastating civil war. This period revealed the fragility of Afghan unity and the ease with which external pressures may aggravate internal strife (Rubin, 1995). The US-led operation in 2001, aimed at dismantling terrorist networks and creating democratic governance, significantly strained Afghanistan's national cohesion. While earlier attempts concentrated on constructing centralised state institutions, they often clashed with traditional power structures and local practices. The imposition of Western political models without proper consideration of Afghanistan's unique social fabric led to governance issues and disenfranchisement among diverse communities (Bizhan, 2024). Internal opposition forces, exemplified by the rise of the Taliban, exploited these divisions. The Taliban's return to power in 2021 emphasised the continuing fractures within Afghan society and the problems of forging a cohesive national identity amidst opposing ideologies and other pressures. Their stringent interpretation of Islamic law and centralisation attempts sometimes alienated non-Pashtun people, further entrenching ethnic and sectarian boundaries (Najam, 2024). In essence, Afghanistan's road toward coherent nationhood has been repeatedly disturbed by the interaction of international operations and internal resistance. Each external engagement has not only failed to unify the nation but has often reinforced existing tensions, leaving a legacy of fragmentation that threatens the entire notion of a unified Afghan identity.

Tribal and Ethnic Loyalties

Tribal and ethnic loyalties are at the heart of Afghanistan's fractured nationhood and have long thwarted attempts to forge a single, cohesive national identity. With Pashtuns, Tajiks, Hazaras, Uzbeks, and a number of minor ethnic groups—all with unique historical, cultural, and linguistic identities—the nation is home to a diverse population. Internal disputes, geopolitical interventions, and government systems that frequently give preference to one group over another have all contributed to these splits. The absence of a dominant national identity that cuts across these differences is one of the main reasons tribal and ethnic allegiances have weakened Afghan nationhood. With the Durrani Pashtun monarchy dominating from the 18th century to the 20th century, the Pashtuns—historically the largest ethnic group—have dominated Afghan politics (Barfield, 2010). Other ethnic groups, especially the Tajiks and Hazaras, who were frequently excluded from political and economic life, became resentful of this domination. Under Abdur Rahman Khan's authority in the late 19th century, the Hazaras, in particular, experienced extreme discrimination, including massacres, which exacerbated ethnic tensions (Kakar, 1979). Political and military groups were based on ethnic allegiances during the Soviet occupation (1979–1989) and the civil war that followed. The Pashtun-dominated Hezb-e-Islami, Tajik-led Jamiat-e-Islami, and Hazara-affiliated Hizb-e-Wahdat were the three main ethnic and tribal divisions among the Mujahideen resistance factions (Rubin, 1995).

These conflicts persisted throughout the post-Soviet period, leading to the establishment of the Taliban, who were mostly supported by Pashtun tribes, and the Northern Alliance, which was primarily made up ofTajiks, Uzbeks, and Hazaras (Giustozzi, 2008). Following the U.S.-led intervention, the post-2001 political order sought to develop an inclusive system of governance. However, political groups and leaders continued to mobilise support based on ethnicity rather than national unity, resulting in ongoing power struggles along ethnic lines (Suhrke, 2011). This was seen in electoral politics, as coalitions between presidential contenders were forged more on the basis of ethnic calculations than on nationalistic or ideological beliefs. Particularly divisive presidential elections occurred in 2014 and 2019, with disagreements mostly based on ethnic factors rather than substantive issues (Hakimi, 2020). The ongoing reliance on tribal systems for governance and conflict resolution is another important aspect contributing to Afghanistan's nationhood's fragmentation. State laws are frequently superseded by the Pashtuns' traditional Pashtunwali code, whilst other ethnic groups depend on informal judicial systems and local authorities (Barfield, 2010).

Effectively implementing national programmes becomes challenging as a result of this undermining of the central government's power. Furthermore, rural communities tend to view the state as an outside force, which strengthens local ties over patriotism. The ethnic and tribal dynamics in Afghanistan have become much more complex since the Taliban came back to power in 2021. The Taliban leadership has made an effort to portray the group as a national movement, but the majority of its supporters are still Pashtun, which worries non-Pashtun communities about possible exclusion. Ethnic division is still a defining issue for Afghan nationhood, according to reports of deliberate violence against Hazaras and persecution of Tajik and Uzbek political leaders (Amnesty International, 2022). Ultimately, Afghanistan's broken nationhood is firmly ingrained in its ethnic and tribal systems, which have moulded its political, military, and social environments. A coherent national identity has not developed from historical power imbalances, ethnic-based factionalism, and the continuation of tribal governments. Although outside interventions and modernisation initiatives have sometimes tried to heal these differences, Afghanistan's unity is constantly challenged by the strongly rooted character of ethnic allegiances.

Islam and the National Identity of Afghanistan

Afghanistan's nationhood has been significantly shaped by Islam, which has impacted its social standards, legal framework, political systems, and resistance activities. Islam, which has historically served as both a unifying and a divisive force in Afghanistan's political and cultural environment, is firmly ingrained in the country's identity as a deeply religious community. From the establishment of the modern Afghan state in the 18th century to the Taliban's current rule, there has been a clear blending of Islam and Afghan nationalism throughout history. With the founding of the Durrani empire in 1747 under Ahmad Shah Durrani, Islam came to define Afghanistan's national character. Durrani's function as a unifier of several

Pashtun tribes under the banner of Islam contributed to his legitimacy as a monarch (Barfield, 2010). The early Afghan state was able to create some degree of unity among its ethnically and tribally diverse populace by consolidating authority according to Islamic precepts. Afghanistan's rulers, notably the monarchs of the 19th century, frequently used Islamic authority to defend their policies, whether they were related to military campaigns, taxation, or legal matters (Kakar, 1979). Islam has been used as a unifying factor in Afghanistan's history during both internal strife and foreign invasions. Islam was a fundamental component of Afghan resistance during the Anglo-Afghan Wars of the late 19th and early 20th centuries, when Afghan commanders united their people against British soldiers under the banner of jihad (Rubin, 1995). Similar to this, Islam emerged as the main ideological instrument used to bring together various Mujahideen factions against the Soviet Union and the communist government during the Soviet invasion of Afghanistan (1979-1989) (Roy, 1990).

The resistance movement was presented as a religious conflict, and the role of Islam in Afghanistan's national identity was further solidified by the backing of Islamic nations, especially Saudi Arabia and Pakistan. Afghanistan's Islamic identity entered a new phase with the rise of the Taliban in the mid-1990s. The movement aimed to create an Islamic emirate founded on a rigorous interpretation of Sharia law and was started by Pashtun religious students who had received their education at Pakistani madrasas (Giustozzi, 2008). They promoted a radical interpretation of Islam during their 1996–2001 leadership, which also repressed ethnic and sectarian variety, restricted women's rights, and enforced religious orthodoxy. Their rhetoric of reinstating Islamic order resonated with sections of the people who were fed up with the anarchy and corruption of the Mujahideen era, even as their governance alienated many Afghans (Coll, 2004). The political regime that emerged after 2001 made an effort to include Islam within a democratic system. Afghanistan was proclaimed an Islamic Republic in 2004 by the Afghan Constitution, which included democratic features like elections and civil rights together with Sharia law as a fundamental legal concept (Suhrke, 2011). Finding a balance between Islamic administration and contemporary political institutions was still difficult, though. Tensions between religious conservatives and reformists resulted from the struggle between traditional

Islamic institutions and Western-backed governance systems. The Taliban's 2021 comeback served as more evidence of how important Islam is to Afghan nationalism. Despite its claims to be more inclusive, the Taliban government nonetheless upholds stringent Islamic laws that have an impact on women's rights, political involvement, and educational opportunities (Amnesty International, 2022). The fight to define Afghanistan's nationhood—whether as an Islamic state, a multi-ethnic republic, or a combination of both—is reflected in their focus on religious authority above ethnic or national identity. Afghanistan's national identity has been significantly shaped by Islam, which has brought forth both unity and discord. It has functioned as a focal point for resistance to foreign invasions, a defence of governance, and a way to legitimise authority. Nonetheless, Afghanistan's political stability and national unity are still impacted by the various interpretations of Islam, which range from moderate to radical. Afghanistan still faces the difficulty of striking a balance between the demands of a modern, inclusive nation-state and its Islamic tradition.

Conclusion

To summarise the discussion, it may be stated that Afghanistan's geopolitical location at the centre of the Great Game and its moniker as the Graveyard of Empires have had a significant impact on the country's identity. These historical accounts emphasise Afghanistan's ongoing fight for independence, fortitude in the face of foreign rule, and internal disintegration. Afghanistan, a buffer state sandwiched between rival superpowers, has consistently been subjected to outside meddling, which has exacerbated internal strife and bolstered its feeling of national resistance. The enduring ethnic, tribal, and ideological divisions that have impeded long-term national unity coexist with the collective identity that has been developed through resistance in Afghanistan as a result of the legacy of these conflicts. Afghanistan's position was that of a pawn in the larger strategic conflict between the Russian and British empires in the late 19th and early 20th centuries, as was characterised by The Great Game. Afghan monarchs had to negotiate a delicate political environment to preserve their independence and balance the interests of their strong neighbours as a result of this foreign competition. In addition to restricting Afghanistan's physical sovereignty, the Durand Line and other artificial borders established during this time planted the seeds for long-lasting ethnic divisions, especially among the Pashtun population.

The rivalry between the empires strengthened Afghanistan's defensive nationalism, which made opposition to outside influence a central aspect of its character. However, rather than a centralised state, tribal and regional leaders frequently spearheaded this resistance, strengthening the decentralised governance systems that still influence Afghanistan's political landscape. The story of the Graveyard of Empires highlights both the cyclical nature of Afghanistan's internal wars and its resilience to foreign occupiers. Foreign interventions have worsened Afghanistan's internal tensions while also frequently failing to impose long-term stability. Although the Americans, British, and Soviets made various attempts to change Afghanistan, they all eventually left, leaving behind a nation riven by conflict and conflicting power systems. Religious ideology became increasingly ingrained in Afghanistan's national identity as a result of the Soviet invasion and subsequent evacuation, which strengthened the influence of Islamic resistance groups. Similar attempts were made to establish a modern Afghan nation-state by the U.S.-led intervention; however, these attempts were thwarted by corruption, reliance on ethnic power brokers, and external dependency.

The Taliban's 2021 comeback served as further evidence that foreign-imposed nationhood could not last and that Afghanistan's internal forces—formed by long-standing grievances and shifting power dynamics—would continue to influence its destiny. These historical factors have shaped Afghanistan's nationhood, which is still complicated and dynamic. A strong resistance identity has been cultivated throughout the nation's history, although this has frequently been reactive rather than proactive, concentrating more on keeping outsiders out than on creating a unified and inclusive national framework. While governance arrangements fluctuate between centralisation and decentralisation based on the ruling power, tribal and ethnic allegiances, nevertheless, struggle with national identity. The enduring nature of these obstacles implies that Afghanistan's national identity will remain characterised by a precarious equilibrium between preserving sovereignty in the face of outside influences and resolving internal conflicts that have traditionally impeded sustained unification. The lessons learned from the Great Game and the Graveyard of Empires are still very applicable as Afghanistan develops.

The durability of the nation is demonstrated by its ability to withstand outside influence, but the continuous fight to create a stable, inclusive, and useful national identity highlights the unresolved conflicts within Afghan society. Afghanistan's ability to create a feeling of nationhood that cuts beyond ethnic, tribal, and ideological barriers while preserving its fiercely autonomous nature will determine whether it can escape the historical cycle of foreign interventions and internal fragmentation.

References

Amnesty International (2022). "Afghanistan: Ethnic and Gender Persecution Under the Taliban".

Barfield, T. J. (2010). *Afghanistan: A Cultural and Political History*. Princeton University Press.

Bizhan, N. (2022). *State Fragility: Case Studies and Comparisons*. Routledge.

Bosworth, C. E. (1977). *The Later Ghaznavids: Splendour and Decay*. Columbia University Press.

Coll, S. (2004). *Ghost Wars: The Secret History of the CIA, Afghanistan, and Bin Laden, from the Soviet Invasion to September 10, 2001*. Penguin.

Dalrymple, W. (2013). *Return of a King: The Battle for Afghanistan, 1839–42*. Bloomsbury Publishing.

Dupree, L. (1973). *Afghanistan*. Princeton University Press.

Frye, R. N. (1992). *The Heritage of Central Asia: From Antiquity to the Turkish Expansion*. Princeton University Press.

Giustozzi, A. (2008). *Empires of Mud: Wars and Warlords in Afghanistan*. Hurst & Company.

Giustozzi, A. (2018). *The Taliban at War, 2001–2018*. Oxford University Press.

Grau, L. W. & Gress, M. A. (2002). *The Soviet-Afghan War: How a Superpower Fought and Lost*. University Press of Kansas.

Gregorian, V. (1969). *The Emergence of Modern Afghanistan: Politics of Reform and Modernization, 1880-1946*. Stanford University Press.

Hakimi, A. (2020). "The Changing Political Order in Afghanistan: Elections and Ethnic Divides". United States Institute of Peace.

Hansen, V. (2017). *The Silk Road: A New History with Documents*. Oxford University Press.

Hopkirk, P. (1992). *The Great Game: The Struggle for Empire in Central Asia*. Kodansha International.

Kakar, M. Hasan. (1979). *Government and Society in Afghanistan: The Reign of Amir 'Abd Al-Rahman Khan*. University of Texas Press.

Najam, D. (October 31, 2024). "Afghanistan's internal fault Lines". *The Express Tribune*. https://tribune.com.pk/story/2506368/afghanistans-internal-fault-lines

Noelle, C. (1997). *State and Tribe in Nineteenth-Century Afghanistan: The Reign of Amir Dost Muhammad Khan (1826-1863)*. Routledge.

Poullada, L. B. (1973). *Reform and Rebellion in Afghanistan, 1919-1929: King Amanullah's Failure to Modernize a Tribal Society*. Cornell University Press.

Robson, B. (2007). *The Road to Kabul: The Second Afghan War 1878-1881*. Osprey Publishing.

Roy, O. (1990). *Islam and Resistance in Afghanistan*. Cambridge University Press.

Rubin, B. R. (1995). *The Fragmentation of Afghanistan: State Formation and Collapse in the International System*. Yale University Press.

Soucek, S. (2000). *A History of Inner Asia*. Cambridge University Press.

Suhrke, A. (2011). *When More Is Less: The International Project in Afghanistan*. Columbia University Press.

Tanner, S. (2009). *Afghanistan: A Military History from Alexander the Great to the War against the Taliban*. Da Capo Press.

5 Afghanistan's Nationhood from the Perspective of Ethnicity

Niranjan Marjani

Introduction

The term 'nation' is a complex phenomenon that is open to varied interpretations. In a simple and broad- based manner, a nation could be defined as a group of people who believe that they consist of a single people based upon historical and cultural criteria, such as shared language (Flint, 2006). In some contexts, membership of a nation is granted if inheritance or blood ties to a particular group can be established (Flint, 2006). Anthony D. Smith, in his book, *National Identity,* has given a more elaborate definition of nation. According to him, a nation can be defined as a named human population, sharing a historic territory, common myths and historical memories, a mass public culture, a common economy and common legal rights and duties for all members (Smith, 1991). Further, he maintains that elements of other kinds of collective identity, such as class, religion, and ethnicity, are also instrumental in forming a national identity.

In their book, *Nations and Nationalism: A Reader,* Philip Spencer and Howard Wollman write that a nation encompassing different ethnicities, religions, and ethnocultural and civic values will have a problem if there is inequality and lame distribution of power (Spencer & Wollman, 2010). This principle implies that multi-ethnic societies will face fragility if there is no equal distribution of power.

Through summarising these basic definitions, it is evident that individual identity, shared culture, and ethnicity form an integral part of a nation and a national identity for its people. This chapter focuses on interactions between diverse ethnicities of Afghanistan and whether the strain in inter-ethnic ties makes nationhood in Afghanistan a contested phenomenon.

Perceiving Afghanistan as a nation from the Western conceptualisation and further, making attempts to establish a government modelled on Western institutions have been common occurrences evident in the West's dealing with Afghanistan. However, these approaches have failed to sustain over a long period of time.

The conceptualisation of Afghanistan as a country or as a monolithic entity, as perceived by the different powers over the course of centuries, is misleading. Beneath the perceived monolithic and geopolitical entity lies a country and a society that encompasses extreme diversities.

While the title of this book suggests studying the concept of nationhood under various Taliban regimes, the phenomenon of challenging the governance structure, whether monarchy or democracy, has been evident in Afghanistan's political history since centuries. This template of challenging the governance structure has always had two underlying motives—either to counter foreign influence or to gain supremacy among various ethnic groups in Afghanistan. The Taliban regime is a representation and a continuation of this phenomenon that is an integral part of Afghanistan's polity. The Taliban has internalised the elements of both the motives—projecting itself as fighting the foreign forces on one hand and also being involved in friction with the minority ethnic groups to wield absolute power over the entire Afghan territory. All these complexities have had an impact on the notion of nationhood and nation-building in Afghanistan.

This chapter focuses on the ethnic conflicts in Afghanistan and how the nationhood remains a contested phenomenon due to these conflicts. Within ethnic conflict, this chapter further explores themes, such as the interplay between ethnicity and religion and the projection and use of force in assuming and maintaining power in Afghanistan. The part of employing force as an instrument is more attributable to the Taliban in its quest for holding on to power in Afghanistan. The analysis of ethnic conflicts is intended to conclude where the concept of nationhood stands with respect to Afghanistan.

While Afghanistan's history is centuries' old, this chapter focuses on the time period from 1747 onwards. The incidents from the mid-18th century to early 20th century are discussed in brief to give a background of the wider analysis. Developments in the 20th century are focused more to study the frictional interaction between diverse ethnicities of Afghanistan. Also, for the purpose of this chapter and for the discussion of minority groups, the principal focus remains on the Tajiks, the Uzbeks, and the Hazaras, the reason being these three groups have been prominently engaged in countering the Pashtun dominance in Afghanistan and also in the fight against the Taliban.

Afghanistan's Ethnic Landscape

Afghanistan, owing to its strategically important location at the crossroads of South, Central, and West Asia, has always played a significant role in shaping the history of these regions for centuries. Afghanistan's location ensured that regional and extra- regional powers have had a perpetual interest in this country. Over the course of several centuries, this interest has been manifested through countless attempts towards establishing control over Afghanistan. From the Persian King Cyrus and Macedonian conqueror Alexander to the United States (US) and NATO forces, various powers have tried to appropriate Afghanistan to suit their respective goals in the region. However, all of them have been consigned to a similar fate of not being able to hold on to Afghanistan for long.

As much as Afghanistan is a proactive participant in the power play between various international actors, it is pertinent to consider the internal dynamics of this country. A broad-based observation suggests that the inability of regional and extra- regional powers to control Afghanistan stems from the relative neglect of the internal fault lines existing within Afghanistan.

Afghanistan's demographic composition is made of diverse ethnic groups. Afghanistan's Constitution of 2004 referred to 14 ethnic groups. Article 4 of the Constitution stated that Pashtun, Tajik, Hazara, Uzbek, Turkmen, Baluch, Pachaie, Nuristani, Aimaq, Arab, Qirghiz, Qizilbash, Gujar, Brahwui, and other tribes shall comprise the nation of Afghanistan (*Deccan Herald,* 2021).

Among these groups, some of the largest groups are the Pashtuns, Tajiks, Uzbeks, Turkmens, Hazaras, Nuristanis, and Balochis. Out of Afghanistan's total population of 41 million, Pashtuns are 42 per cent, Tajiks 27 per cent,

Uzbeks 9 per cent, and Hazaras 9 per cent (Kumar & Malhotra, 2024). The rest 13 per cent of the population comprises Nuristanis, Balochis, Aimaqs, Turkmens, and Arabs. The term 'Afghan' was long equated with the Pashtuns. However, 'Afghan' means a resident of Afghanistan (Feifer, 2010). While Pashto and Dari are official languages, around 30 other languages are spoken by various ethnic groups across Afghanistan.

The Modern State of Afghanistan

The formation of the modern state of Afghanistan is traced back to the 18th century. Again, the Afghan state is mostly equated with the Pashtuns and hence, the evolution of Afghanistan is attributed to the coming together of various Pashtun tribes.

It was in 1747 that the Pashtuns experienced some semblance of unity. The establishment of the modern Afghan state or Afghanistan, as the country stands today, could be attributed to the beginning of the Durrani empire in 1747 under Ahmad Shah Abdali, who assumed the title of Durrani. Afghanistan, under the Durrani empire, roughly constituted the territories that are part of today's Afghanistan.

Afghanistan had always been a restive state, with different groups squabbling with each other for power. Various tribes, such as the Ghilzais, Mohmands, Mehsuds, Wazirs, Khattaks, Afridis and Shinwaris, to name a few, occupied the southern and eastern parts of Afghanistan and were engaged in frequent fights with each other (Khan et al., 2021).

The Durrani empire managed to bring the Pashtuns under the control of one political centre for the first time (Ahady, 1995). Under the Durrani regime, the Pashtuns received preferential treatment compared to other subjects. The Pashtuns were the principal beneficiaries in receipt of state largess in distribution of land and in receiving state expenditures. The Pashtuns enjoyed institutionalised military, political, and economic dominance in Afghanistan during the Durrani empire (Ahady, 1995).

Further attempts towards transforming Afghanistan from a tribal society to a modern state were made by Amir Abdur Rahman Khan, who ruled Afghanistan from 1880 to 1901. In a country always torn by internal conflicts and divisions among different tribes, Abdur Rahman Khan introduced a governance structure where the central government would have a dominant role. This thinking was shaped by Afghanistan's internal fissures as much as external threats (Kakar, 1979/2011).

The 18th and 19th centuries saw some consolidation among the Pashtuns, as also the state of Afghanistan taking shape. However, these developments did little to stem ethnic conflicts in Afghanistan.

Brief Background of the Composition of the Minority Ethnic Groups in Afghanistan

There are several reasons for the diverse and complex ethnic structure of Afghanistan. One of the primary reasons has been the porous borders between Afghanistan and its surrounding regions in the past. Lack of clear demarcation of borders for centuries, leading up to the late 19th century and even early 20th century, meant that populations from the neighbouring regions, comprising the Uzbek, Tajik and Turkmen ethnicities, resided or settled permanently within the territory of modern Afghanistan. This movement of populations from the neighbouring regions contributed to the demographic composition of Afghanistan as it stands today.

Also, during the reign of Amir Abdur Rahman Khan, a dispute arose between Afghanistan and Russia in 1885, known as the Panjdeh incident. This incident was a part of the Great Game between Britain and Russia, both of which were engaged in expanding their frontiers in South and Central Asia. As a part of countering the British, the Russians had previously expanded their frontiers till Turkmenistan in 1884. Beyond Turkmenistan, due to lack of demarcated borders, the Russians approached the Afghan territory. However, a war was averted, and the issue was resolved through diplomatic means. Following this incident, an Afghan Boundary Commission, headed jointly by the Russians and the British, settled the northern boundaries of Afghanistan. However, as a result of this settlement, several Uzbek and Tajik regions to the north of Afghanistan became a part of the Afghan territory (Khan et al., 2021).

Further, in the aftermath of the Russian Revolution, as the Soviet Union brought several regions, such as Bukhara, Tashkent, Khiva, Kokand, etc., which are part of Central Asia today, under the umbrella of the Union of Soviet Socialist Republics, there was a wave of migration of the Tajik, Uzbek, and Turkmen people into Afghanistan. Crossing into the Afghan territory, these groups settled particularly in the northern part of Afghanistan (Abdullaev, 2018). Specifically, many rich peasants from Central Asia settled in Afghanistan following the formation of socialist collective farms in the Soviet Union (Kocaoğlu, 2000).

Apart from the Central Asian origin groups of the Tajik and the Uzbek, the Hazaras are among the prominent minority groups of Afghanistan. The Hazaras, who mostly reside in the central mountainous region of Afghanistan called Hazarajat, are believed to have descended from the soldiers of Genghis Khan. Speaking Hazaragi, a dialect of Dari, and following the Shia denomination of Islam, the Hazaras stand out amid the Pashtuns by way of their ethnicity, language, and religious sect (Minority Rights Group, 2021).

The Struggle among Different Ethnicities

This section discusses how different ethnicities in Afghanistan have had ties underscored by friction. The struggle between ethnicities discussed here could be broadly considered as the majority (the Pashtuns) against the minority (the Tajiks, Uzbeks, Hazaras, etc.). These ethnicities have been at odds with each other for power and for protecting their respective regions as well as fiefdoms. However, the friction among the ethnicities has not been limited to the majority group (the Pashtuns) on one side and the minority groups (the Tajiks, Uzbeks, Hazaras, etc.) on the other. The Pashtuns were (and are, to a certain extent even today) a divided house and had a hostile relationship among themselves. For the purpose of this chapter, only the frictions and struggles between the Pashtuns and other minority groups (mostly the Tajiks, Uzbeks, and Hazaras) are considered. These struggles have often taken the form of civil wars, which has led to regime changes. The template that has characterised Afghanistan's polity for centuries is evident today as well. Further, contrary to the impression that being in the majority facilitated the Pashtuns to remain in power, there have been occasions in Afghan history of the past two centuries when the Pashtuns' hold on power had weakened, which caused some of the minority groups to be in power, although for a short period of time.

The first time the Pashtuns experienced a weakening of their hold on power was in the late 1920s. In 1929, Tajik- origin Habibullah Kalakani became the ruler of Afghanistan. However, his reign was short-lived at just nine months, and he soon lost power to Nader Khan, a Pashtun (Ahady, 1995). Nader Khan established the Pashtun dominance in Afghan politics that was briefly lost to the Tajiks.

The second time when the Pashtuns lost power was in 1992 when Burhanuddin Rabbani, also a Tajik, became the president of Afghanistan. Colonel General Abdul Qadir, a Tajik, was acting president for a brief period in 1978.

The ethnic strife in Afghanistan has been more evident in the past about four decades. Afghanistan's politics during these four decades may seem to encompass mostly struggles against foreign occupation (first, the Soviet Union from 1979 to 1989 and then, the US and NATO forces from 2001 to 2021). However, simultaneous to the power struggle against external actors, Afghanistan's political landscape was also increasingly friction-ridden with ethnic conflicts.

In particular, the period between 1992 and 2001 saw the Pashtun-dominated Taliban receiving resistance from a group called the United Front for the Salvation of Afghanistan, popularly known as the Northern Alliance. This group consisted of ethnic minorities of the northern part of Afghanistan, like the Tajiks, the Uzbeks, and the Hazaras. Leaders like Ahmad Shah Massoud, Abdul Rashid Dostum, Burhanuddin Rabbani, Abdullah, and Karim Khalili have been associated with the Northern Alliance. However, militarily, the Northern Alliance received moderate success, and in 2001, they controlled less than 10 per cent of the Afghan territory. With the Taliban gaining the upper hand in recent years, the struggle between the Pashtuns on one hand and the Tajiks, Uzbeks, Hazaras, and Turkmen on the other continues. Following the takeover of Afghanistan by the Taliban in 2021, there has been very little representation of ethnic minority groups in the Taliban administration (Mohammad, 2024)

Among all the ethnic minorities of Afghanistan, the Hazaras perhaps remains the group that has borne the maximum brunt of the Taliban. The Hazaras are a minority not only in terms of their numbers (9 per cent of the total population) but also in terms of religious denomination. The Hazaras are Shias in a country where the majority follows the Sunni denomination of Islam. Attacks on the Hazaras have been deep- rooted in Afghan history. In the late 19th century, Afghan ruler Amir Abdur Rahman Khan carried out an extended campaign of violence against the Hazara community. Although the exact number is difficult to ascertain, it is estimated that during Amir Abdur Rahman Khan's regime, approximately 60 per cent of the Hazaras were massacred, enslaved, or forcibly displaced from their ancestral homelands (Hakimi, 2024).

Under the Taliban regimes, from 1996 to 2001 and from 2021 to present, the Hazaras have been the target of systematic attacks by the Pashtun-dominated Taliban. After seizing power in 1996, the Taliban declared a jihad on Shia Hazaras (Minority Rights Group, 2021). This declaration was followed by severe repression, persecution, and mass killings of this community. The situation of the Hazaras post-2021 remains the same as they continue to face persecution at the hands of the Taliban.

In their quest to impose their rule over Afghanistan, the Taliban have been employing two prominent instruments—religion as an overarching factor and the use of force.

The Interplay between Ethnicity and Religion

Afghanistan's ethnic mosaic offers an impression that the inter-group rivalry is of ethnic nature. However, there has also been a constant overlap of religion over ethnicity.

The Taliban, being a Pashtun-dominated group, has a natural inclination to impose Pashtunwali, a code of honour followed by the Pashtuns. This code lays down the laws, rules, and regulations to be followed by the Pashtuns. Pashtunwali could also be considered as a binding force among the otherwise fragmented Pashtun sub-groups. However, in case of resistance to the Pashtunwali from the non-Pashtuns or in case of failure of Pashtunwali to impose order within the Afghan society, the Taliban employs Sharia, an Islamic law (Lieven, 2021). Sharia is imposed not just to maintain order but also to prevent fragmentation of the society as also to stem challenges that may arise from different ethnicities trying to secure their respective space in Afghanistan's political landscape.

The Taliban that came to power once again in 2021 has energetically been attempting to impose what is termed as religious nationalism (Salimfar, 2019). Afghanistan has experienced ethnonationalism several times in the past, like Pashtun nationalism (Ruttig, 2012) and Tajik nationalism (Roy, 2003).

However, the Taliban are now imposing a stricter and radical version of Islam, thereby undermining the ethnic diversities.

In the past as well, there was another instance of an ethnic conflict presented as a fight for restoration of religion. The Tajik- origin Afghan ruler, Habibullah Kalakani, came to power in Afghanistan for nine months in 1929. His rule could be interpreted as a weakening of the Pashtun influence, although temporarily, in Afghan politics. However, his ethnic kin believed that Habibullah's rise to power was to protect Islam and oppose the then ruler Amanullah's 'secular and westernized' policies (Moslih, 2016).

While the interplay between ethnicity and religion in Afghanistan remains complex, majority of the times, ethnic supremacy is advanced in the garb of religion. It implies that the Pashtun majority, including the Taliban, remains a deeply ethnic-minded group that pushes forward its ethnic dominance, using the cover of Islam.

The Role of Force in Afghanistan's Polity

Violence is an inseparable part of the struggle among ethnicities. The conflict between the Pashtuns and other ethnicities of Afghanistan is essentially characterised by violent manifestations against each other. The violence or the force factor has been the core aspect of the Taliban ruling Afghanistan. It implies that force has been used as an instrument in attempting to bind together Afghanistan as a nation on the part of the Taliban.

While examining Afghanistan from the nation-state perspective, it is also important to consider the Force Theory of Origin of State. Afghanistan is termed as the graveyard of empires. From a reverse angle, it implies that Afghanistan has been subject to constant invasions from foreign powers. These powers could not consolidate their hold on Afghanistan and subjugate the Afghan people for long and had to leave, which has been interpreted as the defeat of these external powers.

However, as one observes the internal politics of Afghanistan, particularly under the Taliban rule, the force factor seems to succeed. This begs the question as to how the Taliban manages to find support among the people despite use of force.

According to the Force Theory of Origin of State, the State is the result of superior physical force, and it originates in the subjugation of the weaker by the stronger. Edward Jenks, in his book *History of Politics*, argues that there is not the slightest difficulty in proving that all political communities of the modern type owe their existence to successful warfare. This theory states that war begets the State (Jenks, 1900).

The Force Theory considers it natural for a man of exceptional force to overpower his fellow men and exercise some kind of authority over them. This same principle could be applied to the superior tribes and clans and their relationship to other tribes and clans (Asirvatham & Misra, 1936/2015).

According to this principle, the Taliban could be considered as deriving power on the basis of their strengths. Further, the dominance of the Pashtuns within the Taliban puts this group at odds with other ethnicities of Afghanistan, like the Tajiks, the Uzbeks, and the Hazaras.

However, there is a paradox in Afghan politics where the Taliban, despite employing force, manages to find public support. The public support to the Taliban could be attributed to factors like security, governance, and kinship ties (Kaltenthaler et al., 2022). The lengthy presence of foreign forces on Afghan soil had the effect of driving the public opinion in favour of an indigenous alternative. Further, insecurity experienced during the foreign forces' occupation of Afghanistan also caused the public to view the Taliban more favourably, implying that the Taliban was the lesser evil. Also, the Afghan mindset of being averse to a foreign governance model resulted in the Taliban gaining support. Finally, the Taliban derives its power from the ethnic Pashtuns, who are the largest group in Afghanistan.

All these factors ultimately point towards the supremacy of the Pashtuns in the context of nationhood in Afghanistan.

Perception of Nationhood in Afghanistan

While nation and nationhood are complex phenomena, in a country like Afghanistan, these concepts are even more difficult to study. Not only is the population in Afghanistan diverse in terms of ethnicity and language but the majority public in Afghanistan does not perceive the concepts of nation, nationalism, and nationhood as defined by the West.

The perception of Afghanistan as a nation with a nation-state system has been a creation of Western powers in pursuit of their own strategic interests. It was only in the 19th century, during the course of the Great Game, that rival powers British India and Russia created the Afghan state (Schetter, 2003). The British, who supported the Pashtuns in power in Afghanistan, favoured Pashtun elements in the nation-state system in Afghanistan.

The British policy, in a way, extended the policies of the Durrani empire of the 18th century. It was during the Durrani empire that the Pashtuns began to be institutionalised in Afghanistan's politics. Also, the institutionalisation and Pashtun dominance increased to the extent that the term 'Afghan' came to be equated with Pashtun.

As mentioned earlier, Amir Abdur Rahman Khan, too, shaped his reign by employing the template that the Durrani empire and later, the British, had advanced in the Afghan polity. It resulted in further strengthening of the Pashtun dominance in Afghanistan.

However, even as the Pashtuns dominated the Afghan polity, the majority of the Afghan people, particularly in the rural regions, were oblivious to the dynamics of the politics in Kabul. The ordinary Afghan public also had minimal conceptualisation of the nation-state system. Outside of Kabul, in the rural region, people considered the nation-state or government as a hostile factor and an intervention in their social life (Schetter, 2003). The contrast between urban and rural areas and lack of outreach of the government implied that the feeling of nationalism and the concept of nationhood remained blurred among the majority of the Afghans as late as the 19th century.

The application of the concept of nationhood in Afghanistan further assumes complexity since various scholars assign different versions of nation and nationalism to Afghanistan.

The early part of the 20th century is considered to have brought awareness about nationalism and national identity among the people of Afghanistan (Rasikh, 2010). Particularly in the first three decades of the 20th century, the Afghan ruling elite sought to create a national Afghan identity among the Afghan public. This task was undertaken first by Habibullah Khan, who became the king in 1901, and later, by his son, Amanullah Khan, who became the Emir of Afghanistan in 1919. Habibullah Khan and Amanullah Khan attempted to create a national identity for their country through reforming education and government institutions. Both rulers tried to imbibe the Afghan identity through reforms. They imagined that a national identity would propel people to work towards the betterment of the country. They also undertook to convince people that by serving the country, they were carrying out God's command (Rasikh, 2010).

While the West has perceived Afghanistan as one monolithic entity, the people and various ethnic groups of Afghanistan have a relatively fluid conviction about nationhood. Considering the roots of the modern state of Afghanistan inevitably leads towards the beginning of the consolidation of the Pashtuns in the 18th century. This development has been one of the principal causes of fragmentation of the Afghan society where ethnic minorities have been sidelined and even persecuted by the Pashtun majority. It means that a divided society is unlikely to have a unified vision of a nation. Further, the majority of the Afghan population, particularly from the rural areas, harbour a strong aversion to the government run from Kabul. As a consequence, any central government's inability to exert its authority over the entire territory of a country also results in the country's majority public not relating to the idea of one nation.

The Taliban should be viewed more as a phenomenon in Afghanistan rather than just a group of radical extremists. Being a Pashtun-dominated organisation, the Taliban has existed in Afghan politics in various mutations all through the last three centuries when the modern state of Afghanistan started to take shape. Interplaying religion and force to veil ethnic dominance, the Taliban has managed to hold on to power. The Taliban's manoeuvring is facilitated by lack of national vision or the resources and energy to implement it on the part of the ethnic minorities. As such, the Taliban is able to impose its own concept of nationhood over the majority of the Afghan population.

Conclusion

Nationhood is a complex phenomenon that is open to diverse interpretations. In a country like Afghanistan, this phenomenon becomes even more complex as most of the perception of the concept of nation and nationhood is derived from the West. However, Afghanistan, with its ethnic and linguistic diversity, does not fit into the Western theoretical framework of the nation. Afghanistan's nationhood, instead of totally emerging out of shared culture and identity, is based more on kinship ties and protection of indigenous mechanisms that run their respective ethnic societies. Further, the concept of nationhood assumes another layer as different ethnicities in Afghanistan scramble for prominence in the Afghan political landscape. While the Taliban could be considered as a recent development, more of a creation of foreign powers, the phenomenon and the mindset that drives the Taliban has always been deep-rooted in Afghan society. Today's Taliban is a manifestation and a mutation of the previous trends and tendencies that Afghanistan has witnessed at two levels consistently—opposing foreign powers and fighting for dominance within the ethnic structure of Afghanistan. So, nationhood in Afghanistan remains a contested phenomenon as the majority of the Afghan society and various ethnic groups do not view Afghanistan from the Western conceptualisation of the nation.

References

Abdullaev, K. (2018). "Emigration Within, Across, and Beyond Central Asia in the Early Soviet Period from a Perspective of Translocality". In M. Stephen-Emmrich & P. Schröder (Eds.), *Mobilities, Boundaries, and Travelling Ideas Rethinking Translocality: Beyond Central Asia and the Caucasus* (pp. 61–88). Open Book Publishers.

Ahady, A.H. (1995). "The Decline of the Pashtuns in Afghanistan". *Asian Survey, 35*(7), pp. 621-634. https://doi.org/10.2307/2645419

Asirvatham, Dr. E. & Misra, K. K. (2015). *Political Theory*. S. Chand & Company Private Limited. (Original work published 1936)

Deccan Herald (August 18, 2021). "Dominant ethnic groups in Afghanistan". *Deccan Herald*. https://www.deccanherald.com/world/dominant-ethnic-groups-in-afghanistan-1021070.html

Feifer, G. (2010). *The Great Gamble: The Soviet War in Afghanistan*. Harper Perennial.

Flint, C. (2006). *Introduction to Geopolitics*. Routledge.

Hakimi, M. J. (2024). "The Afghan State and the Hazara Genocide". *Harvard Human Rights Journal, 97*, pp. 81–116.

Jenks, E. (1900). *A History of Politics*. The Macmillan Company.

Kakar, H. K. (2011). *Government and Society in Afghanistan: The Reign of Amir Abd Al-rahman Khan*. University of Texas Press. (Original work published 1979)

Kaltenthaler, K., Kruglanski, A. W., & Knuppe, A. J. (2022). "The Paradox of the Heavy-Handed Insurgent: Public Support for the Taliban among Afghan Pashtuns". *Studies in Conflict & Terrorism, 47*(12), pp. 1699–1723. https://doi.org/10.1080/1057610x.2022.2055008

Khan, M. F., Ali, S., & Khan, H. U. (2021). "Ethnic Conflict and the Political Instability in Afghanistan". *Pakistan Journal of International Affairs, 4*(2), pp. 419–434.

Kocaoğlu, T. (2000). "Turkistan Abroad: The Political Migration – From the Soviet and Chinese Central Asia (1918-1997)". In H. Komatsu, C. Obiya, & J. S. Schoeberlein (Eds.), *Migration in Central Asia: Its History and Current Problems* (pp. 113–126). Japan Center for Area Studies.

Kumar, A. & Malhotra, A. (April 17, 2024). "Factoring Ethnicity in Taliban's Quest for Legitimacy". *Georgetown Journal of International Affairs*. https://gjia.georgetown.edu/2024/04/17/factoring-ethnicity-in-talibans-quest-for-legitimacy-an-anthropological-rewiring-of-the-power-structure/

Lieven, A. (2021). "An Afghan Tragedy: The Pashtuns, the Taliban and the State". *Survival, 63*(3), pp. 7–36. https://doi.org/10.1080/00396338.2021.1930403

Minority Rights Group (December 2021). "Hazaras in Afghanistan". https://minorityrights.org/communities/hazaras/

Mohammad. (June 27, 2024). "Minimal Representation of Ethnic Groups in the Taliban Regime: Pro-Taliban Figures Do Not Represent Tajiks, Uzbeks, and Hazaras". *Hasht-e Subh*. https://8am.media/eng/minimal-representation-of-ethnic-groups-in-the-taliban-regime-pro-taliban-figures-do-not-represent-tajiks-uzbeks-and-hazaras/

Moslih, H. (September 2, 2016). "Kabul burial of Tajik King Kalakani stirs tension". *Al Jazeera*. https://www.aljazeera.com/features/2016/9/2/kabul-burial-of-tajik-king-kalakani-stirs-tension

Rasikh, J. S. (2010). *Nationalism in Afghanistan - A Descriptive Analysis*. James Madison University.

Roy, O. (2003). "Islamisme et Nationalisme". *Pouvoirs: Revue d'Etudes Constitutionnelles et Politiques, 104*(1), pp. 45–53.

Ruttig, T. (2012). "How Tribal Are the Taliban?" In S. Bashir & R. D. Crews (Eds.), *Under the Drones Modern Lives in the Afghanistan-Pakistan Borderlands* (pp. 102–135). Harvard University Press.

Salimifar, F. (2019). "Neo- Taliban and Religious Nationalism in Afghanistan". *Iranian Review of Foreign Affairs, 10*(1), pp. 73–97.

Schetter, C. (2003). *Ethnicity and the political reconstruction in Afghanistan*. https://eprints.lse.ac.uk/28376/. Paper presented at State reconstruction and international engagement in Afghanistan, Conference held by London School of Economics and Political Science, May 30-June 1, 2003.

Smith, A. D. (1991). *National Identity*. Penguin Books.

Spencer, P. & Wollman, H. (2010). *Nations and Nationalism: A Reader*. Edinburg University Press.

6 Understanding the Shifting Interplay between Tribes and Ethnic Groups in the Contemporary Political Dynamics of Afghanistan

Rushita Shetty

Introduction

Ethnic and tribal affiliations play a significant role in shaping the identity of individuals and in the formation of social groups, which are based on ethnicity and tribal links. Afghanistan is a country with a set of diverse ethnic and tribal groups, which form the bedrock of Afghan society. Over the years, Afghanistan has witnessed various conflicts and battles fought on its land, which brought in different tribes from neighbouring states into Afghanistan, and these groups today constitute the various ethnic groups that reside in Afghanistan. The geographical location of Afghanistan locates it at the crossroads of great civilisations, allowing it to imbibe culture and traditions from Central Asia, West Asia, and the Indian subcontinent. However, the presence of diverse ethnic groups has resulted in distortion and fragmentation of the Afghan society due to years of conflict and civil war, which has resulted in alienating these groups. Despite the animosity, no ethnic group has endorsed secession at any point in the last century.

Social Identity

Identity plays an integral role in the lives of individuals. Since the day a person is born, they are associated with a certain societal structure, which is ascertained to them since their birth. Once they become part of the society, they derive their identity or their sense of self largely based upon the social categories of which they are a part (Burke, 2000). The sense of belonging and oneness brings together people who share the same identity with one another. This can be in any form—race, gender, language, ethnicity, etc., and this structure allows people to rely on one another. Every individual, over the course of their personal life, becomes a member of unique societal structures and groups. Therefore, the social identities making up the person are a set of unique combinations of groups. Here, identity becomes an object, which is classified, categorised, and recognised in relation with the social categories it is being associated with. Identity has been evoked to generate a sense of sameness amongst the individuals belonging to the same groups or categories. This sameness is expected to manifest itself into solidarity during times of crisis wherein a collective action can take place (Cooper, 2000).

Identities are structured and formed around norms, which provide an outline on how identities must function. These vary from one identity to another. This normative content of identity derives from the social norms, which are emanate from multiple centres of authority. Norms provide a fixed meaning and collective expectations for members of the group. These norms can be social or legal, written or unwritten, and these practices provide recognition to the groups. These norms are the actions through which others recognise the actor as having a particular identity. These constitutive norms help define a social meaning by establishing individual obligations and collective expectations for every member of the group. Therefore, norms define the boundaries and distinctive practices of a group, which distinguishes one group from another (Abdelal & Herrera, 2009).

National Identity

National identity stems from the various social identities that are prevalent in the structured society, out of which a common sense of togetherness and a bond is formed, which is reflected on a larger scale (Grotenhuis, 2016). The nation-building process is a complex task, which begins with bringing various different social identities under one common identity which will represent a nation, wherein the nation is formed by the shared culture, languages, and ethnicities, which, in turn, help create a sense of togetherness amongst the people. In fragile states like Afghanistan where diverse tribal and ethnic groups exist, the notion of national identity is hard to find. Even during a crisis situation in fragile states where NGOs and multilateral agencies have to withdraw their staff from dangerous areas, people tend to rely upon their traditional networks for food, shelter, security, and medical care. The sense of social identity then dominates the larger collective national identity, which plays a crucial role in understanding and knowing how a particular nation functions and what cultures and values it represents. Every nation has its own unique identity, which makes it distinct from another, and in many cases, it borrows from other nations who share similar cultures and beliefs.

National identity has often been related with political self-determination, wherein national groups require a state of their own to survive in a hostile international order (Dahbour, 2002). Political self-determination provides a state with a sense of autonomy and security, which is why national identity becomes important as it allows people with similar beliefs and culture to come together and form a collective identity. National identity acts as a mark of distinction between different nation-states who represent diverse beliefs and culture. National identity here is also understood to promote exclusivity, where every state has its own exclusive identity. The definition of nation has been debated and redefined by various scholars. However, the idea of commonality and similarity has prevailed in all the definitions, wherein the role of ethnic identities also becomes crucial as they act as the base on which national identity is created. Ethnicity, religion, and language are stronger markers of people's identities to find something in common amongst the various social identities. They often act as a roadblock in creating a national identity. Max Weber, in his definition of national identity, links ethnicity and nationality and says, '…both share the same vague connotation that whatever is felt to be distinctively common must derive from common descent'. But Weber does not say that ethnicity and national identity are synonymous with one another. He distinguishes between the two, saying that until the members of the ethnic group recognise the uniqueness of their group, it is merely an ethnic group and not a nation (Dahbour, 2002). Recognising and becoming aware of the uniqueness of a group is integral to the creation of national identity, and the notion of exclusivity is an integral component of national identity. The definition given by Weber emphasises the relation between national identity and an apparent belief in the ethnic commonalities. Ethnicity, therefore, plays a vital role in defining national identity. Max Weber's definition consists of three important concepts. Firstly, the nation is a self- defined entity unlike ethnic groups, which are defined by others. Secondly, the importance of ancestral or kinship ties becomes crucial for national identity, which is where ethnicity becomes significant. Lastly, the emphasis is on the political process, which helps in defining a nation, and every political process requires a political community that has shared beliefs and culture. Therefore, all the three concepts become a necessary aspect of national identity, as defined by Max Weber. Therefore, national identity can be understood to be essentially ethnic identity, which has achieved a political expression.

Village Governance and Social Order of the Afghan Society

Customary governance systems are present in rural Afghanistan, where the indigenous communities set up their own sphere of self-administration and their own organisational structures. These customary governance structures emphasise the role played by villages and the social order that exists within them, which has its implications on the livelihoods of the individuals staying in the villages. The social order in Afghan villages is governed by the organisations that are dependent upon the customary governance, shared between three distinct informal organisations, which are the 'Shuras/Jirgas' (village councils), Mullahs (religious judicial authority), and the Maliks (representatives from communities) (Murtazashvili, 2016). The convergence of these organisations forms an "informal constitution" of village governance. The villages are typically governed by norms, which differ from one village to another. For example, in the Pashtun-dominated villages, they use the Pashtunwali through which they resolve disputes. However, Pashtunwali also has variations since Pashtuns are a diverse community and not monolithic. Similarly, other ethnic groups which are non-Pashtun, like the Tajiks, Hazaras, or Uzbeks, have their own rules and norms to resolve disputes. They rely on rules of Shariat or the unwritten customary norms, wherein every ethnic group has its own interpretation of justice. Therefore, there is no generalised system of governance that is practised in every village.

The village governance also has an impact on the livelihoods of individuals. This is directly correlated with the location of the villages across Afghanistan. As every village has access to different natural resources, it is also partly determined according to the location around the valley in terms of the water supply and the altitude which determines whether the village is prone to drought or flooding. This also signifies the settlement patterns of villages and the conflict that revolves around the procurement of resources (Grace & Pain, 2024). The dependence of villages and individuals upon the diverse assets and income sources that depend on the availability of natural resources also means that villages and their inhabitants are differently affected by the policies, local politics, and power structures. Afghanistan, since its emergence as an identifiable political unit since 1747, has faced a series of crises, including internal political and social upheaval, foreign interventions, and invasions. These crises have had a serious impact on the political entity, leaving it fractured and disrupted. A variety of factors, both internal and external, are responsible for the constant crisis that Afghanistan faces, and one of the primary factors is the mosaic nature of Afghan society. The Afghan society is composed of numerous micro-societies within which key relationships are defined through norms, which vary from one group to another. The state-building and the state-functioning process in Afghanistan has been influenced towards building a coherent coalition of the central and customary governance structures. This is critical in determining the authority, power, and legitimacy of the central government, as Afghanistan is a weak state with a strong society (Saikal, 2005).

The positions of power created in villages highlight the power asymmetry that exists within the governance structures of these villages, since elites accumulate large amounts of resources and revenue. They invariably have a greater role to play in the local politics, which solidifies their positions as leaders or village headmen who take the important decisions in regard to their groups. This asymmetry in power structure has given rise to two sets of scholarly arguments. One set of scholars believe that the traditional and the informal order of governance has been gravely damaged due to war and conflicts, and it holds no value in the present time. The other set of scholars, like Olivier Roy, state that village representatives like the Maliks enjoy better position among the people than the elected Khan. During resistance, the Maliks received more support from the ethnic groups than the elected representatives. Therefore, customary governance systems have always held a powerful position in the Afghan society, where, due to weak state institutions, the dependency upon traditional links has always been more preferred by the Afghans.

Religion and Society in Afghanistan

Afghanistan has been engulfed in violent conflicts for decades, with the Taliban taking control over Afghanistan after the withdrawal of the US armed forces. The Taliban has reinforced its idea of Islam in Afghan society. In order to understand the Taliban's version of Islam, it is necessary to understand the role of religion in the Afghan society and how it becomes a poignant characteristic of building identity. Religion acts a crucial component of the social fabric of Afghanistan and the ethnic groups that form the Afghan society. The majority of the population of Afghanistan follows Islam, with around 85 per cent of them following the Sunni sect of Islam and 15 per cent of them practising the Shia sect of Islam. Shia consists predominantly of the Hazaras (HPCR, 2001). There are a tiny number of followers of other religions in Afghanistan, consisting of the Sikhs, Hindus, and Zoroastrians. Afghan society has been religiously conservative, and as per historical accounts, the rulers and the clergy have shared close ties, and the clerics have often acted as advisors to the ruling class. Rulers who were seen to carry out un-Islamic reforms lost support from the locals and the clergy. Therefore, since the creation of the Afghan society, the reliance on the clergy and focus on practising the principles outlined by Islam have acted as a guide for the society and the ruling class.

The 20th century saw a gradual erosion of the legal scholars of Islam and the Sharia along with the Ulama. The central governments in Kabul tried to maintain a distance from the clergy, which had close ties with the previous monarchs. The central governments tried to keep the religious figures at arm's length to limit or undermine their influence (Sharma, 2009). This distance from the Ulama was short-lived and overturned with the beginning of resistance against the Soviets, which was termed as Jihad, and this was followed by the subsequent civil war between the Mujahideen and Taliban regime. The religious leaders after the 1970s have provided legitimacy to the violent actions that were carried out in the name of Islam. Historically also, the disputes in Afghanistan were resolved by local and religious leaders. Therefore, religious figures have always held an authoritative role in Afghan society, wielding a great degree of power and influence over the ethnic and tribal groups. During the Soviet invasion of Afghanistan in the 1980s, Islam was seen as a unifying factor as it brought together opposing ethnic groups and tribes to fight against the Soviet forces and support the call for Jihad (HPCR, 2001). The Taliban era brought back the religious leaders as the key decision- makers and provided them with enormous power, which placed them in important positions of power in Afghan society.

The ethnic and tribal groups in Afghanistan formed their own resistance forces, which included each of them forming an armed group to carry out violent attacks on the other. For example, the Pashtuns were successful in overthrowing the Soviet armed forces. Along with the Pashtuns, other ethnic groups also joined them in the resistance. However, post the Soviet withdrawal, tensions arose between the different groups. The Tajiks created their resistance group, and Ahmed Shah Massoud was their most charismatic leader, He had a national stature that challenged the Pashtuns while he developed foreign links. Under the leadership of Massoud, the Tajik commanders developed a greater understanding with the urban and rural sectors of their population to support their resistance. The Tajiks were able to accumulate the support from their ethnic group through Jamiat-i-Islami. The Jamiat acted as an important link with Pakistan and other countries, which helped them in procuring arms and generating money for the Tajik resistance (Rais, 2009). Similarly, the Hazaras had their own resistance group. As the Hazaras are followers of the Shia sect of Islam, they comprise the minority community of Afghanistan due to which they have been the most marginalised and persecuted section of Afghan society. The Hizb-i-Wahdat, an umbrella organisation, was created under the influence of Iran. They have been demanding greater regional autonomy for the Hazaras group in the region (Rais, 2009). These political and armed groups, which were based on ethnicity and religion, acted as unifying opposing forces and also instigated violence against one another. In a fragile state like Afghanistan, the social divides between groups based on ethnicity and religion destabilise the growth and development of the states. This invariably has an effect on the state-building process wherein cooperation and provision of equal rights and opportunities for all are essential components.

Role of Ethnicity and Religion in the Taliban Over the Years

The political dynamics in Afghanistan has been a patchwork of different warlords coming into power and establishing their own idea of governance. Since the withdrawal of the Soviet Union from Afghanistan, various rebel groups from diverse ethnicities, which were collectively recognised as the Mujahideen, engaged themselves in a civil war that tormented the Afghan society. These rebel groups demonstrated a united front against the Soviets and were successful in driving them out of Afghanistan. However, post the Soviet withdrawal, there was a disintegration of the rebel groups, and their loyalties shifted according to the circumstances. The Mujahideen was successful in bringing together different ethnic groups, which highlighted a certain sense of national unity among them. However, it was short-lived. Each of the different sects, led by Gulbuddin Hekmatyar, Abdul Rashid Dostum, and Ahmed Shah Massoud, commanded over tens of thousands of hardened fighters, and each of them had their own territorial base through which they wielded their influence in the region. The Mujahideen in Afghanistan saw an amalgamation of different identities, except the minority communities like the Hazaras, who were benefitted by the Communist policies that favoured the minorities. Therefore, the violent rebel groups of Afghanistan, despite having a common agenda of fighting against the Soviet Union, separated, aligning with their ethnic identity.

The Taliban was one such group that was carved out of the resistance forces. It was formed by the Afghan Mujahideen with covert backing from the CIA and the ISI (Terpstra, 2020). They emerged as a cross-border movement, led by Afghan Pashtuns trained in Deobandi madrasas in Pakistan. The madrasas attracted a large number of Afghan refugee boys by offering a free place to stay along with education (Barfield, 2010). The long period for which the Soviet war lasted gave rise to a huge number of refugees, who took shelter in neighbouring countries, and this gave rise to a new class of people who were refugee Afghans born in Pakistan and had never experienced life in Afghanistan. The Taliban was, therefore, different from other Afghan political movements not only because of their exclusive clerical origins but also because of the refugee origins of its followers. The end of the Soviet invasion created a leadership vacuum within Afghanistan, and this gave rise to a civil war, which now pitched Muslims against Muslims. This set the Taliban's goal towards ending the disorder and reforming Afghanistan's religious and cultural practices by turning the country into a pure Islamic state along Salafist lines.

The Taliban was successful in gaining momentum due to the Afghan society being crippled because of the constant in-fighting and the weakened position of the Afghan state in terms of its institutions and political legitimacy, which further questioned the system controlled by Ahmed Shah Massoud and Burhanuddin Rabbani. The armed confrontation amongst the warring factions had begun to shape along the lines of ethnicity and religion. This shattered the hopes for normal and peaceful lives of millions of Afghans who were displaced due to the war. Due to this instability and the civil war, the credibility of the Mujahideen was lost, which further aided the Taliban's motives. The ethnic fault lines of Afghanistan have been prominent ever since its inception, and this was also the case with the rise of the Taliban. The social interaction and exchanges amongst different ethnic groups were seen only in urban settings. The growth of institutions of higher learning situated in Kabul, the bureaucracy, and some clandestine political activity brought together different ethnic groups (Barfield, 2010). There has always been an absence of cultural sensitivity and Afghan nationalism in Afghanistan as the process of state-building was deficient under the rule of both the monarchy and the chaotic Marxist government.

The state institutions under Taliban rule have largely acted as a tool to promote their policies on religion, political concerns, and military imperatives. The policy- making system under the Taliban consists of multiple actors from leadership to commanders to mullahs, each having an influential role in deciding the policies governing the lives of the civilians (Jackson & Amiri, 2019). The decision and policy- making structures play a key role in the working of the state institutions, which are put in place to implement these policies. The Taliban, over the years, have evolved from being a loose- knit guerrilla organisation from the early years of insurgency into a strong political movement. Their driving force of policy-making and mobilisation, however, was largely centred on religion. The Taliban, being predominantly a military-styled group influenced by religion, situated security to be of paramount concern. The functions of the Taliban, in terms of governance, are largely carried out by military commanders. However, other sectors important for state-building, such as health and education, have often posed a challenge for the Taliban. During the early years of insurgency, the Taliban viewed state- run schools to be legitimate targets to carry out attacks. There was clear hostility against state- run educational institutions. Attacks on teachers have been carried out to force them to stop working with the government.

Even post-2001, when the Taliban was forced out of Afghanistan, they held dominant positions in certain regions within the state. However, since their resurgence in 2021, their ideas on education have not evolved. The Taliban believed that state- run and private schools promoted Western ideas and anti-Taliban values. They saw these schools to be an extension of the government and the international communities who helped in building and creating a safe space for education in Afghanistan. The Taliban's view on education was deeply unpopular amongst the locals, who perceived it to be regressive (Jackson & Amiri, 2019). While the Taliban's health policy was seen less as a threat compared to that of education, the Taliban's initial involvement in the health sector was to provide better health care facilities to wounded fighters. The Taliban supported all the initiatives in the health sector. This was largely driven by the necessity to provide healthcare to fighters and also to satisfy the demands of the local population. After being ousted from power in 2001, the Taliban greatly relied on the services provided by NGOs and international aid agencies. It was a two-way process. Since these NGOs had to carry out their duties in Taliban- controlled areas, they had to negotiate with the Taliban, and since the Taliban had to satisfy the population under their control, it became necessary for them to cooperate with these aid agencies (Jackson & Amiri, 2019). Therefore, the Taliban has never relied on state institutions or worked towards the state-building process, since their system of governance depends upon a hierarchy- based system, controlled by commanders and their Islamic ideology, which has no space for building a self-sufficient state of Afghanistan. Therefore, while looking into the state institutions and their working under the Taliban, it becomes important to understand that the foundation of the Taliban lies in religion, which is reflected in their governance system.

Conclusion

Identity has always played a pivotal role in how a state conducts and formulates its legislature, executive, and judiciary. The role of identity becomes even more important in the absence of these state organs, especially in the case of weak and fragile states, which are characterised by the lack or absence of state authority, state legitimacy, and state capacity. Afghanistan has faced conflict and violence throughout its history, which places it under the set of fragile states. Governance in Afghanistan has ranged from monarchy, communist regime and violent rule under the Taliban to democracy and then again, back to the Taliban. The constant political turmoil and the absence of national leaders failed to unify the country as a single entity. Despite decades-long war and conflict, no ethnic or tribal group from Afghanistan has made any secessionist claims. This has been one of the greatest advantages of Afghanistan, wherein the idea of a sovereign and independent state is accepted and acknowledged by the Afghans. The general belief among the global population that Afghanistan and its people are inherently ungovernable has turned into an unfortunate conventional wisdom, which is also reflected in the state-building policies.

The lack of understanding about the village- governing patterns that existed in Afghanistan became one of the primary reasons why the central government began to lose its legitimacy. The structure of a country's ethnic cleavages is not just a social fact but also a historical product, which has been shaped over centuries. Understanding the ethnic landscape of a country becomes essential as the dynamics of ethnic competition that takes place and the conflicts that give rise to ethnic tensions are not because of the presence of different groups but due to the pattern of their relative size and geographical distribution. The real challenge in a society like Afghanistan is to reintegrate the various microsocial communities, which are run by different warlords, who came into power post the collapse of the Afghan state. The Afghan society is a mosaic of numerous ethnic tribes, and attempts to develop a common identity amongst these groups have not been successful. The magnitude of Afghanistan's social diversity is so high that individuals are more loyal towards their tribal and ethnic identities rather than associating themselves with a larger national identity. Over the course of its history, Afghanistan has been invaded by different rulers due to the geopolitical significance of its location. As a result, Afghanistan has grown to develop diverse social groups, which makes the process of constructing a unified national identity a difficult and sensitive task. The multi- ethnic structure of the Afghan society plays a significant and characteristic role in the political and social framework of the country. Therefore, ethnicity and tribalism form the foremost aspect of the identity of the populace, wherein they recognise themselves as Afghans only when they are away from the homeland.

References

Abdelal, R. & Herrera, Y. M. (eds.), (2009). *Measuring Identity: A Guide for Social Scientists*. Cambridge University Press.

Barfield, T. (2010). *Afghanistan: A Cultural and Political History*. Princeton University Press.

Burke, J. E. (2000). "Identity Theory and Social Identity Theory". *Social Psychology Quarterly*, *63*(3), pp. 224–237.

Cooper, R. B. (2000). "Beyond Identity". *Theory and Society*, *29*(1), pp. 1–47.

Dahbour, O. (2002). "National Identity: An Argument for the Strict Definition". *Public Affairs Quarterly*, *16*(1), pp. 17–37.

Grace, J. & Pain, A. (2024). *Rethinking Rural Livelihoods in Afghanistan*. Afghanistan Research and Evaluation Unit Organization. https://areu.org.af/publication/424/

Grotenhuis, R. (2016). "National identity: A model and its content". In *Nation-Building as Necessary Effort in Fragile States* (pp. 125–151). Amsterdam University Press.

HPCR (2001). *The Role of Islam in Shaping the Future of Afghanistan*. Harvard University. https://hhi.harvard.edu/publications/role-islam-shaping-future-afghanistan

Jackson, A. & Amiri, R. (2019). "Insurgent Bureaucracy: How the Taliban Makes Policy". United States Institute of Peace. https://www.usip.org/sites/default/files/2021-08/pw_153-insurgent_bureaucracy_how_the_taliban_makes_policy.pdf

Murtazashvili, J. B. (2016). *Informal Order and the State in Afghanistan*. Cambridge University Press.

Rais, R. B. (2009). *Recovering the Frontier State: War, Ethnicity and State in Afghanistan*. Lexington Books.

Saikal, A. (2005). "Afghanistan's weak state and strong society". In S. Chesterman, M. Ignatieff, & R. Thakur (eds.), *Making States Work: State Failure and the Crisis of Governance* (pp. 193–209). Institute of Samoan Studies.

Sharma, P. (2009). "Role of Religion in Afghan Politics: Evolution and Key Trends". In A. Pandya & E. Laipson (eds.), *Islam and Politics: Renewal and Resistance in the Muslim World* (pp. 33–42). Stimson Center.

Terpstra, N. (2020). "Rebel governance, rebel legitimacy, and external intervention: assessing three phases of Taliban rule in Afghanistan". *Small Wars & Insurgencies*, *31*(6), pp. 1143–1173. https://doi.org/10.1080/09592318.2020.1757916

7 Analysing Pashtun Nationalism in Afghanistan

Kshipra Vasudeo

Nationalism, like the air we breathe, is ever-present yet difficult to grasp (Bieber, 2018). It shapes global systems, influences state policies, and affects individual behaviour. It can act as both a stabilising force that upholds traditions and a disruptive force that challenges existing structures. Although many have predicted the decline of nationalism, history has shown its persistent nature. The post-Cold War period, instead of marking its end, witnessed a surge in nationalist sentiments, visible in conflicts and upheavals in various regions.

In recent years, nationalism has re-emerged across the globe. Political shifts, such as Donald Trump's election as President of the United States, Brexit, and the policies of leaders in Japan, India, and Turkey, reflect this trend. The rise of far-right parties in parts of Europe further demonstrates the growing appeal of nationalist ideologies. Media attention has highlighted this phenomenon in Western countries and regions like Asia and Africa, indicating that nationalism remains a powerful force in shaping the modern world.

Salman Rafi Sheikh (2016) highlights that the issue of Pashtun nationalism has been interpreted through various perspectives. Some view it as concerning the broader framework of Muslim nationalism and British colonial rule in the Indian subcontinent, while others see it as a reaction to the political marginalisation of the Pashtuns following the partition of India. In the post-9/11 era, particularly with the rise of the Taliban, many explanations have linked the phenomenon of 'Talibanisation' to Pashtun nationalism, portraying it either as a new form of nationalist expression or as an anti-nationalist movement. However, such interpretations overlook the distinct origins and circumstances surrounding both movements. Pashtun nationalism and Talibanisation stem from separate socio-political foundations, making them two fundamentally different phenomena.

According to Devasher (2023), the region inhabited by the Pashtuns, often referred to as Pashtunistan, spans over 100,000 square miles, extending from the Indus River to the Hindu Kush mountains. This ancient land has witnessed numerous conflicts and power struggles throughout history. Before the Sikh conquests in the 19th century and later British rule, the Pashtuns were politically unified under the Afghan empire, which stretched eastward to the Indus. However, the creation of Pakistan in 1947 and the earlier formation of Afghanistan in 1747 divided the Pashtuns along the 2,640-kilometre-long Durand Line, a disputed border between the two countries.

Despite this division, Pashtuns on both sides of the border share common ancestry, culture, language, and historical experiences. Most Pashtuns follow the Sunni Hanafi school of Islam, though some Shia communities also exist. Their shared religious and cultural ties create a strong sense of unity, making them feel like one community despite political borders. The Pashto phrase 'Lar O Bar, Yaw Afghan', meaning 'Afghans from both lowlands and highlands are one', expresses this deep-rooted identity and sense of belonging (Devasher, 2023).

The geographical location of the Pashtun region has served as both an advantage and a vulnerability. Its position along the land route to the riches of India made it a target for numerous invasions throughout history. However, the rugged mountainous terrain of the region became a source of strength for the Pashtun people. This challenging landscape not only provided natural protection but also shaped their resilient and determined character, enabling them to resist and confront invaders with great strength.

According to Effendi (2004), "You cannot defeat people who have no concept of defeat in the classical sense. They only believe in survival. They know when to fight, when to run and hide, and when to talk. Military operations against such adversaries can only have one objective: to bring them to the negotiating table."

In medieval times, Pashtunistan acted as a frontier region, often caught between the competing empires of India, Iran, and Central Asia. Over the last two centuries, the region suffered invasions by the world's leading powers of the time. During the 19th century, the Pashtuns were drawn into the Great Game, where they became unwilling participants in the struggle between Great Britain and Russia. In the 20th century, the Cold War brought further turmoil, with the Soviet Union's invasion turning the Pashtuns into victims of the rivalry between the United States and the USSR. They endured a brutal internal conflict, and in the 21st century, the United States became heavily involved as the Pashtuns emerged as pivotal players in the war on terror and its subsequent developments.

Arthur Swinson has remarked that few regions of a similar scale have experienced such relentless conflict, sacrifice, and a mix of both noble and ignoble qualities throughout history. Pashtunistan has been a crossroads for powerful conquerors—figures like Alexander the Great, Timur, Babur, and Nadir Shah have all left their mark here. In more modern times, the region has witnessed the influence of military and political leaders, such as Pollock, Napier, Nicholson, Roberts, Churchill, Wavell, Lytton, Curzon, Gandhi, Nehru, Attlee, Jinnah, and Mountbatten (Swinson, 1969).

Among these historical references, the Khyber Pass stands out as a symbol of the region's tumultuous past. James Spain describes it as a place where history is almost tangible, its stones bearing the imprints of numerous empires. The pass has been shaped by the legacies of Persian opulence, Greek strength, Tartar resilience, Mogul grandeur, Afghan refinement, and British power, each leaving a lasting influence through both their achievements and sacrifices (Spain, 1972).

Contextualising the Pashtuns

The first question is, who are the Pashtuns? How can they be defined? There is often confusion surrounding the terms 'Pashtun', 'Pakhtun', 'Pathan', and 'Afghan'. This ambiguity largely arises from historical usage, as Persians once used the name 'Afghan' to refer to the people we now call Pashtuns—a naming practice that has endured over time. Later, during the British colonial era, efforts were made to distinguish between these identities. The British labelled those influenced by Persian culture and speakers of Dari as Afghans, while they used 'Pashtun' or 'Pathan' to refer to others. Despite these attempts, the distinctions between the terms have remained blurred. Historically, during interactions with India, they communicated in Pashto. In the northern parts of the region, the people tend to identify as Pakhtun, whereas in the south, the term 'Pashtun' is more commonly used. This distinction also extends to the language, which is referred to as Pakhto in the north and Pashto in the south. Scholars continue to disagree on both the origins of the Pashtuns and the timeline of their settlement in the region now known as Pashtunistan.

Afghanistan has historically not been a stateless territory, as ruling elites managed to establish relationships with various social groups and local leaders. These connections allowed them to maintain control over people, land, and resources while gaining recognition from neighbouring states, thus aligning with the definition of a state.

In the late 19th century, Afghan society was diverse, made up of small towns, tribal communities, feudal landlords, independent farmers, and those working under landlords. Over the 20th century, cities grew, farmers faced increasing debt, and traditional tribal structures weakened. Despite these changes, Afghanistan remained socially and culturally divided, with different legal systems, political beliefs, and languages.

Local communities had strong ties and could organise themselves through tribal leaders, militias, and community gatherings. However, their military power was mostly limited to their own regions unless they received external support. The Afghan state also depended on these local militias to build its armies.

Two key networks facilitated broader collective action: tribal and religious networks. Tribal networks were stable but rarely unified, while religious networks were more adaptable and capable of bridging divisions. The ulema (Islamic scholars) became increasingly political, especially during the 1980s, due to influences from the radicalised Deobandi school in Pakistan (Giustozzi, 2008).

Table 7.1: Segmentation of Afghan Society in 1979

Category	**Percentage**
Urban Population	15.4%
Rural Population	84.6%
First Language	**All Spoken Languages**
Pashto	48%
Dari	40%
Uzbek	8%
Turkmen	2%
Others	2%
Ethnic and Social Groups	**Percentage**
Tribal Pashtun	15%
Semi-detribalised Pashtuns	26%
Detribalised Pashtuns	5%
Urbanised Pashtuns	5%
Urbanised Tajiks	3.5%
Tajik Rural Communities	16%
Shia Tajiks and Qizilbash	0.5%
Uzbeks	9%
Turkmen	2%

Source: Giustozzi, 2008.

The perception that the Pashtuns are inherently religious extremists is misleading and unfounded. Extremist attitudes and behaviours cannot be attributed to an entire ethnic group, as this would imply that all its members think and act alike. While some may hold strong religious affiliations, it is incorrect to assume that this naturally leads to violence. It is unjust to blame an entire community for the actions of a few individuals. Extremism among the Pashtuns did not originate from within but was rather shaped by external influences and geopolitical circumstances. The role of proxy wars in the region cannot be ignored, and the manner in which conflict was imposed on Pashtun territories raises concerns about foreign intervention and hidden agendas (Babakhel, 2016).

There are various theories regarding the origins of the Pashtuns, with hypotheses ranging from Semitic and Indo-Aryan to Turko-Iranian and Arab roots. It highlights that while some traditions trace the Pashtuns' ancestry back to legendary figures like Afghana or Qays bin Rashid—whose conversion to Islam marks the beginning of their recorded history—scholars continue to debate these origins. Additionally, the text notes efforts to codify Pashtun genealogies, such as the compilation of the Makhzan-i-Afghani during the Mughal era. Demographically, there are approximately 31 million Pashtuns in Pakistan and 15 million in Afghanistan, with Karachi hosting the largest concentration worldwide. A central element of Pashtun identity is the tribal code of Pashtunwali, which governs their social conduct through principles of honour, revenge, hospitality, and the protection of family dignity, particularly in relation to women. The narrative also reflects on how early Western accounts, notably those by British administrators like Mountstuart Elphinstone, have shaped the modern image of the Pashtuns by comparing them to other well-known groups and emphasising both their admirable qualities and perceived vices.

The Pashtuns, a historically prominent ethnic group, mostly inhabit Afghanistan and Pakistan. Their identity is influenced by a strong tribal framework, the Pashto language, and the Pashtunwali code, which prioritises honour, hospitality, and justice (Ahmed, 2013). Notwithstanding geographical boundaries, the Pashtuns preserve a profound feeling of oneness via common cultural and historical experiences. Their influence in regional politics has persisted for centuries, spanning from the Afghan empire to modern wars (Giustozzi, 2008). Comprehending Pashtun identity is essential for examining the wider socio-political dynamics of South Asia and its adjacent areas.

Emergence of Pashtun Nationalism in Afghanistan

The Afghan state initially functioned as an imperial entity, characterised by a patrimonial system that relied heavily on coercion and military conquest. Defining its revenue-raising mechanism is challenging due to the diverse practices involved. However, before major reforms, the dominant method depended on tribal and community elders, who were responsible for collecting taxes while retaining a significant portion for personal gain. This system closely resembled “tax farming”, where intermediaries profited from tax collection rather than a centralised administrative structure (Kakar, 1979).

Afghanistan’s complex ethnic diversity has long contributed to its instability and conflict, as noted by Mountstuart Elphinstone, who observed the nation's turbulent power dynamics shaped by old rivalries and emerging interests (Saikal, 2004, p. 1). This fragmentation extends beyond politics into the legal system, which has historically balanced religious, tribal, and modern laws. While Sharia law dominated cities, tribal codes remained strong in rural areas. Efforts by Amir Abdur Rahman to centralise religious law faced resistance, and Amanullah's Western-style legal reforms in 1920 saw limited success outside urban centres. By the 1970s, many rural areas still relied on traditional laws. After 1978, the collapse of state courts further reinforced tribal and religious legal systems. The Taliban later imposed Sharia law over tribal codes, intensifying tensions with local communities (Giustozzi, 2008).

Today, many Pashtuns view themselves as belonging to a Semitic lineage, believing that their ancestors were among Prophet Muhammad's companions. In doing so, they seek to validate their ethnic sanctity through religious ties. This strong attachment to both their ethnic identity and religious heritage significantly reinforces their nationalist sentiments (Rashid, 2008, p. 7).

Benedict Anderson, in his influential work, *Imagined Communities*, argues that nations are "imagined" because even in the smallest countries, most members will never meet or know each other, yet they share a deep sense of belonging. In a similar way, a typical Pashtun is unlikely to know more than a few fellow Pashtuns personally (Anderson, 2006, p. 7).

Pashtun nationalism grew from tribal ambitions to establish a state and gain political power. In this view, forming a nation was seen as the only way to secure authority. However, the Pashtun-led governments in Afghanistan have often presented skewed and speculative figures regarding the Pashtun population to claim a majority, despite the absence of any scientific, objective census since Afghanistan became a political entity (Adamec, 2005, pp. 23–26). In a truly civic and democratic nation-state, the focus is on individual citizenship rather than on the ethnic or religious composition of the population. The modern idea of a nation-state, which distinguishes between old agrarian societies and modern industrial ones, has had little impact on Afghanistan. The country has remained largely tribal and has been minimally influenced by modern democratic and civil processes. Consequently, the traditional tribal, religious, and ethnically driven nationalist movements in Afghanistan, spanning from 1747 to the present, are not significantly shaped by the contemporary concept of a nation-state (Ehsan, 2017).

In 1747, all the Pashtun tribes gathered in Kandahar for a nine-day Loya Jirga, during which Ahmad Shah Abdali was selected as king. He later adopted the surname Durrani for himself and his dynasty, earning the title, "father of the Afghan nation". In 1772, Durrani moved the capital from Kandahar to Kabul and extended his rule into northern Afghanistan, incorporating various ethnic groups into the emerging Afghan nation. Despite enduring internal conflicts among the Ghilzai and Durrani Pashtuns, as well as tensions between Pashtun and non-Pashtun communities, the country has managed to survive through the centuries, maintaining a certain level of sovereignty and territorial cohesion. In the 19th century, British India attempted to conquer Afghanistan on three occasions but failed each time, leading them to designate Afghanistan as a client state rather than an integral part of their empire. At the same time, Tsarist Russia expanded into Central Asia and northern Afghanistan, garnering local support to counter British influence. This rivalry between the two empires was marked by covert tactics, including espionage, bribery, and subtle manoeuvring, for control over Kabul.

By the late 19th century, the two empires reached an agreement to define Afghanistan's borders: to the north with Russia, to the east with India, and to the west with Persia. The British compelled Afghanistan to sign the Treaty of Gandamak in May 1879, and in 1893, the frontier known as the Durand Line was established. Meanwhile, the Russians set boundaries along the Amu Darya in 1888 and in the Pamir region in 1895, with both settlements later confirmed by the 1907 St. Petersburg Anglo-Russian agreement (Ehsan, 2017).

The borders drawn for Afghanistan were established for strategic reasons and did not take into account the ethnic or historical realities of the region. This approach essentially created Afghanistan as a nation-state from what was largely a buffer zone. During his rule from 1880 to 1901, King Abdul Rahman—who received British financial support to build the country's first modern army and administration—employed severe measures to bring other ethnic groups, such as the Tajiks, Hazaras, and Uzbeks, under centralised control. He also forcibly relocated many Pashtuns, including prominent members of the Ghilzai tribe who opposed him, from south-central regions to the northern areas beyond the Hindu Kush. His policies were aimed not only at neutralizing internal rivals but also at reducing the influence of non-Pashtun groups and seizing their lands. These repressive strategies were later continued by his successors, including Habibullah, Amanullah, Nadir Shah, and Zahir Shah (Ehsan, 2017).

There are two main interpretations of what defines the Afghan state. One view emphasises the territorial and dynastic aspect, associating Afghanistan with the lands once governed by Abdul Rahman and highlighting its tribal roots. The other perspective focuses on religion, characterising the country as the region that has remained steadfastly Muslim despite being surrounded by non-Muslim powers, like Britain and Russia, or by those considered heretical, such as certain Shia Persians. In this framework, Afghanistan is seen as a "Millat" (a religious community as defined under Ottoman law), with the Amir strengthening his authority by mobilising the people to defend their Muslim identity against external threats (Roy, 1990, p. 17).

Since 1924, European recognition of Afghanistan has increasingly been based on a vision of nationalism that is seen as uniquely Afghan. The 1923 constitution established Afghanistan as a nation-state where every resident was granted citizenship regardless of their religious background, deliberately omitting any reference to a "Muslim Millat". In the process of forging a national identity, various elements of folklore were introduced—even if they did not have strong indigenous roots. For instance, the sport, Bozkashi, of Turkish origin, was adopted as the national sport, and the dance known as Atan, from Paktia, was adopted as the national dance. Over time, state leaders have placed a significant emphasis on "ethno-symbolism", relying on myths, symbols, and traditional customs to shape a cohesive national narrative.

Olivier Roy argues that Afghanistan has long oscillated between two ideas of nationhood. One concept is that of an abstract nation defined by its sovereign identity, while the other is a historical notion of a Pashtun nation based on ethnic identity, even though this ethnic group never fully achieved nationhood. Interestingly, neither concept had a significant impact on the various groups within the country. The latter idea, however, particularly benefitted the Pashtuns who were not part of the Durrani tribal aristocracy. These groups, many of whom came from the Ghilzai tribe, embraced Pashtun nationalism as a means to enhance their social and political standing and to challenge the existing power monopoly. This movement gained considerable support among the young, educated elite and eventually contributed to the rise of the Khalq faction within the communist party, representing a phase of extreme Pashtun nationalism (Roy, 1990).

Afghan and Pashtun leaders have, on one hand, attempted to adopt Western political models to modernise the country. On the other hand, they have also utilised the nation-state framework to strengthen their ethnic identity by promoting their language and cultural symbols and even modifying military titles to reflect their heritage (Barfield, 2010; Rubin, 2002). For instance, renaming regions and districts from Farsi and Turkish to Pashto clearly demonstrates this effort (Gregorian, 1969). The challenge of balancing Pashtun ethnic dominance with the principles of a democratic, civic nation has persisted since the early nation-building attempts in Afghanistan (Rubin, 2002).

Pashtun political leaders have adopted nationalist rhetoric and symbols to project an image of unity and justify their ongoing power. In contrast, other ethnic groups have found themselves increasingly sidelined, experiencing systematic suppression of their cultural heritage, language, myths, and territorial claims, along with unequal access to power and resources. These persistent discriminatory practices based on ethnicity, religion, and language have fostered deep resentment and disillusionment among these communities, a frustration that notably erupted during the 1990s. According to anthropologist Ernest Gellner, pre-modern societies were primarily organised around kinship and patronage ties; in such societies, strong clan-based systems prevailed because loyalty was rooted in family rather than in a modern nation-state (Cole & Kandiyoti, 2002).

Afghanistan remains a country where religion and ethnicity are deeply intertwined with political life. Afghan and Pashtun nationalist ambitions have not only shaped domestic policies but also significantly influenced the nation's foreign policy. For example, the Afghan government once introduced a radical reform aimed at promoting Pashtunism as the cornerstone of a broader Afghan nationalism, an effort designed to impact Pashtuns on the Pakistani side of the border. This policy contributed to separatist movements among Pakistani Pashtuns—evidenced in 1949 when Afridi tribes declared an independent Pashtunistan, a state recognised solely by Afghanistan, thereby straining relations with Pakistan.

In the 1950s, Afghanistan's refusal to join regional alliances, such as the Middle East Treaty Organization (MEDO), the Central Treaty Organization (CENTO), and the Southeast Asia Treaty Organization (SEATO) —all of which included Pakistan—was influenced by its ongoing border disputes, particularly over the Durand Line and territorial disagreements with Iran. This stance led the United States to withhold military aid, which, in turn, contributed to Prime Minister Daoud Khan's pivot towards the Soviet Union. His pursuit of ethnicity-based policies, coupled with increasing Soviet economic and military assistance, gradually eroded Afghanistan's neutrality and deepened its dependence on Moscow.

The subsequent civil war in the 1990s, fuelled by ethno-political divisions, ultimately gave rise to the Taliban. The Taliban's takeover, driven by strong Pashtun chauvinism, was marked by severe persecution of non-Pashtun groups, cultural destruction, and religious intolerance—actions that eroded their legitimacy as a unifying national force. After 2001, there was a move towards greater national integration, with government roles distributed among major ethnic groups. However, despite significant international support for building a democratic system, President Karzai's administration continued to be dominated by traditional, tribal, and factional politics.

The major challenge ahead lies in establishing a robust legal and institutional framework that ensures governance based on public participation, transparency, accountability, and merit rather than on family ties or ethnic affiliation.

State-building is a deliberate political process, influenced by a range of social and economic factors rather than occurring naturally. No modern nation is entirely homogeneous in terms of ethnicity or religion; every state comprises diverse groups with varied cultural, ethnic, and religious backgrounds. Theories of political modernisation by Tilly (1994), Mann (1995), and Hechter (2000) focus on how governance systems evolved over time. From the 16th century, continuous wars between European states led to more efficient government control and resource management. Earlier, rulers relied on local elites to govern (indirect rule), but later, a centralised and hierarchical bureaucracy took over (direct rule).

This change led to two major paths toward the nation-state. In autonomous states like France, national leaders unified the population and promoted nationalism to justify their rule (Hechter, 2000; Tilly, 1994). Mann (1995) explained that nationalism also emerged from ordinary people demanding democratic representation from an increasingly powerful state.

However, a more common result of direct rule was the rise of nationalist movements seeking independence. In multiethnic empires like the Habsburg, Ottoman, and later, Yugoslav states, local elites resisted being ruled by outsiders and fought for self-rule. Whether these movements succeeded depended on various factors, including international support. Based on these ideas, it can be proposed that the stronger the central control over a region, the higher the chances of it becoming a nation-state.

In the context of Afghanistan, the challenge of constructing a cohesive nation-state has been attributed to several factors, including its challenging geography, persistent ethnic and sectarian divisions, and entrenched tribal structures. However, it is also contended that the policies of successive central governments have exacerbated these divisions. Rather than promoting genuine national unity, these governments have frequently reinforced existing ethnic and tribal cleavages by allocating power to prominent ethnic leaders and their kin. This approach has resulted in a system where civic participation is limited and democratic integration is undermined.

Furthermore, as noted by organisations such as the International Crisis Group, the prospects for achieving moderation and democracy in Afghanistan depend on the government's ability to encourage inclusive public participation and to adopt innovative engagement strategies. For Afghanistan to evolve into a unified nation-state, it is imperative that all ethnic and religious communities are granted opportunities for political involvement, that the rule of law is firmly established, and that a robust civil society is developed. Ultimately, the formation of a national government that genuinely reflects the country's diverse population is essential for its successful democratisation and long-term stability (Rotberg, 2007).

Afghanistan's experience with nationalism after colonialism is complex due to its deep ethnic divisions and weak national identity. Instead of a unified Afghan nationalism, different ethnic groups—the Tajiks, Uzbeks, Hazaras, Turkmens, Aimaqs, Nuristanis, and Baluchis—held competing ideas of the nation. Afghanistan's history reflects both external colonialism by Britain and the USSR and internal colonialism, where Pashtun tribal elites dominated minority groups. The ongoing process of nation-building remains unstable, with ethnic tensions worsening due to power struggles and war since 1978 (Hyman, 2002).

Decades of conflict have shattered Afghanistan's fragile unity. Rival leaders have failed to establish a stable government, leading to the fragmentation of the state. The Taliban and northern warlords competed for control, deepening ethnic and sectarian divisions. Meanwhile, nationalism in Afghanistan remained weak, mainly appealing to a small urban elite detached from the predominantly rural and tribal population. As a result, Afghanistan lacks a unified national identity, with many people remaining more loyal to local or ethnic affiliations than to the state itself (Hyman, 2002).

Conclusion

The trajectory of Pashtun nationalism has been significantly influenced by a combination of historical, political, and religious factors, which have shaped the socio-political realities of the Pashtun people. The rise of the Taliban brought about a drastic shift in traditional Pashtun values, particularly undermining the Pashtunwali code, which emphasised hospitality, honour, and communal justice. The Taliban's rigid interpretations of Islam not only restricted women's rights and mobility but also disrupted cultural institutions, such as the Hujra (traditional guesthouses for communal discourse) and Lashkars (community defence forces), weakening the foundations of Pashtun society (Babakhel, 2016; Khattak, 2009). These changes, coupled with Pakistan's military operations in tribal regions and policies that treated the Pashtuns as strategic assets in conflicts such as the Kashmir wars and the Soviet-Afghan War, further marginalised the community. The promotion of religious extremism during General Zia-ul-Haq's regime and the subsequent proliferation of madrasas in place of secular educational institutions contributed to the decline of Pashtun political consciousness and cultural identity (Bibi & Khan, 2020).

The aftermath of the Soviet withdrawal, followed by the War on Terror, saw Pashtun regions becoming conflict zones where the community suffered immense socio-economic losses, displacement, and psychological trauma. Decades of conflict left the Pashtuns caught between extremist groups and state military operations, further alienating them from mainstream political processes. Media portrayals perpetuated stereotypes, depicting the Pashtuns as Taliban sympathisers rather than victims of radicalisation and state policies. Economic hardships, urbanisation, and forced migration also led to a dilution of traditional values, further eroding the unity of the Pashtun nationalist movement (Khattak, 2009).

Despite these challenges, contemporary Pashtun nationalism is undergoing a revival, driven by younger generations who seek to reclaim their identity and assert their constitutional rights. Movements such as the Pashtun Long March exemplify the growing political consciousness within the community, as activists demand justice, better governance, and an end to state repression. This resurgence reflects a shift away from tribal affiliations and historical grievances towards a collective push for socio-political reforms and human rights (Sood, 2018). The resilience of the Pashtun people in the face of decades of violence and oppression underscores their determination to preserve their cultural heritage while advocating for a more inclusive and democratic political framework. If this momentum continues, Pashtun nationalism could evolve into a formidable socio-political force that not only reclaims lost cultural and political space but also strengthens democratic discourse within Pakistan and the broader region.

References

Adamec, L. (2005). *The political history of Afghanistan: From Amir Abdul Rahman era till independence*. Kabub Payez Publisher. (A. M. Zama, Trans.; pp. 23–26).

Ahmed, A. S. (2013). *The Thistle and the Drone: How America's War on Terror Became a Global War on Tribal Islam*. Brookings Institution Press.

Anderson, B. (2006). *Imagined Communities: Reflections on the Origin and Spread of Nationalism*. Verso.

Babakhel, M. A. (May 29, 2016). "Extremism in books". *Dawn*. https://www.dawn.com/news/1261474/extremism-in-books

Barfield, T. (2010). *Afghanistan: A Cultural and Political History*. Princeton University Press.

Bibi, H. & Khan, S. (2020). "An Analysis of Various Factors having Direct or Indirect Impacts on Pashtun Nationalism". *Sir Syed Journal of Education & Social Research*, *3*(2), pp. 346–353. https://doi.org/10.36902/sjesr-vol3-iss2-2020(346-353)

Bieber, F. (2018). "Is Nationalism on the Rise? Assessing Global Trends". *Ethnopolitics*, *17*(5), pp. 519–540. https://doi.org/10.1080/17449057.2018.1532633

Cole, J. R. I. & Kandiyoti, D. (2002). "Nationalism and the Colonial Legacy in the Middle East and Central Asia: Introduction". *International Journal of Middle East Studies*, *34*(2), pp. 189–203. https://doi.org/10.1017/S0020743802002027

Devasher, T. (2023). "The Pashtuns: Understanding History and Culture". *Defence and Diplomacy Journal*, *12*(2), pp. 15–27.

Effendi, M. Y. (2004). "Watch and ward on the frontier (1849-1947)". Report presented at the seminar on Federally Administered Tribal Areas of Pakistan, Area Study Centre, University of Peshawar, and Hanns Seidel Foundation.

Ehsan, M. (2017). "Ethnicity, Religion and Nationalism in Afghanistan". *Himalayan and Central Asian Studies*, *21*(2-3), pp. 118–132.

Hechter, M. (2000). *Containing Nationalism*. Oxford University Press.

Hyman, A. (2002). "Nationalism in Afghanistan". *International Journal of Middle East Studies*, 34(2), pp. 299-315.

Gregorian, V. (1969). *The Emergence of Modern Afghanistan: Politics of Reform and Modernization, 1880-1946*. Stanford University Press.

Giustozzi, A. (2008). "Development as State Making: Afghanistan—Transition Without End, An Analytical Narrative on State-Making" (Working Paper 40). Crisis States Research Centre. https://www.lse.ac.uk/international-development/Assets/Documents/PDFs/csrc-working-papers-phase-two/wp40.2-afghanistan-transition-without-end.pdf.

Khattak, D. (August 14, 2009). "In Pakistan, Taliban tearing apart a culture: Pashtun residents say militants have imposed extremist views on the population, displacing centuries-old traditions". *Christian Science Monitor*.

Kakar, H. (1979). *Government and Society in Afghanistan: The Reign of Amir Abd al-Rahman Khan*. University of Texas Press.

Mann, M. (1995). *The Sources of Social Power, Volume 2: The Rise of Classes and Nation-States, 1760-1914*. Cambridge University Press.

Rashid, A. (2008). *Descent Into Chaos: How the War Against Islamic Extremism is Being Lost in Pakistan, Afghanistan and Central Asia*. Penguin.

Rotberg, R. I. (2007). *Building a New Afghanistan*. Brookings Institution Press.

Roy, O. (1990). *Islam and Resistance in Afghanistan* (2nd ed.). Cambridge University Press.

Rubin, B. R. (2002). *The Fragmentation of Afghanistan: State Formation and Collapse in the International System*. Yale University Press.

Saikal, A. (2004). *Modern Afghanistan: A History of Struggle and Survival*. I.B. Tauris.

Sheikh, S. R. (2016). "Pashtun nationalism: Politics and Talibanization". *Pakistan Horizon*, 69(1), pp. 71–86. Pakistan Institute of International Affairs.

Sood, V. (March 6, 2018). "The Pashtun awakening". Observer Research Foundation. Retrieved from https://www.orfonline.org/research/pashtun-awakening

Spain, J. W. (1972). *The Way of the Pathans*. Oxford University Press.

Swinson, A. (1969). *North-West Frontier: People and Events 1839-1947*. Corgi.

Tilly, C. (1994). *Coercion, Capital, and European States, AD 990-1992*. Blackwell.

8 Impact of the Tajik Ethnicity Factor on Tajikistan's Ties with Afghanistan

Aditi Bhaduri

Afghanistan is home to many ethnic groups. The ethnic factor was well managed by the Afghan monarchy. It became a critical issue only after the Afghan jihad ended and Afghanistan became a theatre for internecine bloodletting. The Taliban, in particular, fed on Pashtun pride and nationalism and let loose a reign of terror, especially against the Hazara and the Tajik minorities. While the US- backed governments of both President Hamid Karzai and President Ashraf Ghani had been accommodative of the many ethnic groups inhabiting the country, the current Taliban government has been failing on this front, despite being in power for more than four years.

This paper will look into how the Tajik minority community in Afghanistan has helped shape the policies of the neighbouring state of Tajikistan towards Afghanistan.

Almost all of Afghanistan's immediate neighbours, and even others in the region, have established relations with the Taliban and have been engaging with it. This also includes India, which had been holding back for the longest time and has only recently begun to engage with the Taliban. Tajikistan alone has, till now, refused to establish any relations with the Taliban. It also continues to host the previous Afghan government's representative, Mohammad Zahir Aghbar, who now has switched allegiance to the Tajik-dominated Resistance Front.

Who are the Tajiks?

Afghanistan is home to a number of ethnic groups. The Pashtuns form the largest group—38-44 per cent of the population; the Tajiks form 25 per cent of the population; the Hazaras form 10 per cent of the population; and the Uzbeks form 6–8 per cent of the population. Besides these main ethno-linguistic groups, there are several smaller ethnic groups: the Aimaq, Baluchis, who are located in the west and southwest of the country and the Nuristanis, located in the east of the country.

The Tajiks are an ethnic group that speak a dialect of Persian (Dari) and live in the area extending from western China to Iran. The Tajiks are of Iranian background and may have been the first Persian inhabitants of modern day Afghanistan. Contemporary Tajiks are the descendants of ancient Eastern Iranian inhabitants of Central Asia, notably the Sogdians and the Bactrians. They are predominantly Sunni Muslims of the Hanafi School of law.

The Tajiks are the largest ethnic group in Tajikistan, comprising nearly 80 per cent of the population of 7.3 million. The Tajiks are the second-largest ethnic group in Afghanistan, with roughly 8.8 million people (Minority Rights Group, n.d.). Credible numbers about the demographic composition of Afghanistan are not available. The last census conducted in the country was in the 1970s.

In Afghanistan, the Tajik population is concentrated in the northeast of the country along the border with Tajikistan, but communities are also found in the centre and west of the country. Large Tajik populations in Afghanistan are also located in major cities, such as Kabul, Herat, and Mazar-e Sharif.

While the origins of the Tajik populations in Afghanistan and Tajikistan and aspects of their language are similar, with cultural overlap, the diverse political trajectories of the two countries have created visible distinctions between them.

The largest concentrations of Tajiks in Afghanistan are found in the mountainous terrain of the Panjshir Valley in the northeast and in the surrounding provinces of Parham, Takhar, Badakhshan, Baghlan, Samangan, and Bakhi. The Panjshir Valley is seen as a 'spiritual home' for Afghan Tajiks, and many of the most influential of the Tajik leaders within the Northern Alliance are originally from there. Tajiks also reside in western Afghanistan, primarily in and around the city of Herat. A sizeable Tajik population lives in and around Kabul, where they have, to a large degree, assimilated with the urban and other ethnic populations.

Among Afghanistan's Tajiks, the tribal organisation has essentially disappeared and has been substituted by familial and village organisations. Thus, unlike Afghan Pashtuns, there are no tribal affiliations but a strong sense of Tajik community.

Relations between the Tajiks and Pashtuns are complex, often being tense and confrontational. The rivalry between the Tajiks and Pashtuns and the inability of these two groups to share power has been a strong and driving force in the domestic politics and conflicts of Afghanistan.

Tajiks have served as administrators and bureaucrats in Afghanistan, but they have been essentially shut out of the high-ranking leadership positions and the military officer class. These positions are primarily dominated by the Pashtun tribes. Tajiks have only held any significant national power within Afghanistan twice in the country's history. The first instance was under the short- lived rule of Habibullah Khan in 1929 (Institute for the Study of War, n.d.).

The second instance was under Afghanistan's Mujahideen government of 1992 under Tajik Burhanuddin Rabbani, who was elected President of the Islamic Council for one year by the Mujahideen executive council. Rabbani held onto power in Kabul for four years before he was toppled by the Taliban in September 1996. During Taliban rule (1996-2001), President Rabbani served as the head of the Afghan government that held Afghanistan's seat at the United Nations and which was recognised by the international community, including India. Rabbani also served as the political figurehead of the main military opposition to the Taliban, the Tajik-dominated Northern Alliance.

The Northern Alliance was united, however, by the common Taliban enemy and by the leadership of General Ahmed Shah Masood, known as 'The Lion of the Panjshir'. Masood, like the majority of the core of the Northern Alliance, was a Tajik. General Masood was the most prominent Tajik leader in Afghanistan since 1996 and the primary source of military and political authority among the Afghan Tajiks.

Tajikistan and Afghanistan

Tajikistan sits on Afghanistan's northeastern border, lying adjacent to the Afghan provinces of Badakhshan, Takhar, Kunduz, and Balkh. Tajikistan shares the longest border with Afghanistan, measuring 1357 km. Much of Tajikistan's southeastern border with Afghanistan lies in the Pamir Mountain range—the junction of the Hindu Kush and the Karakoram Mountains and home to some of the highest peaks in the world.

Tajikistan and the Afghan Jihad

When the Afghan jihad broke out following the 1979 invasion by the erstwhile Union of Soviet Socialist Republics (USSR) into Afghanistan, the Republic of Tajikistan was a part of the USSR, one of the Soviet Republics. By virtue of sharing a long border with Afghanistan, Tajikistan is ethnically, linguistically, and culturally connected to the Tajik population on the other side of the border in Afghanistan. As a bordering republic, therefore, logistically, it played an important role for transportation and supplies. Many of the military and civil personnel sent to Afghanistan from the USSR also constituted Tajiks, as did personnel from other Soviet Republics, like Uzbekistan and Turkmenistan, that not only shared a border with Afghanistan but also linguistic and cultural linkages.

According to scholars, researchers, and Soviet/Russian Afghan war veterans, the Afghan jihad had a two-fold impact on Tajik Soviets.

Witnessing first-hand the socio-economic levels of the Afghans, many Soviet Tajiks felt a sense of pride in the Soviet Union, which reinforced their sense of loyalty to the USSR.

For yet other Soviet Tajiks, long exposure to the Afghan Tajiks ignited in them a sense of loss of their cultural and linguistic heritage. As a result, after returning to their homeland, they pushed for cultural, linguistic, and religious revival in Tajikistan.

Many of the Soviet Tajiks who worked in state institutions, and particularly in the humanities, in the Republic of Afghanistan, became nationalists in Tajikistan. They supported the revival of the Tajik language, the revival of Tajik culture, and the revival of the Islamic religion in Tajikistan. For example, Tohrir Abdudžabbor, Mirbobo Mirrahim, and many others supported this (Göransson, 2016). Many others played a leading role in the passing of the Law on Language and in the movement for the independence of the Tajik republic (Klimentov, 2022). Inevitably, this interface also ignited another fervour, more explosive in scope—religious. Many of these Tajiks were introduced to Islamism in Afghanistan. The jihad invoked in many of them feelings of empathy for Afghan Tajiks, reinforcing ethno-cultural bonds and pride in a shared heritage, which while alive in Afghanistan, seemed to have been usurped in Tajikistan. The jihad also coincided with Perestroika and Glasnost back home under then President Mikhail Gorbachev. This resulted in loosening of censorship, relaxation of strict rules imposed to clamp down on assemblies, religiosity, and the revival of religion. Thousands of Tajiks (as also Uzbeks and Kyrgyz) secretly joined the Afghan jihad, fighting with Afghan-Tajik mujahideen leaders Ahmad Shah Massoud and Burhanuddin Rabbani and their Jamiat-e Islami, and thus, these Tajiks were introduced to Islamism and Tajik nationalism.

Victor Spolnikov, former KGB station chief in Kabul who went on to become a researcher at Moscow's Oriental Studies Institute, was of the view that 'unofficial Islam' in Central Asia had long worried the KGB. He argued that the Soviet-Afghan War had triggered the creation of the Tajik Islamist movement (Spolnikov, 1994).

The roots of the Tajik Civil War, therefore, can be traced back to the end of the Soviet–Afghan War. Inevitably, with the breakdown of the USSR, a struggling economy, and the return of Tajik Islamists to Tajikistan, chaos and conflict ensued. State institutions broke down, leading to the Tajik Civil War, which lasted from 1992 to 1997. The main opposition group—the Islamic Renaissance Party (IRP)—was born in the crucible of the Afghan jihad. Terrorists like Juma Namangani were baptised in jihad in Afghanistan and went on to found groups like the Islamic Movement of Uzbekistan (IMU). The IMU, while having lost its potency, still continues to exist, with the potential to emerge as a threat.

During the Tajik civil war, opposition groups like the IRP, which later with other opposition groups morphed into the United Tajik Opposition (UTO), were not only supported with arms and resources by the Afghan Mujahideen but were often given refuge on Afghan territory from where they continued their armed struggle.

Ultimately, in 1997, peace accords were signed between the Tajik government of President Emamoli Rahmanov and the Tajik opposition in Moscow, facilitated by the Russian Federation and the United States of America.

Along with Islamism and jihad, Tajikistan also suffered from drug trafficking through its territory from Afghanistan to Russia and further to Europe.

By the time the Tajik civil war ended, the Taliban had seized power in Kabul. Concluding that the Taliban, with their madrasa-learned puritanical Deobandi Islam, constituted a bigger threat than the Mujahideen did, Tajikistan, together with Russia, Iran, and India, began supporting the Tajik- dominated Northern Alliance of General Ahmed Shah Masood. The Northern Alliance was physically concentrated in and their influence limited to the Panjshir Valley. Tajikistan became the conduit for supplies and support from Russia, Iran, and India to the Northern Alliance.

What also needs to be remembered is the fact that hundreds of Tajiks had then fled to Afghanistan and had found shelter there. After their return to their homeland, they could not be indifferent to the fate of the Tajiks on the other side of the border. Emotions, therefore, run high when adversity befalls the Tajik community in Afghanistan. When the Taliban took over Kabul in 1996 and the Tajik- dominated Northern Alliance mounted a strong resistance to it, they were supported by Tajikistan, which became the conduit for supplies and support from Russia, Iran, and India to the Northern Alliance.

It was in Tajikistan that Indian envoy Bharath Raj Muthu Kumar met Ahmed Shah Massoud to chalk out logistics for Indian aid. As the Taliban began taking over Afghanistan, again hundreds of Afghans fled to Tajikistan.

When the war on terror and Operation Enduring Freedom began, Tajikistan extended all help and support to the US forces.

Tajikistan and Taliban 2.0

The day Kabul fell, on August 15, 2021, as the US and the NATO forces withdrew, an observer in Dushanbe told this author that an era had just started. "The Tajiks will never ever accept to be ruled by the Taliban," he said. "Either they will continue to fight or they will insist on a federation," the observer further added.

As events unfolded, President Ashraf Ghani fled, allegedly with a helicopter full of money. His vice president, Amrullah Saleh, it was rumoured, had also fled. Some accounts said he was in neighbouring Tajikistan. But he soon resurfaced in the Panjshir valley—famous for its unyielding and autonomous spirit. Together with Ahmad Massoud, son of the late Mujahideen and Northern Alliance leader Ahmed Shah Massoud, they are leading the last resistance to the Taliban. The rest of the Mujahideen and acclaimed warlords have all fallen, most having fled to other countries.

When Saleh resurfaced, claiming the mantle of the caretaker president—as per Afghanistan's constitution—the loudest cheer came from the Afghan ambassador in Dushanbe. Mohammad Zahir Aghbar, representing the Islamic Republic of Afghanistan, removed the photo of President Ghani from the Embassy's wall and hung up one of Saleh in a widely circulated photo, which he also posted on his Facebook page. He also held a press conference where he proclaimed Saleh to be the 'legitimate caretaker president' and came out strongly against 'corrupt' President Ashraf Ghani, who he said had fled with $169 million, and called for Interpol to arrest him and the accomplices who fled with him—Hamidullah Moheb and Fazal Mahmood Fazli. He also refused to acknowledge the Taliban government, calling for the formation of an inclusive government.

Considering Tajikistan's authoritative rule, it is obvious that Aghbar could not have done all this without some kind of endorsement by the Tajik government.

With Tajikistan sharing the longest border with Afghanistan and with cross border ethno-cultural, linguistic, and religious linkages, what happens in Afghanistan does not remain in Afghanistan but spills over into Tajik territory and vice versa.

As the Taliban began taking over Afghanistan, again hundreds of Afghans fled to Tajikistan, though there is no official data available. However, the authorities of Gorno Badakhshan province, on July 7, 2021 (about a month before the Taliban took over Afghanistan), announced that about a thousand Afghans had fled there. Almost 15,000 Afghan soldiers were also reported to have fled there out of fear, but authorities were said to have ensured their safe return home. Tajikistan had also made provisions to shelter 100,000 Afghan evacuees in the wake of the Taliban takeover.

It is no surprise, therefore, that of all of Afghanistan's neighbours, it is Tajikistan that has not yet had any official engagement with the Taliban.

According to journalist Sirojiddin Tolibov, since the Taliban took over Kabul, the people of Tajikistan have been mostly dismayed, feeling that this would give a fillip to the rise of similar groups in Tajikistan. The elites particularly see this as a Pashtun-orientated Taliban, which will seek revenge on the Tajik and other non-Pashtun minorities in Afghanistan. Only the religious people are happy seeing the Taliban rise to power and their threats of dealing firmly with corruption as an inspiration for Tajiks to deal with their political elites (Bhaduri, 2021).

While border security had been reinforced, with the Tajik army holding numerous military drills with Russia, Uzbekistan, and also procuring arms, popular sentiment in Tajikistan is, by and large, with Ahmed Massoud in Panjshir. The leader of the Democratic Party of Tajikistan, Saidjafar Usmonzoda, in a statement, called the Taliban a 'terrorist group', which was conducting a genocide on the non-Pashtun Tajik people of Afghanistan, devastating their lands and stealing their women and called on the international community, and even the government, to shut down the embassies of Qatar and Pakistan for having facilitated the return of the Taliban. Once again, this could not have happened had there not been a wink and a nod from the authorities. Following this, about 2000 Tajik youth announced their readiness to volunteer militarily with Ahmed Massoud's forces in Panjshir.

On September 8, 2021, the Taliban announced its interim government under Mullah Hibatullah Akhundzada and declared the country an 'Islamic Emirate'. It was exclusively male, Pashtun, with Taliban hardliners dominating all posts. Around the same time, Dushanbe began celebrating the 30th anniversary of Tajikistan's independence. President Emamoli Rahmon, in an address to the nation, delivered the first salvo. Without naming Pakistan, he stressed that the instability and tragedy of Afghanistan was the result of foreign interference in the country, which was continuing till now. The Tajik president also expressed concern over the situation in Afghanistan becoming more complicated and tragic, which would be a cause of great concern for the region and for the countries around the world.

The National Resistance Movement, headed by Ahmed Massoud and former Afghan Vice President Amrullah Saleh, denounced the government.

Instead, it announced that it would continue the resistance, and, four years later, Panjshir has not yet submitted to the Taliban.

President Rahmon expressed regret at the way the Afghans had been abandoned by powers who used them and called again for international organisations to protect the human rights of the Afghan people and for 'immediate and collective' measures for the formation of a government of 'national reconciliation, taking into account the interests of all peoples and minorities living in Afghanistan'.

Coming soon after the Taliban's announcement of its government, this seemed to be nothing but a rejection of the Taliban's government.

But this was not all. Coming on the heels of the President's speech was a press conference by the Afghan ambassador in Dushanbe, Mohammad Zahir Aghbar. Rejecting the Taliban government, which he said had taken the country by force, he stressed that the resistance in Panjshir would continue, and that both Ahmed Massoud and Amrullah Saleh were still present in Panjshir. The war was not one between fellow Afghans but one which had been foisted on the Afghans by external forces, he said, in an obvious reference to Pakistan whose spy chief had to fly in to Kabul to get the government formation going and which is accused of sending its air power to quash the resistance in Panjshir.

The ambassador further signalled that it was more than likely that a council may be constituted in Afghanistan, which would include those like Ahmed Massoud, Amrullah Saleh, Marshall Rashid Dostum, and others under the flag of the NRF and which could fight the Taliban. He stressed that the NRF did not consist only of Tajiks but included Uzbeks, Pashtuns and Hazaras, enjoying the confidence of all the Afghan people.

Soon after, Pakistan's foreign minister, Shah Mehmood Qureshi, made a tour of regional and neighbouring capitals to drum up support for the newly formed Taliban government in Kabul. This included a meeting with President Emamoli Rahmon. However, the meeting turned out to be an embarrassment of sorts for Qureshi. Instead of persuading Rahmon to support the Taliban, Qureshi got an earful from Rahmon regarding the fact that the Taliban were not fulfilling their promise of forming an inclusive government with Tajik representation. The Taliban, therefore, remained unrecognised by Tajikistan.

Following this announcement, Rahmon's popularity has shot up. While pre-empting the conflict from spilling over onto Tajik territory, this announcement also served to shore up the President's standing. However, Rahmon had also underscored the fact that Dushanbe did not mind an efficient national reconciliation in the neighbouring country where ethnic Tajiks constitute almost 45 per cent of the population, though not at any cost, and only on specific decent terms for the entire ethnic community of the local Tajiks.

Rahmon also posthumously awarded the leaders of the anti-Taliban movement (ethnic Tajiks)—the legendary commander of the Mujahideen, Ahmad Shah Massoud, and the ex-President of Afghanistan, Burhanuddin Rabbani—with the Order of Ismoili Somoni, Tajikistan's highest distinction.

It is also amply clear that Tajikistan also supports the remaining opponents of the Taliban—the Afghan National Resistance Front in the Panjshir province (more than 98 per cent of the province's population are ethnic Tajiks). This is the only territory that the Taliban have not yet fully taken over (Umarov, 2021).

Why did Tajikistan take such an anti-Taliban Position?

Four years after the fall of Kabul to the Taliban, the Islamic Emirate of Afghanistan has established representative offices in Tehran, Abu Dhabi, Doha, Moscow, Beijing, and Ashkhabad. Taliban- ruled Afghanistan continues trade and official relations with Tashkent and Astana. Taliban representatives are also present in Delhi.

On March 20, 2025, much of Asia celebrated Nowruz—the old Persian New Year that coincides with the spring equinox. It remains a major festival of Tajikistan and was celebrated with fervour. One of the institutions that also marked the festival with celebrations was the Afghan Embassy in Dushanbe that represents the Afghan National Resistance Front, more commonly known as the Northern Alliance. The Embassy is headed by Ambassador Mohammad Zahir Aghbar, who had earlier represented the Islamic Republic of Afghanistan till the fall of Kabul to the Taliban on August 15, 2021. Celebrating an ancient tradition is a symbolic act on the part of the Afghan National Resistance Front to oppose the narrow-minded and radical version of Islam that the Taliban has imposed in Afghanistan.

Cultural affinity is one of the aspects that is often employed to oppose the current Taliban regime in Afghanistan by the Tajiks and the Afghans opposed to the Taliban. This aspect is also deployed by the Tajik government to refuse to recognise the current Taliban government in Kabul till it forms an "inclusive government", which here is understood as power-sharing with the Tajiks of Afghanistan.

Tajikistan, thus, stands out as the only country in the region which has still not extended any kind of recognition to the Taliban regime in Kabul. On the other hand, it openly supports the Afghan resistance, while at the same time, advocating for an inclusive government in Kabul, as it had earlier, too.

Initially, the tough anti-Taliban rhetoric of the President of Tajikistan was widely attributed to a two-layered logic. The first was for internal consumption in Tajikistan—(to project himself as a strong man) the Father of the Nation must always be strong and determined to protect the nation world-wide. For this, there was a strong base as common Tajik sentiment in the country is firmly hinged on solidarity with their Tajik brethren in Afghanistan.

The second was in the external message that Tajiks everywhere, and especially in Afghanistan, must be sure that they always can count on the support of their kin, people, and the state (of Tajikistan).

However, security remains the most important aspect. Tajikistan shares not just the longest border with Afghanistan but one that is also mountainous and difficult to control. While Tajikistan is a member of the Moscow-led Collective Security Treaty Organisation (CSTO) and houses a large Russian military base, the Tajik army is considered as the weakest in Central Asia.

From the time it became imminent that the Taliban would take over Kabul, Tajikistan hosted and participated in a number of military drills with the CSTO as well as bilaterally and multilaterally with countries like Uzbekistan. Prior to the Taliban takeover of Kabul, there were border skirmishes between Tajikistan's border forces and Tajik members of the Taliban on the Afghan side.

Moreover, much of the drug traffic from Afghanistan to Russia and Europe passes through Tajikistan.

In recent years, terrorist attacks have occurred in the country more than once. There is growing religious radicalisation in the country. Tajik nationals, along with other Muslim citizens of Russia and countries of the Commonwealth of Independent States (CIS), constituted one of the main pillars of the Islamic State Caliphate that had temporarily emerged in Syria and Iraq. Even police officers from Tajikistan had migrated to join the Islamic State.

Even after the decimation of the Islamic Caliphate, in recent times, Tajik nationals have been found involved in terror attacks in places as far as Tehran and Germany. The horrific terror attacks on the Moscow mall, Crocus, was carried out by Tajik nationals in the name of the Islamic State Khorasan Province (ISKP). The ISKP is rapidly expanding its footprint in Central Asia, including in Tajikistan, as also actively recruiting from Tajik migrant workers living outside Tajikistan in foreign countries like Russia, Germany, and Türkiye. The ISKP constitutes a nightmare and Tajikistan's worst security threat. In order to combat this phenomenon, the Tajik government recently took measures like banning the hijab and participation of children in religious festivities.

Officially, President Emomali Rahmon justified this position by saying that the Taliban cannot be trusted because they violate the rights of national and religious minorities. At meetings with world leaders and at international venues, Rahmon never tires of repeating, "Tajikistan will not recognize any other government formed in this country through oppression and persecution, without taking into account the position of the entire Afghan people, especially all of its national minorities" (*ANI*, 2021).

This strong position is striking, diverging as it does, not only with that of its regional neighbours but even with Russia, with whom Tajikistan shares the closest ties. However, for a secular Soviet- trained political elite, which had battled Islamists in a long scarring civil war and stares at the growing spectre of the ISKP in the country, this position is inevitable.

Conclusion

Tajikistan has remained steadfast to the Tajik community in Afghanistan. However, two factors may be causing a slow rethink in Dushanbe: one is the Afghan Taliban's entrenchment in Afghanistan and its slow but sure recognition by more and more countries, both in the region as well as by extra-regional powers; and the second is the growing threat of the Islamic State of Khorasan or the ISKP.

The first reported contact occurred after militants from the Islamic State of Khorasan (ISK) launched several rockets from northern Afghanistan into Tajikistan on May 7, 2022. Former Tajik security officer Samariddin Chuyanzoda travelled to Kabul on May 14, 2022, to meet with Taliban representatives. The Taliban were facing sporadic attacks from the ISK before foreign troops departed Afghanistan, and those attacks continue to this day. The Taliban claim that among the ISK militants they have killed or captured in the last three years, some are citizens of Tajikistan (Pannier, 2024).

In August 2024, Saimumin Yatimov, the leader of Tajikistan's security service, visited Kabul to reportedly discuss strengthening ties between Tajikistan and the Taliban. Even earlier, Tajik officials had held discussions regarding the Jamaat Ansarullah (a terrorist group originating in Tajikistan that allied itself with the Taliban during the final years foreign forces were in Afghanistan) fighters.

Tajikistan has also been allowing humanitarian aid to reach Afghanistan through its territory and has also sent humanitarian aid to the war-torn country.

However, in summer 2024, Tajikistan also upgraded its relations with Pakistan to a Strategic Partnership. On December 30, 2024, Muhammad Asim Malik, General Director of Pakistan's Inter-Services Intelligence, travelled to Dushanbe and met with President Emamoli Rahmon. Coming against the backdrop of Pakistan's intensifying conflict, the meeting fuelled speculation that an anti-Taliban coalition may be in the works. Rahmon's office, however, released a statement saying that issues of current bilateral relations and prospects for their further development, as well as issues of regional peace, security, and stability, were discussed (Pressa, 2024).

Tajikistan may, therefore, like other countries in the region, be engaging de-facto with the Taliban. How the trajectory of bilateral relations continues will also depend on regional developments and the Taliban's relations with regional powers. But for any kind of official recognition or sustained engagement, the Tajik factor will, no doubt, play the decisive role.

References

Bhaduri, A. (August 27, 2021). "Tajikistan in global limelight as Afghanistan explodes". India Narrative. https://www.indianarrative.com/opinion-news/tajikistan-in-global-limelight-as-afghanistan-explodes-24320.html

Göransson, M. (2016). "Tajikistan and the Ambiguous Impact of the Soviet-Afghan War. The Political Mobilisation of Former Participants of the Soviet-Afghan War in 1989". *Cahiers d'Asie Centrale, 26*, pp. 113–142. http://journals.openedition.org/asiecentrale/3277

Klimentov, V. (2022). "The Tajik Civil War and Russia's Islamist moment". *Central Asian Survey, 42*(2), pp. 341–358. https://doi.org/10.1080/02634937.2022.2134298

Minority Rights Group (n.d.). "Tajiks in Afghanistan". https://minorityrights.org/communities/tajiks/

Pannier, B. (November 25, 2024). "Tajikistan's Afghan Conundrum". Foreign Policy Research Institute. https://www.fpri.org/article/2024/11/tajikistans-afghan-conundrum/

Pressa. (December 30, 2024). "Tajikistan and Pakistan Discuss Prospects of Political Relations". https://pressa.tj/tadzhikistan-i-pakistan-obsudili-perspektivy-politicheskih-otnoshenij/

Spolnikov, V. (1994). "Impact of Afghanistan's War on the Former Soviet Republics of Central Asia". In H. Malik (Ed.), *Central Asia, Its Strategic Importance and Future Prospects*. Macmillan.

Umarov, T. (October 26, 2021). "Why Tajikistan Is Taking a Stand Against the Taliban". Carnegie Endowment for International Peace. https://carnegieendowment.org/posts/2021/10/why-tajikistan-is-taking-a-stand-against-the-taliban?lang=en

9 Fractured Nationhood

Taliban's Exclusionary Practices and the Marginalisation of the Hazara Community in Post-2021 Afghanistan

Ziba Akbari

Introduction

The Taliban's return to power in Afghanistan has reignited discussions on the essence of Afghan nationhood and the challenges of building an inclusive nation-state. This chapter delves into the complex issue of nationhood in a multi-ethnic country, with a particular focus on the Hazara community. The period from 2001 to 2021 marked a phase where the Hazaras saw a more stable political engagement, with their ethnic identity playing a significant role in national politics (Ibrahimi, 2017). However, the Taliban's resurgence has altered this landscape, promoting a vision that sidelines non-Pashtun groups.

Afghanistan's ethnic diversity is both a cultural asset and a political challenge, with the potential to either unite or divide the nation (Ishtiaq et al., 2024). The Taliban's exclusionary policies have particularly alienated marginalised groups, prompting them to hold onto their unique identities. This has complicated the process of forging a cohesive national identity, risking increased resistance and conflict.

The Hazara Shia community has faced longstanding discrimination and violence, tracing back to the formation of Afghanistan in 1747 (Bhura, 2023). Historically, various Afghan leaders have manipulated constitutional frameworks to consolidate power and promote Pashtun identity, often to the detriment of other ethnic groups (Leake, 2023). The Taliban, emerging from the post-Soviet chaos in 1989, gained support primarily among the Pashtuns through a strict interpretation of Islamic law. During their initial rule from 1996 to 2001, minorities, including the Hazaras, faced severe repression and exclusion (Human Rights Watch, 2022; Nojumi, 2016).

The social fabric of Afghanistan has been marked by ethnic tensions, with the Hazara community particularly vulnerable. Despite some political and social advancement from 2001 to 2021, the Hazaras continued to face systemic challenges and discrimination (Rosen, 2022; Simon & Lam, 2021). The Taliban's return in 2021 has exacerbated the plight of minority groups, especially the Hazaras, with resurgence in discriminatory practices and violence (Omarkhail et al., 2024). The combination of a rigid Sunni interpretation of Islam and deep-seated ethnic biases has severely restricted the rights of the Hazaras, as recent attacks have highlighted (Akbari, 2022; Hakimi, 2023).

This chapter will explore the increasing marginalisation of the Hazara community under Taliban rule since 2021, examining the broader implications for nation-building in Afghanistan. By analysing existing literature and reports, this paper aims to shed light on the challenges of fostering an inclusive Afghan identity amidst complex socio-political dynamics. Additionally, it will highlight the resilience and organisational efforts of the Hazara community despite growing exclusion, contrasting the relatively inclusive past with the current exclusionary practices. These dynamics not only hinder the process of nation-building but also escalate the potential for conflict and resistance.

Theocratic Nationalism and the Hazaras Under Taliban's Exclusionary Practices

Theocratic nationalism, a political ideology merging religious principles with nationalist aspirations, seeks to establish a state governed by religious law. It often intertwines a particular religious identity with the state's national identity, resulting in exclusionary policies. Scholars like Juergensmeyer (1993) and Asad (2003) highlight that this ideology is prominent in regimes where Islamic principles form the basis of state policies and national identity. These frameworks frequently marginalise ethnic and religious minorities who do not conform to the dominant national narrative (Smith, 2003).

In Afghanistan, the decision to make Pashto the national language reflects a broader effort similar to other decolonising nations, which often use language as a tool for nation-building. However, this decision has marginalised non-Pashtun communities, contributing to a narrow interpretation of national identity (Leake, 2023). The concept of a nation-state, defined as a political entity characterised by a unified identity and governance, remains underdeveloped in Afghanistan. Among the Pashtuns, this concept is often viewed as a foreign imposition that threatens traditional tribal and Sharia-based structures. The Taliban's portrayal of themselves as the embodiment of a national discourse grounded in Sharia law aligns with the broader Islamic Ummah—the global Muslim community that transcends national boundaries (Marsden, 1998).

Exclusionary practices are strategic mechanisms employed by theocratic states to maintain ideological purity and consolidate power. According to Brubaker (2009), these practices establish clear boundaries of national membership, ensuring that resources and rights are confined to those deemed legitimate members of the nation. This often manifests through discriminatory policies, socio-economic disenfranchisement, and rhetoric that delegitimises certain groups. Scholars like Mamdani (2001) and Young (2000) argue that such practices reinforce social hierarchies, perpetuating cycles of marginalisation and resistance, which undermine social cohesion and contribute to instability.

The Taliban's rhetoric and media often depict the Hazaras as outsiders, undermining their historical and cultural ties to Afghanistan. This portrayal aligns with reports documenting how Taliban leaders denounce the Shia faith of the Hazaras, labelling it incompatible with the state's Sunni-centric ideology (Abbasi, 2024). Such exclusionary language fosters intolerance and hostility, promoting the Taliban's vision of a homogenous Islamic society that does not tolerate deviations from their strict interpretation of Sunni Islam.

The Taliban's governance exemplifies a blend of religious fundamentalism and ethnonationalism—a form of nationalism defined by shared heritage, language, faith, and a focus on a particular ethnic group. According to Ibrahimi (2023a), the Taliban's policies toward the Hazara community are driven by both religious and ethnic prejudices, leading to their political, cultural, and economic marginalisation. This systemic discrimination exacerbates social divisions, perpetuating a cycle of exclusion and repression. The Taliban's ideology, rooted in an extremist Sunni interpretation of Islam, positions the Hazaras as both religious and ethnic outsiders. Akbari (2022) notes that this has resulted in a resurgence of discriminatory practices against the Hazaras under Taliban rule.

The Hazara community has been systematically excluded from significant political roles within the Taliban-led government, including key positions such as cabinet members, governors, and police chiefs (Bhura, 2023). Reports indicate that Hazara officials and civil servants have been systematically removed from their positions and replaced with individuals loyal to the Taliban's ideology, ensuring that the Hazaras are excluded from political decision-making processes. This exclusion is documented by Human Rights Watch (2022) and further manifested in restricted access to education and healthcare services in Hazara-dominated regions. The United States Commission on International Religious Freedom (USCIRF, 2022) reports that educational institutions in these areas have faced closures, with Hazara students and educators experiencing intimidation and violence, severely limiting their educational opportunities.

The resurgence of the Taliban has led to increased threats and systemic discrimination against ethnic and religious minorities, particularly the Hazaras. This is evident in the return of Pashtun nomads to Hazara areas, facilitated by Taliban officials, resulting in land disputes and a continuation of historical subjugation (Ibrahimi, 2023a, 2023b). The targeted killings of Hazara elites and civilians illustrate an intent to diminish the community's political and social influence, actions that may be considered genocidal (Khan, 2024). The forced displacement of Hazaras is indicative of ethnic cleansing, portraying them as 'a neglected people at risk of genocide'. This community faces systematic attempts at marginalisation and destruction, including killings and forced displacement (Hakimi, 2023; Razai et al., 2023).

Understanding the experiences and perceptions of marginalised groups like the Hazaras is crucial for addressing these challenges and exploring paths toward greater inclusivity and stability. The next section will delve deeper into these issues, focusing on the complex relationship between national identity, exclusion, and the quest for belonging.

Hazara Marginalisation and Consequences

The Taliban's exclusionary practices have profoundly impacted the Hazara community, reshaping their identity and sense of belonging and fuelling counter-narratives that resist mainstream narratives. This marginalisation has contributed to a significant identity crisis in Afghanistan, particularly among non-Pashtun communities who feel disconnected from a cohesive Afghan national identity. This disconnect complicates efforts to foster national unity (Ishtiaq et al., 2024).

Religious exclusion has been a key tool in nation-building, often marginalising minority groups. Afghanistan's history of attempting to homogenise its population has often marginalised ethnic and cultural diversity, fostering mistrust and alienation among minority groups. The persistence of counter-narratives among groups like the Hazaras highlights their resilience in maintaining their cultural and religious identity despite systemic exclusion (Ibrahimi, 2023a).

The persecution of the Hazaras due to their ethnic and religious identity has left lasting trauma, influencing their current socio-political stance (Akbari, 2022). The Taliban continues this tradition, systematically excluding the Hazara community and eroding their sense of belonging within the country (Aktürk, 2022). This exclusion manifests in practices, such as forced displacement, land confiscation, and political disenfranchisement, all of which deepen the Hazaras' perception of being marginalised. The derogatory labelling of the Hazaras as "infidels" exacerbates this alienation, further distancing them from a shared Afghan identity (George Washington University, 2021).

This systemic exclusion of the Hazaras from key political and administrative roles since 2021 has intensified ethnic divisions and heightened feelings of disenfranchisement (Murtazashvili, 2024). The ongoing exclusion of the Hazara community from political and social spheres exacerbates ethnic divisions and increases their sense of isolation (Bhura, 2023). The Taliban's control over cultural expressions and historical narratives further marginalises non-Pashtun groups, erasing their presence from the national identity narrative (Malik et al., 2023).

The construction of national identity in Afghanistan has been fraught with challenges, particularly for marginalised groups such as the Hazaras. In this context, the development of counter-narratives serves as a form of resistance against systemic exclusion. The Hazara community has increasingly emphasised its Shia practices and cultural heritage, constructing a distinct identity in opposition to the Taliban's Sunni-centric ideology. This reflects Anderson's (2006) concept of "Imagined Communities", wherein shared narratives are crucial for forming a collective identity.

The exclusion of non-Pashtun, non-Sunni groups by the Taliban has catalysed the Hazaras' assertion of a unique identity, distinct from the dominant national narrative (Nojumi, 2016; Ibrahimi, 2017). This assertion is not merely cultural but also political, as evidenced by the activities of organisations like the National Council of the Sunni Hazaras (NCSHA). Founded in May 2015, the NCSHA seeks to promote a multi-religious ethnic identity and to bridge traditional sectarian divisions. It provides a platform for the political representation and symbolic recognition of Sunni Hazaras, who have historically been marginalised and often subsumed under broader ethnic categories (Ibrahimi, 2023b).

Recent research highlights the significance of the NCSHA's efforts, emphasising the importance of political inclusion and equitable representation in preventing instability (Ishtiaq et al., 2024). The organisation's mission underscores the broader struggle for identity and rights among marginalised groups in Afghanistan, illustrating a narrative of exclusion and a call for revival. In such a landscape, marginalised groups are more likely to align themselves primarily with their ethnic or religious communities rather than with the nation as a whole, further complicating the nation's quest for a cohesive identity (Wimmer, 2018).

Apart from the formation of these counter-narratives, another potential consequence of systemic marginalisation and persecution is the emergence of conflict and radical resistance. Radicalisation can emerge from the exclusion of diverse religious practices (Roy, 2017). The Taliban's strict Sunni Islamic identity marginalises non-conforming groups, creating conditions ripe for radicalisation as a response to exclusion (Aktürk, 2022; Roy, 2017).

Gurr's theory of relative deprivation suggests that when there is a significant gap between expected and actual living conditions, frustration can escalate into political violence. This theory provides insight into the potential for radical resistance among marginalised groups. The continuous denial of basic rights and frequent violent attacks heighten this sense of deprivation, increasing the likelihood of violent resistance as a means of asserting identity and resisting oppression (Gurr, 2015). Globally, marginalised groups facing systemic exclusion have often resorted to radical resistance. For example, the Rohingya Muslim minority in Myanmar has experienced severe persecution, leading to the rise of armed resistance groups like the Arakan Rohingya Salvation Army (ARSA) (International Crisis Group, 2022). Similarly, the Kurds in Türkiye have faced systemic exclusion and violence, prompting groups like the Kurdistan Workers' Party (PKK) to engage in armed struggle (Gunter, 2016). In Palestine, exclusion and marginalisation have also led to the formation of various militant groups. These examples underscore how systemic exclusion can foster conditions conducive to radical resistance (Milton-Edwards, 2013).

In the context of the Hazaras in Afghanistan, the ongoing marginalisation and frequent violent attacks amplify their sense of deprivation, making violent resistance more likely as a form of identity assertion and opposition to oppression. Amnesty International and the United States Holocaust Memorial Museum have documented numerous incidents of severe violence against the Hazara community, highlighting their vulnerability and underscoring the systemic nature of these threats (Mullen & Donine, 2021; Amnesty International, 2021, 2022).

Given this environment of terror and direct violence, the Hazara community, in response, has developed a range of strategies, from peaceful advocacy to armed resistance. The Enlightenment Movement is a significant example of peaceful protest. This movement, committed to justice and recognition through non-violent means, emerged in response to the Afghan government's decision to reroute the TUTAP power project away from the Hazara-majority region of Bamiyan. The movement included large-scale peaceful demonstrations, such as the tragic event on July 23, 2016, where a protest in Kabul was targeted by a terrorist attack, resulting in significant casualties (Saeedi, 2019). Similarly, the National Council of the Sunni Hazaras of Afghanistan (NCSHA), established in May 2015, has actively promoted non-violent resistance by advocating for the rights and recognition of Sunni Hazaras through peaceful means. The NCSHA has focused on fostering a multi-religious ethnic identity and advocating for political representation and resource allocation without resorting to violence. This organisation's efforts underscore the broader Hazara community's commitment to achieving justice and equity through peaceful advocacy, reflecting a continued preference for non-violent strategies amidst systemic marginalisation (Ibrahimi, 2023b, pp. 677-679).

In addition to peaceful efforts, there is evidence of defensive militarisation within the Hazara community in response to systemic exclusion and violence. The stringent Sunni Islamic identity imposed by the Taliban marginalises the Hazaras' distinct Shia beliefs, leading to defiance against this marginalisation. The Hazaras often feel compelled to consider armed resistance as a necessary means of survival. This collective defence strategy could evolve into a substantial opposition force against the Taliban's regime (Shay, 2021; Sakhi, 2022).

Leaders like Zulfiqar Omid have played pivotal roles in civil movements and later, in forming resistance groups. Initially involved in peaceful advocacy through the Labor and Development Party and the Enlightenment Movement, Omid eventually established a resistance movement in response to continued violence and discrimination against the Hazaras (Zawar, 2021). As the security situation in Afghanistan deteriorated, particularly with the Taliban's resurgence, peaceful methods became increasingly ineffective (Sakhi, 2022). Faced with ongoing attacks and the threat of genocide, Omid established a resistance force in Daikundi province, known as Dai-4, to defend Hazara civilians against violent aggression from the Taliban and other extremist factions (Republic of Silence, 2021; DW, 2021).

This transition from peaceful activism to armed resistance highlights the complex and dire circumstances faced by the Hazara community. It illustrates how long-standing peaceful activism can evolve into armed resistance when confronted with existential threats. The duality of responses—from seeking justice through non-violent means to taking up arms as self-defence—reflects the diverse spectrum of resistance strategies employed by marginalised groups like the Hazaras. This spectrum, encompassing peaceful advocacy and armed resistance, underscores the complex landscape of resistance strategies among marginalised groups.

Navigating National Identity Amidst Division

The concept of nationhood in Afghanistan faces significant challenges due to the complex interplay of diverse ethnic and religious identities. The Taliban's authoritarian regime, with its emphasis on a homogenous, exclusionary identity, has significantly hindered the nation-building process. This approach has marginalised minorities, like the Hazaras, leading to resistance and the development of counter-narratives that question the legitimacy of the state (Murtazashvili, 2024). The continued exclusion of specific ethnic groups threatens to repeat Afghanistan's history of marginalisation and conflict, undermining efforts toward a cohesive national identity (Bhura, 2023).

As noted by Aktürk (2022), exclusionary national religious configurations complicate nation-building efforts by marginalising significant portions of the population. This marginalisation is not merely a social or cultural issue but has significant political implications. It erodes the sense of national belonging and encourages the development of counter-narratives that challenge the dominant discourse of Afghan identity as promoted by the Taliban. The absence of representation for marginalised groups in the central government further exacerbates these divisions. As Wimmer (2018) highlights, without political representation, national identification remains weak, and the sense of belonging to the nation is diminished. In deeply divided societies, such as Afghanistan, the legitimacy of the state is often questioned due to the perception that it serves the interests of specific ethnic groups rather than the entire citizenry. This pervasive mistrust among ethnonational groups significantly undermines social cohesion and fuels the ethnopolitical conflict over state legitimacy (Milan, 2022). The discussion on the complexities of integrating diverse identities into a cohesive national narrative in Afghanistan highlights the failure of liberal intervention, particularly in fostering a unified nation. This failure underscores the intricate challenges faced by the Afghan state in reconciling the diverse ethnic and religious landscape within a national framework (Younus, 2024). The Taliban's emphasis on a homogenous identity has further fragmented the national consciousness, destabilising efforts towards societal cohesion and perpetuating conflict. The cycle of exclusion and potential radicalisation presents a substantial challenge to creating a cohesive and inclusive national identity. The consociational model, which has been implemented in various divided societies to ensure proportional representation of major ethnic groups, can also perpetuate ethnic divisions by emphasising collective rights over individual rights. This model often curtails the emergence of alternative political identities and reinforces the primacy of ethnic identity in political representation (Milan, 2022).

The oppressive measures and restrictions enforced by the Taliban have generated fear and frustration among the populace, hindering their ability to exercise fundamental freedoms, such as accessing education, expressing opinions freely, and contributing to societal development. This regime fails to create the necessary conditions for ensuring material well-being and security, exacerbating the divide between the government and the people, ultimately leading to resistance and insurgency (Sakhi, 2022). As Wimmer (2018) concludes, skilled leadership and inclusive nationalist ideologies are vital in creating an integrated political arena that can support a cohesive national identity, even in the face of historical and structural challenges.

In sum, the current socio-political landscape in Afghanistan, dominated by the Taliban's rule, presents a complex and evolving challenge to the idea of a unified Afghan nation. The marginalisation of minority groups like the Hazaras underscores the fragility of national unity. However, the persistence of diverse ethnic identities and the ongoing struggle for inclusivity reflect a nationhood in flux—one that continues to be negotiated and contested. The future of Afghanistan's national identity will depend on the balance between exclusionary forces and the resilience of its diverse populace.

Conclusion

The resurgence of the Taliban in Afghanistan has marked a profound shift in the socio-political landscape of the country, with significant repercussions for marginalised communities, particularly the Hazaras. This chapter has examined the Taliban's exclusionary practices, revealing their role in eroding a sense of national belonging and fostering counter-narratives that risk escalating conflict and radical resistance. The marginalisation of the Hazara community not only exacerbates their socio-political alienation but also complicates the broader process of nation-building. An inclusive national identity, crucial for Afghanistan's stability, requires the integration and recognition of all societal groups, fostering a shared sense of belonging and collective purpose. The systemic discrimination and targeted violence faced by the Hazaras have led them to assert their distinct cultural and religious identity as a form of resistance, underscoring their resilience. However, the exclusionary governance of the Taliban increases the risk of radicalisation and threatens the nation's cohesion. Afghanistan's complex history and socio-political context make the challenge of forging a unified national identity particularly formidable. The failure to address these issues perpetuates divisions and instability, hindering the nation's progress towards peace. Ultimately, the path to a stable and inclusive Afghanistan lies in acknowledging and addressing the grievances of all its people, with the experiences of the Hazara community highlighting the critical need for an inclusive approach to nation-building.

References

Abbasi, F. (May 3, 2024). "Attacks Target Afghanistan's Hazaras". Human Rights Watch. https://www.hrw.org/news/2024/05/03/attacks-target-afghanistans-hazaras

Akbari, F. (March 7, 2022). "The Risks Facing Hazaras in Taliban-ruled Afghanistan". George Washington University. https://extremism.gwu.edu/risks-facing-hazaras-in-taliban-ruled-afghanistan

Aktürk, Ş. (2021). "Nationalism and Religion in Comparative Perspective: A New Typology of National-Religious Configurations". *Nationalities Papers, 50*(2), pp. 1–14. https://doi.org/10.1017/nps.2021.17

Amnesty International (August 19, 2021). "Afghanistan: Taliban responsible for brutal massacre of Hazara men". https://www.amnesty.org/en/latest/news/2021/08/afghanistan-taliban-responsible-for-brutal-massacre-of-hazara-men-new-investigation/

Amnesty International (August 9, 2022). "Afghanistan: Taliban must immediately step-up measures to protect the Hazara Shia communities". https://www.amnesty.org.au/afghanistan-taliban-must-immediately-step-up-measures-to-protect-the-hazara-shia-communities/

Anderson, B. (2006). *Imagined Communities: Reflections on the Origin and Spread of Nationalism*. Verso.

Asad, T. (2003). *Formations of the Secular: Christianity, Islam, Modernity*. Stanford University Press.

Bhura, S. (2023). "Targeted and Forgotten: The Hazara Shia Community's Struggle in Afghanistan". Society for the Study of Peace and Conflict. https://sspconline.org/sites/default/files/2023-05/IB_SSPC-Spandana-Hazara-May-262023.pdf

Brubaker, R. (2009). *Citizenship and Nationhood in France and Germany*. Harvard University Press.

DW (September 1, 2021). "Afghanistan's repressed minority faces a hostile Taliban". https://www.dw.com/en/afghanistans-repressed-minority-faces-a-hostile-taliban/a-59039636

Gunter, M. M. (2016). *The Kurds*. Markus Wiener Publishers.

Gurr, T. R. (2015). *Why Men Rebel*. Routledge.

Hakimi, M. J. (2023). "The Genocide of Hazaras". *Virginia Journal of International Law Online, 63*.

Human Rights Watch (June 10, 2022). "Afghanistan: Taliban Torture Civilians in Panjshir". https://www.hrw.org/news/2022/06/10/afghanistan-taliban-torture-civilians-panjshir

Ibrahimi, N. (2017). *The Hazaras and the Afghan State: Rebellion, Exclusion, and the Struggle for Recognition*. Hurst & Co.

Ibrahimi, N. (2023a). "A Violent Nexus: Ethnonationalism, Religious Fundamentalism, and the Taliban". *Review of Faith & International Affairs, 21*(3), pp. 22–37. https://doi.org/10.1080/15570274.2023.2235809

Ibrahimi, N. (2023b). "The state, identity politics and ethnic boundaries in Afghanistan: The case of Sunni Hazaras". *Nations and Nationalism, 29*(2), pp. 669–685. https://doi.org/10.1111/nana.12933

International Crisis Group (December 7, 2017). "Myanmar's Rohingya Crisis Enters a Dangerous New Phase". https://www.crisisgroup.org/asia/south-east-asia/myanmar/292-myanmars-rohingya-crisis-enters-dangerous-new-phase

Ishtiaq, T., Asghar, A., Raza, S., & Achakzai, N. K. (2024). "Fragmented Identities: The Impact of Ethnic Divides on Afghanistan's Political Instability". *Journal of Management Practices Humanities and Social Sciences, 8*(3). https://doi.org/10.33152/jmphss-8.3.14

Juergensmeyer, M. (2008). *Global rebellion: religious challenges to the secular state, from Christian militias to al Qaeda*. University of California Press.

Khan, R. & Stuffers, M. (2024). "Afghanistan's Hazaras: An Unknown Genocide?" NIOD Institute for War, Holocaust and Genocide Studies. https://www.niod.nl/en/longreads/afghanistans-hazaras-unknown-genocide

Leake, E. (2023). "Constitutions and Modernity in Post-Colonial Afghanistan: Ethnolinguistic Nationalism and the Making of an Afghan Nation-State". *Law and History Review, 41*(2), pp. 295–315. https://doi.org/10.1017/s0738248022000530

Malik, T., Jan, F., & Ullah, Z. (2023). "The epistemicide in Afghanistan: an analysis of Taliban's policies towards national and cultural symbols". *Liberal Arts and Social Sciences International Journal*, 7(2), pp. 61–80. https://doi.org/10.47264/idea.lassij/7.2.4

Mamdani, M. (2001). *When Victims Become Killers: Colonialism, Nativism, and the Genocide in Rwanda*. Princeton University Press.

Marsden, P. (1998). *The Taliban: War, religion and the new order in Afghanistan*. Oxford University Press.

Milton-Edwards, B. (2008). *The Israeli-Palestinian Conflict: A People's War*. Routledge.

Mullen, T. & Donine, T. (September 13, 2021). "Women and Hazara in Afghanistan at Risk of Mass Atrocities". United States Holocaust Memorial Museum. https://www.ushmm.org/genocide-prevention/blog/women-and-hazara-face-heightened-risk-of-mass-atrocities

Murtazashvili, J. B. (2024). "The experimented society: interventions, social science, and the failure of post-conflict reconstruction in Afghanistan". UNU WIDER. https://www.wider.unu.edu/publication/experimented-society-interventions-social-science-and-failure-post-conflict

Nojumi, N. (2016). *The rise of the Taliban in Afghanistan: Mass mobilization, civil war, and the future of the region*. Springer.

Omarkhail, I., Guozhu, L., & Asap, A. (2024). "The Decline of Pashtuns and the Rise of Fundamentalism in Afghanistan". *Ethnopolitics*, pp. 1–19. https://doi.org/10.1080/17449057.2024.2355416

Razai, M. S., Mahmood, A., Alizada, B., & Hargreaves, S. (2023). "Two years on from Taliban takeover of Afghanistan, the Hazaras community is a neglected people at risk of genocide". *BMJ*, *382*, p. 1888. https://doi.org/10.1136/bmj.p1888

Rosen, B. (November 13, 2022). "Taliban Takeover in Afghanistan Leaves Hazaras Uniquely Vulnerable". *Brown Political Review*. https://brownpoliticalreview.org/2022/11/taliban-violence-toward-hazara-people/

Roy, O. (2017). *The Failure of Political Islam*. Harvard University Press.

Saeedi, S. Z. (July 26, 2019). "Ghani's Missed Opportunity: The Hazara Enlightenment Movement". *The Diplomat*. https://thediplomat.com/2019/07/ghanis-missed-opportunity-the-hazara-enlightenment-movement/

Sakhi, N. (2022). "The Taliban Takeover in Afghanistan and Security Paradox". *Journal of Asian Security and International Affairs*, *9*(3), pp. 383–401. https://doi.org/10.1177/23477970221130882

Shay, S. (2021). "The armed resistance to the Taliban regime in Afghanistan". *Security Science Journal*, *2*(2), pp. 7–21. https://doi.org/10.37458/ssj.2.2.1

Smith, A. D. (2003). *Chosen Peoples*. Oxford University Press.

Simon, D. J. & Lam, J. (August 26, 2021). "Protecting Afghanistan's Hazara People Under Taliban Rule". The MacMillan Center. https://macmillan.yale.edu/news/protecting-afghanistans-hazara-people-under-taliban-rule

United States Commission on International Religious Freedom (USCIRF) (April 25, 2022). "2022 Annual Report: Key Findings and Recommendations". https://www.uscirf.gov/events/2022-annual-report-key-findings-and-recommendations

Wimmer, A. (2018). *Nation Building: Why Some Countries Come Together While Others Fall Apart*. Princeton University Press.

Young, I. M. (2000). *Inclusion and Democracy*. Oxford University Press.

Younus, A. (2024). "The Failure of Liberal Interventionism: Deconstructing Afghan Identity Discourses of 'Modern' and 'Tradition'". *Politics and Governance, 12*. https://doi.org/10.17645/pag.7380

Zawar, H. (April 15, 2021). "Hazara World - Zulfiqar Omid: Why a Peaceful Politician is Pushed to Pick up Arms to Defend his People?!" Hazara World. https://hazaraworld.com/zulfiqar-omid-why-a-peaceful-politician-is-pushed-to-pick-up-arm-to-defend-his-people/

10 Gender Violence in Afghanistan

Sanchita Bhattacharya

Introduction

Gender violence is often due to a dissimilar equation of authority and dominance between two genders. The criminal offenders, sadly, in most of the cases, are close paternal relatives: husband, father, brother, son, nephew, uncles, male cousin, etc. Gender violence has a persistent model and becomes a habit with the passage of time. Habitual offenders are triggered into violent behaviour at the slightest provocation. As a result, the woman, whether a daughter, sister or wife, becomes the target of aggression.

Violence against women is extensive in Afghanistan, a country experiencing conflict and turmoil since more than 40 years. The violence perpetrated against women is entrenched in the religious, social, and cultural practices of the country. Afghan women hardly have any freedom or even a choice of escape from tyranny and abuse. Women in Afghanistan are also exposed to the viciousness characteristic of any country undergoing conflict, and the situation has worsened after 2021, with Taliban 2.0 coming to power. Violence against Afghan women is closely linked to an intensely ingrained trend of impunity that is, in part, a consequence of years of struggle. The factors causing women's weakness and the continuation of violence against women in Afghanistan are: inadequate financial resources; the traditional gender rules giving legitimacy to patriarchy; the destruction of protective social order; and the weak rule of law.

The United Nations Conventions on Elimination of Discrimination against Women claims that any damage inflicted to a woman because she is a woman is considered the basis for Gender Based Violence (GBV). The General Recommendation 19 of the Committee goes further to state that such harm could be categorised as inflicting physical, sexual, psychological harm to a woman, even the threats of committing such suffering, and dispossession of freedoms (Izumi, 2007).

Afghan women have suffered enormous hardships, aggravated by prevailing social biases and discrimination that further compound the consequences of violence. Furthermore, Afghanistan, particularly outside major urban areas, continues to be deeply rooted in a patriarchal society, where religion and complicated tribal customs command social communications. These religious values and cultural codes and patterns profoundly shape the roles and status of women in Afghanistan (Girowal, 2024).

No doubt, even under the previous internationally backed government, between 2001 and 2021, violence against women was widespread and common in Afghanistan. The difference, nevertheless, was the presence of legal frameworks and institutions that could offer some degree of protection and accountability. The justice system, although faulty, was showing signs of progress, while instruments, such as the Elimination of Violence Against Women Law, Family Response Units, the Prosecutor's Office, and other protective mechanisms, made a genuine difference. These mechanisms indicted perpetrators, provided safe houses, and gave other protections to Afghan women. Ominously, since the Taliban took power, it has dismantled the complete legal framework. Today, women victims of violence and injustices have nowhere to go; they are now left to fend for themselves (Mosadiq, 2024).

Violence, and indeed the fear of violence, is a major barrier when it comes to education and contribution in decision-making processes and keeps women bound in poverty. In Afghanistan, women who want to participate or are trying to articulate their thoughts are mostly seen to be challenging religious and tribal norms, which puts them in the frontline of danger and abuse. Within Taliban society, male supremacy outside the household has resulted in changes within the home, creating an insight among men and boys that women and girls have neither the capacity nor need for financial, social, and political opportunities and supporting a belief that women and girls should remain inside the house in a position of enslavement.

Edicts and decrees of the Taliban

The eradication of hard-won rights for women under the Taliban is methodical and should be seen as an overt attack on the rights of women and their personhood. The Taliban's edicts, declarations, and overall outlook are the product of a lethal blend of tribal codes of conduct and harshest interpretation of Islam. A woman is, therefore, considered as a possession of the male members of her family, clan, and tribe. There is no space for a woman to proclaim her own self due to an overpowering patriarchal mindset and social mores. A girl or a woman is labelled as the bearer of 'honour', giving the male- obsessed Afghan society every right to prosecute her existence.

Women's presence and voice are considered to be potential instruments of vice, and resultantly, they are never allowed to be heard or seen without cover in public under the Taliban regime's strict rules and regulations. They cannot talk; work; play; read; sing; travel; or assert themselves in the toxic environment of Taliban's Afghanistan.

The Taliban's anti-women laws, combined with a bolstered patriarchal structure, have made Afghanistan the lowest-ranked country in the 2023 Women, Peace and Security Index with 177 countries. After the fall of Kabul in August 2021, the Taliban began rolling back the over two decades of advances Afghan women had attained in education, employment, politics, health, governance, etc. (GIWPS, 2024).

Three years of edicts, statements, and decrees by the Taliban have targeted the rights, lives, and bodies of women and girls, closing spaces for them in their own homes and communities and at the national level. Not one decree on women and girls has been reversed.

A few such edicts are as follows:

September 17, 2021: Ban on girls' secondary education and removal of the Ministry of Women's Affairs.

November 22, 2021: Ban on dramas, soap operas, and entertainment shows broadcasting women.

December 29, 2021: Ban on women taking long-distance road trips alone.

February 2, 2022: Ban on women government employees from entering government offices without hijab.

March 24, 2022: Closure of schools for girls above the 6th grade.

May 7, 2022: All Afghan women ordered by the Taliban to wear head-to-toe clothing in public.

May 19, 2022: Forced face- covering for women TV presenters and other women on screen.

December 20, 2022: University education suspended for all female students.

January 29, 2023: Female employees of local clinics and health centres ordered by officials of the Taliban Ministry of Vice and Virtue in Kandahar Province to refrain from going to work without being accompanied by a *Mahram* (male guardian).

March 23, 2024: Avowal by Taliban's Supreme Leader, Mullah Hibatullah Akhundzada, to start stoning women to death in public.

Deobandi-Hanafi background of the Taliban

It is vital to understand that the Taliban's hardline Islamic system is entrenched in the 19th-century Deobandi[1] movement of British colonial India, a prominent strain among Islamists in contemporary Pakistan and Afghanistan that is based on Hanafi[2] *Fiqh* (jurisprudence) within the Sunni sect. The other three *Fiqh* are Maliki, Hanbali, and Shafi'I (Bhattacharya, 2022). The Taliban arose from the doctrines of Deobandism, obtaining a significant portion of their theological teachings from teachings in Deobandi seminaries. Since an extreme focus and predisposition toward politics form the core of these teachings, the theology of the Taliban can be considered typologically as a form of political theology. In the political theology of the Taliban, 'politics' is the end, and 'theological teachings' serve as the means to this end. In spite of the Taliban's claim that their goal in following political power is to reinforce religious values and establish 'God's law', they utilise religious morals to rise to positions of power (Salehi, 2024).

Moreover, the Wahhabism-inspired Deobandi vigilante ideology that lies at the heart of the Taliban movement inspires believers to pick up arms and apply their conception of order in the society. This aligns with the historical roots of Wahhabism where the cleric, Muhammad ibn Abd al-Wahhab, in the

18th century, formed an alliance with the local emir, Muhammad ibn Saud. Together, under the spiritual leadership of the former, they began winning lands in Arabia through ibn Saud's *ikhwan* (brothers in Arabic), leading to the founding of an administration based on rules they both deemed 'Islamic'. Mullah Omar, who founded the Taliban in 1994, was a student of Deobandi education during the Islamist struggle against the Soviet and Afghan governments and later joined it. As a veteran of the Afghan jihad, he commanded reverence among his followers for his apparent devoutness (Khan, 2024).

The Deobandi movement became the most popular school of Islamic thought among the Pashtuns living on both sides of the Durand Line. Many significant Pashtun community leaders established Deobandi seminaries in these areas. Khan Abdul Gaffar Khan, also known as the Frontier Gandhi, was involved in starting several schools based on Deobandi curriculum in the Pashtun belt (Puri, 2009).

Sadly, after many decades, these seminaries, as they are, spread across South Asia following the partition of India, particularly across the Pak-Afghan border, where they provided ideological support to the radicals. As the ideological battle between the United States and the Soviets, and later, Iran and Saudi Arabia, intensified, particularly following the Soviet invasion of Afghanistan in 1979, these Deobandi madrasas (Islamic seminaries) received enormous amounts of reserves and funding from Saudi Arabia, Pakistan, and the United States. This was because both the US and Pakistan needed a source of recruits to fight in Afghanistan and Kashmir, and the Saudis wanted to spread their version of Islam, Wahhabism, in the region to counter Iran's influence (Mehran, 2024).

Talibanism is perhaps a combination of post-intellectual Deobandism with conservative Pashtun tribal norms, packaged as a normative Islamic ethic. In this sense, understanding Deobandism carefully irradiates the ideological roots of the Taliban but does not completely elucidate their current beliefs and practices (White, 2012). Therefore, the Taliban Code of Law is a dangerous concoction of Hanafi jurisprudence and tribal code of conduct. The Taliban's enforcement of their criminal laws and their resolution of private disputes are a mixture of the Hanafi *Fiqh* and tribal codes. Sadly, these customs and laws are extremely anti-women in nature (Bhattacharya, 2022).

Pashtunwali- the way of Pashtun life

Pashtunwali serves as a manual for the Pashtun population's way of life, social order, rights and obligations, morals, and code of honour. Nevertheless, among Persian-speaking Afghans, and specifically among the Turkic and Hazara peoples of northern and central Afghanistan, the isolation of women is invested with less symbolic meaning than it is among the Pashtuns. In most of northern Afghanistan, women take on a more active and public role in decision-making, and there is open acknowledgement of the economic and social power that women exercise (Gibbon, 2021).

Dignity, honour, and shame are central concepts in Pashtunwali. However, 'shame' is primarily connected to the behaviour of women. This code also restricts the spatial existence of women in Afghanistan. It is thought that women cannot increase the standing (accumulate honour) of a family or a group; in truth, they can only contribute to reducing it. The behaviour of women impacts the whole group or family's status, mainly that of male relatives. Women are meant to be modest and reputable, and men are responsible for their behaviour and have an absolute obligation to protect the women of the group. Women are considered irrational beings with low self-discipline and little control over their impulses. At the same time, as women must be protected against outsiders, they must be controlled and protected against their own weaknesses and predisposition to engage in indecent/immoral behaviour (Landinfo, 2011)

As the dominant group in Afghanistan since its entry into modern statehood, many Pashtuns have often prided themselves for their superior levels of female seclusion and their uncompromising standards of honour. Originally transmitted orally, Pashtunwali was later documented and analysed by colonial scholars, anthropologists, nationalists, and folklorists, sometimes with the result that what were more flexible ideals became reified as a singular tribal code determining the behaviour of all Pashtuns (Wimpelmann, 2013).

The code of Pashtunwali is based on chivalry (*ghayrat* or *nang*), honour (*izzat*), hospitality (*melmastia*), gender boundaries (*purdah* or *namus*), and council (*Jirga*), the legislative authority in the public domain. *Purdah* and *namus* are compulsory components of Pashtunwali that are related to the honour of the family, especially, of women. According to the code, the sexual honour and general conduct of females are crucial elements of male honour.

Regrettably, under the pretext of protecting and honouring these norms and customary laws, the Taliban have once again started a storm to proclaim their power and presence over the female population of Afghanistan. The faces of Afghan women are gradually vanishing, both literally and metaphorically, from the public domain (Bhattacharya, 2024).

Pashtunwali is so well rooted within the Pashtun society since ages that from early childhood, girls are told that they will bring shame to themselves and their families should they violate the rules of *purdah* and seclusion. While *purdah* is publicly defined as a way to shield women from outside dangers, there is a powerful subtext articulated through it, which considers women as treacherous creatures, only half-civilised and out of control, and unless their field of action is limited by *purdah*, they will shame the family (Gibbon, 2021).

Economic Violence

Economic violence includes depriving women of their inheritance, not providing alimony (*nafaqa*), preventing a role in family expenditures, selling their belongings without their consent, and preventing them from working. Other cases of violence included 385 different cases of ousting from home, early marriage, forced marriage, exchanging women, and preventing women and girls from going to school (Bhattacharya, 2021).

The Taliban have systematically denied economic opportunities to Afghan women. In 2024, Afghanistan ranked 178 out of 180 in the World Bank's annual report on female economic participation and empowerment. In 2023, the UN Secretary-General directly addressed the Taliban, calling on the regime to lift its restrictions on women's work and education (Pepin, 2024). Women have been forced out of public administration roles, their existence in the private sector has been considerably curtailed, and many women-owned businesses have been forcibly closed. In December 2022, the Taliban imposed a ban on women working for national and international NGOs, a restriction that was extended to Afghan women employed by the UN in April 2023. By July 2023, even beauty salons, a vital source of income and autonomy for many women, were ordered to shut down (UN Women, 2024). Additionally, the salaries of those who are working have been drastically reduced by the Taliban. For instance, in June 2024, the Taliban-led government issued a decree that set the monthly salaries of all female government employees at

5,000 afghanis, or around USD 70, regardless of their job, qualifications, or experience. Incidentally, for many women, it means a drop of up to 75% in their salaries at a time when Afghanistan is grappling with mass joblessness and increasing poverty (Siddique, 2024).

As the Taliban have enforced restrictions in education and health[3], the female staff is decreasing by the day. Due to various restraining edits on women, organisations also are no longer interested in hiring them, so as to avoid legal punishment and the wrath of Taliban militia. The economic discrimination is taking the sheer amount of abuse women are experiencing under the Taliban to another level.

As women are not given space in the public domain, regrettably, many who claim to be their families' sole providers, have resorted to begging as their only means of survival. Women are the breadwinners of thousands of families. But women have had their job opportunities taken away from them, and there are no policies to support them. Resultantly, in the capital city of Kabul and in other provinces, there has been an unprecedented increase in the number of female beggars. They are begging for just a little bread for themselves and their children (Nehan & Escobales, 2023). However, contrary to the ground realities and economic misfortune of women, the Taliban approved legislation to prevent begging and remove beggars from cities, as announced in May, 2024, by the Taliban-run Justice Ministry. The legislation consists of three sections and 27 principles, according to a statement from the ministry (Amu TV, 2024).

Mental Health Challenge

The mental health emergency of Afghan women unfolding now is directly linked to decades of war and violence. In Afghanistan's profoundly patriarchal society, one worn out by four decades of war, the UN estimates that one in two people—most of them women—suffered from psychological suffering even before the Taliban takeover in 2021.

It is a noteworthy aspect of the ongoing political, social, and economic turmoil in Afghanistan. It is essential that the extent of the problem unfolding now is understood as a new stage of the catastrophe, resulting from the political and social changes since August 2021. The harm inflicted since then cannot be resolved quickly and if left unaddressed, will threaten the welfare of future generations of Afghan women and the ability of Afghan society to rebuild itself. The various job-related restrictions have led to many women not wanting to go to work. The lack of employment opportunities and increasing poverty were cited as foremost reasons for worsening mental health among women (Safi and Rivas, 2023).

The past 20 years saw groundbreaking initiatives to establish systems of healthcare to address the mental health needs in Afghan populations. Notably, a public mental healthcare system was established to train new cadres of mental health professionals and psychological counsellors who would join the nation's basic healthcare system. In 2000, women who were located in Taliban-controlled areas were found significantly more likely to report signs of depression, suicidal ideation, and actual suicidal attempts compared with women residing in non-Taliban-controlled areas.

Afghan women are suffering from psychological problems, including anxiety, depression, insomnia, isolation, loss of hope and motivation, fear, aggression, ever more reclusive behaviour, and thoughts of suicide. The women are desperately seeking support, counselling, and psychological services (Faiez, 2023). With no reproductive rights, maternal healthcare, and basic civil rights, destitution of women in Afghanistan is beyond imagination. Women are forced to give birth at home deprived of basic maternal care. Not only this, the Taliban, in 2023, prohibited the sale and purchase of contraceptives, intimidating shopkeepers from selling them, thus depriving women of their reproductive rights. Refuting UN concerns over the current ban on women in Afghanistan, the spokesperson of the Taliban responded, "If any non-Muslim expresses concern or rejects these laws, they should first educate themselves about Islamic laws and respect Islamic values. We consider such objections to Islamic Sharia as disrespectful" (Mishra, 2024).

Taliban decrees have caused a devastating sense of fear and psychological suffering among Afghan women. The mental health crisis affecting Afghan women has reached unparalleled levels, and the effect on future generations could be permanent. Domestic violence also causes mental health issues since, typically, due to the absence of knowledge on mental health issues, male members of the family subject women to domestic violence while women are already suffering mental issues. Unhealthy domestic environment and religion- sanctioned violence against women have normalised such brutality, especially creating fear in the minds of young girls. The situation is disastrous and grave. The Taliban is not allowing any documentation or official record of the same.

Gender differences in depression and anxiety are visibly noticeable in Afghanistan. These are accredited to the methodical and official discrimination experienced by Afghan women, including the system of *purdah*, the practice of excluding women from public spaces. Gender difference in mental health issues may also be related to the cultural 'straitjacket' governing the public appearance of emotions, discouraging women to disclose forms of desolation and men to show terror, sorrow, or hesitation, as this would bring disgrace on the family (Chiovenda, 2019). Perpetual confinement at home without education or a future is taking a definite toll on young females.

Conclusion

The Taliban militia is mostly composed of Sunni Muslim conservative clerics and their followers from the Pashtun tribes of southern Afghanistan. These men cause havoc under the justification of preserving religion and their way of life. For the women of Afghanistan, the situation is tragic because since the last 20 years, they have been exposed to the outside world; therefore, they are now in a worse situation than in the 1990s.

Moreover, the Taliban's way of governance or justice strengthens the inherent 'trigger-happy' culture within the tribal set-up of Afghanistan. Decades of conflict have completely destroyed the country, which is very well demonstrated in the atrocious treatment of women. Violence against women has been completely legalised by the Taliban, with the introduction of various decrees and edicts all over the country.

In a tragic way, the official presence of the Taliban will normalise violence against women. It is hard to measure the degree of exploitation and harassment of women across this country. Dreadful incidents may be isolated, but now, tension pervades the daily lives of many Afghan women.

Notes

1. Deobandism began in India as a movement seeking to re-establish a Muslim religio-political order in South Asia. After 80 years of cultivating a religious intellectual vanguard and aligning with the majority Hindu community in secular nationalist

politics to achieve independence from British colonial rule, a major chunk of Deobandis embraced Muslim separatism. Once that goal was realised in the form of the independent nation-state of Pakistan, the locus of Deobandism shifted to Islamising the new Muslim polity. The ascent of an Islamist-leaning military regime coupled with regional geopolitics at the tail end of the Cold War fragmented and militarised the Deobandi phenomenon whose locus yet again shifted westward. After the 1980s, the movement increasingly reverted to its British-era jihadist roots through terrorism and insurgency. That process has culminated in the Taliban's empowerment in Afghanistan and now threatens to destabilise the entire South Asian region (Bokhari, 2021).

2. 'Hanafi' refers to one of the major schools of law (*madhab* or *mazhab*) in Islamic jurisprudence (*fiqh*), named after the famed Persian scholar, Imam Abu Hanifa (d. 767 CE). First, and most simply, the Hanafi school is dominant in particular geographic areas. Adopted by the Abbasids, the Ottomans, and the Mughals, Hanafism remains the dominant tradition in the Levant, Iraq, Afghanistan, South Asia, Central Asia, Turkey, western China, and the Balkans. The divergence in Hanafi practices speaks to the fact that the traditional *fiqh* literature covers a relatively small range of subjects and leaves a great many political, devotional, and social topics open for interpretation (White, 2012).
3. The Taliban has barred women employed by the previous government from continuing with their jobs. Only women, whose jobs cannot be done by men because of hardline interpretation of Sharia by the Taliban, comprising doctors, nurses, and teachers, are allowed to work, but with severe restrictions.

References

Alemi, Q., Panter-Brick, C., Oriya, S., Ahmady, M., Alimi, A. Q., Faiz, H., Hakim, N., Hashemi, S. A. S., Manaly, M. A., Naseri, R., Parwiz, K., Sadat, S. J., Sharifi, M. Z., Shinwari, Z., Ahmadi, S. J., Amin, R., Azimi, S., Hewad, A., Musavi, Z., & Siddiqi, A. M. (2023). "Afghan mental health and psychosocial well-being: thematic review of four decades of research and interventions". *BJPsych Open*, *9*(4). https://doi.org/10.1192/bjo.2023.502

AMU TV (2024). "Taliban leader approves law to curb begging". https://amu.tv/98246/

Bhattacharya, S. (September 4, 2021). "No good future for Afghan women under the Taliban". *East Asia Forum*. https://eastasiaforum.org/2021/09/04/no-good-future-for-afghan-women-under-the-taliban/

Bhattacharya, S. (March 15, 2022). "Women always faced horrid times under Taliban, this time even female mannequins are not safe". *Firstpost*. https://www.firstpost.com/world/women-always-faced-horrid-times-under-taliban-this-time-even-female-mannequins-are-not-safe-10460951.html

Bhattacharya, S. (June 27, 2024). "Afghan Women Forced Into Obscurity By Taliban 2.0". *The Friday Times*. https://thefridaytimes.com/27-Jun-2024/afghan-women-forced-into-obscurity-by-taliban-2-0

Bokhari, K. (November 23, 2021). "The Long Shadow of Deobandism in South Asia". *New Lines Magazine*. https://newlinesmag.com/essays/the-long-shadow-of-deobandism-in-south-asia/

Chiovenda, A. (2019). *Crafting Masculine Selves: Culture, War, and Psychodynamics in Afghanistan*. Oxford University Press.

Faiez, R. (September 19, 2023). "Mental health among Afghan women deteriorating across the country, UN report finds". *AP News*. https://apnews.com/article/mental-health-afghan-women-un-report-c0db1ebeb1506746c961c92fd67174c1

Gibbon, K. F. (August 28, 2021). "Pashtunwali: Pashtun Traditional Tribal Law in Afghanistan". *Cultural Property News*. https://culturalpropertynews.org/pashtunwali-pashtun-traditional-tribal-law-in-afghanistan/

Girowal, H. (March 14, 2024). "The Vicious Cycle of Women's Rights Violations in Afghanistan and the Need for Accountability—Afghanistan". ReliefWeb. https://reliefweb.int/report/afghanistan/vicious-cycle-womens-rights-violations-afghanistan-and-need-accountability

GIWPS (2019). "Women, Peace, and Security Index". https://giwps.georgetown.edu/the-index/

Izumi, K. (2007). "Gender-Based Violence and Property Grabbing in Africa: A Denial of Women's Liberty and Security". In G. Terry & J. Hoare (Eds.), *Gender Based Violence*. Oxfam GB.

Khan, N. (February 15, 2024). "Sifting Facts from Fiction: The Underpinnings of the Taliban's "Islamic Emirate"". *The SAIS Review of International Affairs*. https://saisreview.sais.jhu.edu/sifting-facts-from-fiction-the-underpinnings-of-the-talibans-islamic-emirate/

Landinfo (2011). "Afghanistan: Blood feuds, traditional law (pashtunwali) and traditional conflict resolution". https://www.ecoi.net/en/file/local/1104068/1788_1327313532_1940-1.pdf

Mehran, M. (2024). "Where Does the Taliban's Educational Ideology Come From?" *Hasht-e-Subh*. https://8am.media/eng/where-does-the-talibans-educational-ideology-come-from/

Mishra, A. (August 27, 2024). "Taliban ruled Afghanistan: Acute Mental health crisis in women rising while the world watches". TheHealthSite. https://www.thehealthsite.com/diseases-conditions/mental-health/acute-mental-health-crisis-in-women-on-rise-in-afghanistan-while-the-world-watches-1120192/

Mosadiq, H. (March 7, 2024). "Twice under the Taliban: The repeated nightmare of my generation". Atlantic Council. https://www.atlanticcouncil.org/content-series/inside-the-talibans-gender-apartheid/twice-under-the-taliban-the-repeated-nightmare-of-my-generation/

Nehan, N. & Escobales, R. (October 20, 2023). "Women are begging on the streets of Kabul". Chatham House. https://www.chathamhouse.org/publications/the-world-today/2023-08/nargis-nehan-women-are-begging-streets-kabul

Pepin, T. (2024). "Sticks and Stones: The Taliban's War Against Women". *The Cairo Review of Global Affairs, 51.* https://www.thecairoreview.com/essays/sticks-and-stones-the-talibans-war-against-women/

Puri, L. (2009). "The Past and Future of Deobandi Islam". *CTC Sentinel, 2*(1), pp. 19–22.

Safi, M. & Rivas, A.M. (2023). "The mental health crisis among Afghan women and girls". ODI. https://media.odi.org/documents/The_mental_health_crisis_among_Afghan_women_and_girls_mh6O2uX.pdf

Salehi, A. (2024). "An Inquiry into Taliban Theology: Deobandism with a Pashtunwali Flavor". Afghan Institute for Strategic Studies. https://aissonline.org/Uploads/PublicationEnglishFiles/an-inquiry-into-taliban-theology-english-7368.pdf

Siddique, A. (2024). ""Systematic Discrimination": Taliban's Drastic Cut In Salaries of Female State Employees Triggers Anger". *RadioFreeEurope/RadioLiberty*. https://www.rferl.org/a/afghanistan-taliban-women-employees-salaries/32998050.html

UN Women (2024). "FAQs: Afghan women three years after the Taliban takeover". https://eca.unwomen.org/en/stories/explainer/2024/08/faqs-afghan-women-three-years-after-the-taliban-takeover-0#:~:text=In%20December%202022%2C%20the%20Taliban,were%20ordered%20to%20shut%20down

White, J. T. (2012). "Understanding the Taliban: Assessing Religious Categories of Analysis". Danish Institute for International Studies. https://www.diis.dk/files/media/publications/import/understanding_the_taliban.pdf

Wimpelmann, T. (2013). *The Price of Protection Gender, violence and power in Afghanistan* [Ph.D. Thesis]. https://eprints.soas.ac.uk/16802/1/Wimpelmann_3513.pdf

11 Ethnic Conflict in Afghanistan

The Struggle for Inclusive Governance under the Taliban

Puspa Kumari

Introduction

The Afghan society is one of the most complex societies among existing tribal systems in the world. Not only is it divided into different ethnic groups, but each ethnic group is further divided into sub-groups. It is important to note that the term 'ethnic group' was unknown in the 19th century, and many authors used different categories and references in their endeavours to describe and define the population of Afghanistan. Henry Bellew, in his report, "The races of Afghanistan: Being a brief account of the principal nations inhabiting the country", equated races and nation (Schetter, 2005). It was not until the mid-20th century that foreign academics and the government mapped the division of Afghan society systematically into ethnic categories by differences in language, sectarianism, culture, etc. The French anthropologist, Dollot, was the first researcher to have used the term 'groupe ethnique' for Afghanistan and categorised the Afghan people into several ethnic units (Schetter, 2005). Afghanistan, for many centuries, was not a united country. Many kingdoms have ruled over different regions of Afghanistan over a period of time. It was not until the 18th century that Afghanistan became a modern united nation under the leadership of Abdul Rahman Khan. Later, people have used their ethnic identity to politically benefit and gain power among other groups. In this chapter, we will try to understand how ethnic identity has come into play in the political arena, and what role it has played in shaping the current dynamics of Afghanistan.

Major Ethnic Groups in Afghanistan

There are nine major ethnic groups spread over Afghanistan, which include the Pashtuns, Tajiks, Hazaras, Uzbeks, Turkmens, Balochs, Nuristanis, Aimaks, and Pashayis. Maintaining harmony among these groups is one of the biggest problems confronting Afghanistan. It is also a key determinant of whether the country's future is to be one of peace and reconciliation or conflict and discord. This section gives a detailed overview of all the communities, geographical distribution, and their history of existence in Afghanistan.

The Pashtuns

Concentrated in the southern and eastern parts of Afghanistan, the Pashtuns are generally considered to be the country's largest ethnic group since the mid-18th century and comprise almost 40-42 per cent of the country's total population (Ali, 2015). An even larger number of Pashtuns reside on the other side of the border with Pakistan, mainly in the North-West Frontier Province (NFWP) and northern parts of Balochistan. If we talk about their existence geographically, they reside majorly in cities like Jalalabad, Kandahar, Khost, Kohat, Lashkar Gah, Mardan, Mingora, Peshawar, and Quetta, among others.

There remains a lack of unanimity amongst scholars about the origin of the Pashtuns. They are said to be composed of lineages that trace their origin to Qais bin Rashid, who is said to be the founding father of the Pashtuns. These lineages unite into larger clans, such as Durrani, Ghilzai, Abdali, Gurghust, and Karlanri. The Pashtuns have ruled Afghanistan for over 200 years. In the 18th century, they were handed the reins of leadership by the British after the drawing of the Durand Line. This was when Abdul Khan Abdali of Kandahar established the Durrani empire (Lamer & Foster, 2011). Pashtun dominance in Afghanistan arguably continues till today. Since the country's creation in 1747, central leadership has been in the hands of Pashtuns, except in the cases of Habibullah Kalakani and Burhanuddin Rabbani (Aikins, 2011).

Unlike any other tribal group in Afghanistan, the Pashtuns have their own code of conduct, known as "Pashtunwali", which they follow strictly with discipline (Devasher, 2022). It is the way of life of the Pashtuns. This is a concept which can be interpreted as an ethnic self- portrait of the Pashtuns. The code of conduct is what distinguishes them from other tribal groups: their tribal spirit, moral and ethical rules of behaviour, the demand for martial bravery, reasonable actions and consultation, a system of customary legal norms, and faith in Islam.

The Tajiks

The Tajiks are the second-largest ethnic group in Afghanistan. They comprise almost 25-30 per cent of the total population of Afghanistan (Ali, 2015). The Tajiks mostly reside in the north-eastern regions of Badakhshan, Parham, Takham, Baghlan, and Samangan, as well as in the Panjshir Valley. A considerable number of Tajiks also reside in the western regions, the central highlands, and the northern parts of the country. The Panjshir Valley is seen as a 'spiritual home' for Afghan Tajiks, and many of the most influential Tajik leaders within the Northern Alliance are originally from the Valley.

The Tajiks are of Iranian background, and historically, they may have been the first Persian inhabitants of modern day Afghanistan. The Tajiks have been living in Central Asia for over 2500 years. They are said to be the descendants of the Soghdians and the Bactrians. The Tajiks do not have a strong ethnic or tribal identity, and they do not have a specific social structure like the Pashtuns. They have adopted the social and cultural patterns of people from neighbouring countries. Afghan Tajiks are primarily Dari language speakers. The majority of the population of Afghanistan and most Afghan Tajiks are Sunni Muslims of the Hanafi school of thought. A small minority of Tajiks living in the rough terrain of the mountains of northeast Afghanistan, near the border with Tajikistan, belong to the Ismaili sect of Shia Islam.

The Tajiks constituted the core of the Northern Alliance military force, which had been the biggest group opposing the Taliban. They held the government of Afghanistan from 1992-1996 before being unseated by the Taliban in 1996. After the attack of September 11 in the United States of America, the Northern Alliance served as the main US ally in Afghanistan for defeating the Taliban during the fall of 2001. The Tajiks have served as administrators and bureaucrats in Afghanistan, but they have not been given any high-ranking leadership positions. These positions are primarily dominated by the Pashtun tribes. In 1929, Tajik leader Habibullah Khan seized power from the Pashtun king, Amanullah Khan, but he was overthrown after ruling for nine months by five prominent Pashtun brothers (the Musahiban brothers). The Tajiks did not gain control of Afghanistan until Burhanuddin Rabbani was elected President of the Islamic Council for a year by the Mujahideen executive council in 1992. He held power in Kabul for four years until the Taliban occupied the capital in September 1996. The famous leader of the Northern Alliance, Ahmad Shah Masood, who is also known as 'The Lion of Panjshir', belonged to the Tajik tribe as well. Masood was later assassinated on September 9, 2001, by a suicide bomber belonging to Al Qaeda.

The Hazaras

The Hazaras are an ethnolinguistic group originally from the mountainous region of central Afghanistan. They account for up to 10 per cent of Afghanistan's population (Sawe, 2019). The Hazaras are said to be the descendants of Genghis Khan, the founder of the Mongol empire, who swept through the region in the 13th century (Hucal, 2016). The Hazaras speak an eastern variety of Persian called Hazaragi with many Mongolian and Turkic words. While most Afghan Muslims are from the Sunni branch of Islam, most of the Hazaras are Shia Muslims. They are arguably the most persecuted and marginalised group in Afghanistan (Hucal, 2016).

At the end of the 19th century, after an unsuccessful revolt against the Afghan government, the Hazaras migrated to Quetta in Balochistan and Meshed in Iran. However, many returned and settled in Afghan Turkestan, north of the Hindu Kush, where they were granted land. The Hazaras' homeland lies in the central range of the Hindu Kush, a region known as Hazarajat. This region historically remained isolated due to its rugged terrain and harsh climate, allowing its culture to develop independently but preventing the area from developing in tune with surrounding regions.

According to anthropologist Thomas Barfield, during the late 19th century, Afghanistan's Emir, Abdur Rahman Khan, sought to centralise power and unify the country. He launched a fierce campaign against various ethnic and tribal groups, including the Hazaras, in order to "Pashtunise" Afghanistan (Hakimi, 2024). This period is known as 'The Hazara Genocide', during which thousands of Hazaras were killed and many others were forcibly displaced and enslaved. It was not until 1919 that the Hazaras were ridden of their label as slaves by King Amanullah Khan (*Britannica*, 1998). The 20th century saw continued discrimination against the Hazaras. During the country's civil war in the 1990s and the subsequent capture of Kabul by the Taliban in 1996, the Taliban declared war on the Hazara ethnic group. The Hazaras were singled out and murdered, most notably in the massacre of Mazar-e-Sharif in 1998 (Hakimi, 2024).

The Balochs

Often overlooked, the Afghan Baloch are just one among the many groups that make up the colourful ethnic mosaic of Afghanistan. Divided between three countries—Pakistan, Iran, and Afghanistan—the Baluchis are one of Asia's classical cross- border minorities. The original Baloch homeland probably lay on the Iranian plateau (*Britannica*, 2024). The total population of Balochis in Afghanistan is estimated at approximately six lakhs. Afghan Balochs live primarily in four southern and southwestern provinces—Helmand, Nimruz, Farah, and Kandahar. Their language is known as Balochi, but Afghan Balochs mostly speak Bruhui, Dari, and Pashto. The Baloch people have maintained their tribal and nomadic way of life, relying on agriculture and livestock. They have migrated from their homeland to neighbouring countries to seek refuge or to escape the sufferings of the decades-long war between local and foreign powers. During the 19th century, the British empire's expansion into South Asia had a significant impact on the Baloch people, including those in Afghanistan. They were divided into three countries: British India (currently Pakistan), Iran, and Afghanistan (*Britannica*, 2024). The Durand line, a border drawn by the British between Afghanistan and Pakistan, divided Baloch tribal territories.

The majority of Baloch people in Afghanistan are Sunni Muslim, some belonging to the Deobandi movement and others to the Barelvi movement (*Britannica*, 2024). For years, Afghanistan was seen as a place of refuge for the Baloch people. But following the return of the Islamist Taliban to power in Kabul in August 2021, members of the group fear that they have lost their sanctuary.

The Uzbeks and Turkmens

The Uzbeks and Turkmens form the Turkic ethnic group in Afghanistan and constitute nine per cent of the total population in Afghanistan. They are Sunni Muslims and occupy the northern region of Afghanistan, which includes east of Herat and west of Hazarajat. Often known as 'Chahar Aimaq', their major divisions include the Jamshidi, Firozkohi, Taimani, and Taimuri. The related Turkmen tribes are found in the northwest border with Turkmenistan and Iran. Both the groups speak Uzbek and Turkic languages. It is very likely that the Uzbeks migrated with a wave of Turkic invaders and intermingled with local Iranian tribes over time to become the ethnic group they are today. The Uzbeks did not have any representation in the government until the event of 9/11 when Abdul Rashid Dostum rose to power and supported the Americans in defeating the Taliban.

History of Ethnic Violence in Afghanistan

Afghanistan's strategic location made it a crossroads for various invasions and migrations, contributing to its ethnic diversity. Early conquerors included the Persians, Greeks, Mauryans, and Central Asian tribes, each leaving an impact on the region's demographics. Ethnicity in Afghanistan is essentially pre-nationalist, with ethnic groups holding similar economic and political interests but no common ideology or separatist aspirations (Barfield, 2011). Today's ethnic groups' relations and aspirations were shaped and greatly influenced during the emergence of modern Afghanistan at the time of Amir Abdul Rahman (1880-1901). Thereafter, till 1978, until the end of Sardar Daud's rule, the same Pashtun clan alternately ruled the country. The Pashtuns lost their overwhelming majority at the time, because the Amir ceded their territories to British India, under the Durand Line treaty agreement of 1893 (Devasher, 2022).

The conflicts in Afghanistan were never exclusively ethnic throughout the 20th century. They were more focused on alliance- building by factions and powerbrokers. During the second half of the 20th century, Afghanistan had a stable, centralised, mostly Pashtun-dominated government, which relied on foreign assistance to bring about gradual modernisation. This period saw concerted government efforts to grant rights to all citizens to establish more equality among them. The relative political freedoms granted under the 1964 constitution allowed the formation of leftist and Islamist groups, but ethnicity played a more prominent role in political alignments. The communist military coup in 1978 marked the end of the Pashtuns' long held power after the downfall of the Durrani dynasty and opened the political arena to all aspirants. But the communist government did not last long, and soon, the battle to gain power started among different factions.

Ethnicity became a political military force to reckon with when the Afghan war broke out in 1979 (Devasher, 2022). Pakistan and Iran used the ethnic potential for conflicts. On the grounds of Shiite loyalties, Iran established the Hizb-i-Wahadat, which was strong amongst the Shiite Hazaras. During the 1980s, the Jamiat-i-Islami, the oldest resistance movement, developed into a representation for the Tajiks. Pakistan supported the Taliban, which followed a radical Islam, but this was also Pashtun-dominated (Schetter, 2005). The leaders of the warring factions made their supporters aware of their social and economic deprivation on the basis of their ethnic belonging in the past and present. All warring factions justified their political demands, referring to the size of their ethnic group and their territorial roots. They also used ethnicity in their military actions.

In 1994, local Mujahideens formed a group of madrasa- educated people, now known as "the Taliban", and managed to gain control of most of Afghanistan till 1996. The Taliban's rise was fuelled by rural Pashtun support for its agenda of ending warlord-generated insecurity and corruption, bringing back Pashtun prominence (Sinno, 2021). During the establishment of their first Emirate from 1996-2001 in Afghanistan, the Taliban ruled forcefully and imposed many radical restrictions on the local populace. Whoever tried to oppose them was punished, especially the Shiite Hazaras, who were subjected to brutal retaliatory attacks. This forcefully imposed rule soon ended after the attack of 9/11 when the US invaded Afghanistan in search of Osama bin Laden, the mastermind behind the attack and the leader of Al Qaeda.

Causes for Ethnic Conflicts

Pashto, one of the two official languages of Afghanistan, could not develop much due to its lack of literary history, even though the Pashtuns have dominated politically and ruled the major part of Afghanistan for centuries.

The 'inferior status' of Pashto is another reason that has long infuriated many Pashtun leaders and has been an element of movements, including the Taliban. Many Afghans think that the Taliban's insistence on Pashto is a form of revenge—an expression of a cultural and ethnic bitterness—for the traditional dominance of the Dari language.

The century- long war between different ethnicities for power has been fuelled by many anti-Taliban factions. This is another reason for the instability in the country. The ISKP (Islamic State of Khorasan Province) portrays the Taliban as being a Pashtun mono-ethnic, nationalist, democratic, Hanafi supremacist, and un-Islamic movement. They allege the Taliban oppress non-Pashtun ethnicities and even accuse them of group killings of Tajiks, Uzbeks, and Hazaras. Below are several important reasons for ethnic conflicts in Afghanistan:

Power Struggle

The competition for political power and resources among different ethnic groups and factions has been a major driver of ethnic violence in Afghanistan. During the reign of Ahmad Shah Durrani, Pashtuns started getting prominent roles in Afghanistan's political landscape. After Ahmad Shah, his descendants, Abdur Rahman Khan, Habibullah, Amanullah Khan (who declared independence in Afghanistan in 1919), Nadir Khan, Doud Khan, and many such Pashtuns, have acceded to the throne and ruled Afghanistan. Power has mostly been in the hands of one community, and others felt that they had not been given proper representation to show their capability. The Pashtuns were privileged in all areas and dominated the military. The Tajiks were left with the economic sector and the educational institutions, whereas the Hazaras were marginalised in general.

Economic Disparities

Afghanistan has been rich in natural resources, such as copper, gold, oil, natural gas, uranium, bauxite, coal, iron ore, lithium, chromium, lead, zinc, gemstones, sulphur, gypsum, and marble, which are worth almost US$ 3 trillion. The opium trade also has always been majorly controlled by the Taliban who are radical Pashtuns. They benefit from it by exporting opium, which is worth millions, to neighbouring countries and use the money to further strengthen their army or create influence over the others. They control poppy production in their region and have become drug lords in various aspects of the drug trade. This power struggle has always created competition and tension among ethnicities.

Foreign Interventions

Afghanistan has never been an independent state or excluded from foreign interventions. Foreign powers, like the USA, the former Soviet Union, and Britain, have invaded Afghanistan either with the promise to bring peace and stabilise the economy or to use the country as a buffer zone to spread their influence in Central or South Asia. Even if the tribals try to share power, foreign invaders support a specific group to benefit personally, which has resulted in creating tension among other ethnicities about being marginalised or being actively discriminated against by dominant groups.

Marginalisation of Small Ethnic Groups

Undoubtedly, state-building and institution-building processes have to be reflective of ethnic harmony. If we look at the history of Afghanistan, the Pashtuns have ruled for centuries, and in recent decades, the Pashtun-dominated Taliban- led interim government has tried to impose its strict interpretation of Islam. After coming back to power in 2021, the Taliban have been systematically excluding other minority groups, especially Shia Muslims, first from the political sphere and then from public spaces. Groups like the Tajiks, Uzbeks, and Turkmens have been raising their voice against not getting enough representation in the political sphere, considering their significant numbers in the country. The Taliban are trying to favour their loyalists and fill their internal political sphere with like-minded radicals who support their strict ideology of Sharia (Bahrami, 2018). Ethnic deprivation of minority groups is a constant feature of any multi-ethnic state and society, and Afghanistan is not an exception.

Ethnic Groups under the Taliban Regime

After the event of 9/11, in order to capture bin Laden and due to the Taliban's refusal to hand him over, the US military invaded Afghanistan and allied with minority groups' local leaders and some Pashtun warlords to oust the Taliban. These warlords ended up filling most key posts in the regime the US-led coalition established in Kabul (Sinno, 2021). Therefore, the Afghan population went back to suffering from the warlords' predatory behaviour and open corruption. However, after the US withdrawal, and consequently, the Taliban takeover of Kabul in August 2021, the new cabinet shows a stark lack of inclusivity, with key positions overwhelmingly dominated by Pashtun leaders. According to a report published by the Middle East Research Institute (MERI), a very small percentage of non-Pashtun ethnic groups are present in the Taliban regime. The findings show that out of 1,137 high-ranking Taliban officials, only 87 are Tajiks, Uzbeks, and Hazaras, reflecting minimal representation, with the minorities having no decision-making power (Mohammad, 2024c). The Deputy Prime Minister, Malawi Abdul Salam Hanafi, who is an Uzbek leader, has secured the second topmost leadership position in the Afghan government. However, the actual decision-making power is in the hands of the supreme leader, Mullah Hibatullah Akhundzada.

Politically, the Taliban's cabinet and Supreme Court lack Hazara and Shia representation, and the regime has abolished the Shia personal status law and Ja'fari jurisprudence from the education system, dismissing Shia judges (Danish, 2024). Afghanistan's 2004 constitution permitted Shias to use their Ja'fari jurisprudence in court cases. But the constitution has since been suspended indefinitely by the Taliban, and minorities are ordered to follow the rules made by the Taliban (Ellinwood, 2023).

In the declining economy, since the Taliban takeover, the World Health Organisation reported that over 28 million people, representing about 73 per cent of the population, are in urgent need of humanitarian assistance (World Health Organisation, 2023). Health facilities remain understaffed and under-resourced, grappling with shortages of essential medicines and supplies, impeding the delivery of critical healthcare services. The situation is catastrophic for everyone but is particularly grave for the Hazara population, as they predominantly reside in the country's most deprived and least developed regions. This geographical remoteness exacerbates the challenges they face. There have been several deadly attacks on Shia/Hazara civilians since the Taliban takeover. While the Islamic State of Khorasan Province (ISKP) has claimed responsibility for most attacks, the Taliban's response has been very tepid (Bjelica, 2022). In public, the Taliban ministers promise to safeguard religious minorities in Afghanistan, but there are no tangible actions on the ground. It is also very important to note the condition of women in Afghanistan, who are being treated as the unwanted minorities in the country, although they constitute almost 50 per cent of the country's population. Hundreds of restrictions on their movement, education, and work has led to an international outcry about mistreatment and systematic oppression by the current regime.

The exclusion of other ethnic groups is not limited to the political sphere; it also extends to actions on the ground, where the Hazaras have been forced to submit property ownership documents, face illegal land seizures, and endure forced relocations (Mohammad, 2024a). Transferring and arrest of non-Pashtun Taliban commanders has led to a public outcry about detention on the basis of ethnicity and linguistic differences. Internally, ethnic discrimination has led to discontent among non-Pashtun Taliban commanders, resulting in resignations like that of Tajik commander Abdul Hamid Khorasani (Mohammad, 2024c).

The Taliban's heavy-handed approach towards the ethnic minorities has played a crucial role in aiding the recruitment of non-Pashtuns into the Islamic State of Khorasan Province (ISKP) ranks (Wahlang, 2023). The ISKP actively exploits the Taliban's oppressive actions towards minority groups to recruit new members and expand its cadre. By positioning itself as a more inclusive alternative in terms of ethnicity, the ISKP capitalises on the Taliban's repressive measures against ethnic minorities to strengthen its ranks. This dynamic illustrates how ethnic inequality in Afghanistan also fuels the spread of terrorism in the region.

In a more recent event, the Taliban authorities have imposed new restrictions on the occasion of Ashura, the tenth day of Muharram. According to these restrictions, the installation of special gates and flags for Muharram on the streets, the opening of water stations for passers-by, and the movement of mourning groups from one congregation hall to another at night have been banned by the Taliban (Mohammad, 2024b). Overall, the Taliban's treatment of ethnic minorities is characterised by systematic exclusion, legal and social discrimination, and inadequate protection against violence, exacerbating the hardships and vulnerabilities of these communities.

Conclusion

The process of defining Afghanistan's conflict as an ethnic one is a complex issue. There is no single cause of violence in the ongoing situation in Afghanistan. While it is often assumed that persistent violence in Afghanistan can be attributed solely to ethnic groups, other factors are also involved. Not to be discounted is the Taliban, which has evolved mostly from the Pashtun ethnic group. Suppression of other ethnic minorities, excluding them from major political affairs and decision-making bodies, and imposing one way of Islam on all Afghans, irrespective of their beliefs, has and will always be a major factor behind the instability and decentralisation of governance in Afghanistan. More often than not, the underlying struggle is about political power and access to resources, and thinking of the conflict in ethnic terms limits rather than enhances understanding of the root causes of the violence.

Including minority groups' representatives in the decision- making bodies and giving them a safe space to speak for their community is the only way to bring internal harmony among the local population. An inclusive government that represents all the ethnic groups can foster a sense of belonging and unity among the population. It can mitigate the risk of civil unrest and rebellion by addressing the grievances of all factions. Inclusivity meets global expectations and shows the ruling government's capability to govern, which, in result, can attract much needed aid and investment in the country, essential for post-conflict healing and comprehensive peace processes.

References

Aikins, M. (September 20, 2011). "Profile: Burhanuddin Rabbani". *The Guardian*. https://www.theguardian.com/world/2011/sep/20/profile-burhanuddin-rabbani

Ali, F. (2015). "Afghanistan: the rise of ethnic consciousness through history; a comprehensive overview of the origin of the Afghan conflict". Leibniz Institute for Social Sciences. https://nbn-resolving.org/urn:nbn:de:0168-ssoar-438323

Bahrami, A. (July 7, 2018). "Main Causes of Ethnic Conflict in Afghanistan and Solutions". *Daily Outlook Afghanistan*, the Leading Independent Newspaper. http://www.outlookafghanistan.net/editorialdetail.php?post_id=21283

Barfield, T. (2011). "Afghanistan's Ethnic Puzzle: Decentralizing Power Before the U.S. Withdrawal". *Foreign Affairs*, *90*(5), pp. 54–65. https://www.jstor.org/stable/23041776

Bjelica, J. (January 16, 2022). "A Community Under Attack: How successive governments failed west Kabul and the Hazaras who live there". Afghanistan Analysts Network. https://www.afghanistan-analysts.org/en/reports/war-and-peace/a-community-under-attack-how-successive-governments-failed-west-kabul-and-the-hazaras-who-live-there/

Britannica (July 20, 1998). "Abdur Rahman Khan | Emir, Afghanistan, & History". https://www.britannica.com/biography/Abdur-Rahman-Khan

Britannica (July 2, 2024). "Baloch | People, history, & culture". https://www.britannica.com/topic/Baloch

Danish, T. (May 14, 2024). "Hazaras and Shias: Violence, Discrimination, and Exclusion Under the Taliban". *Jurist News.* https://www.jurist.org/commentary/2024/05/hazaras-and-shias-violence-discrimination-and-exclusion-under-taliban/

Devasher, T. (2022). *The Pashtuns: A Contested History.* HarperCollins India.

Ellingwood, A. (August 29, 2023). "Ethnic and Religious Minorities Face Systemic Discrimination Under Taliban Rule in Afghanistan". Feminist Majority Foundation. https://feminist.org/news/ethnic-and-religious-minorities-face-systemic-discrimination-under-taliban-rule-in-afghanistan/

Hakimi, M. J. (2024). "The Afghan State and the Hazara Genocide". *Harvard Human Rights Journal, 37,* pp. 81–115. https://journals.law.harvard.edu/hrj/wp-content/uploads/sites/83/2024/06/03_HLH_37_1_Hakimi81-116.pdf

Hucal, S. (June 27, 2016). "Afghanistan: Who are the Hazaras?" *Al Jazeera.* https://www.aljazeera.com/features/2016/6/27/afghanistan-who-are-the-hazaras

Lamer, W. & Foster, E. (2011). "Afghan Ethnic Groups: A Brief Investigation". Civil Military Fusion Centre. https://reliefweb.int/report/afghanistan/afghan-ethnic-groups-brief-investigation

Mohammad. (June 9, 2024a). "Land Seizure Allegations: Taliban Declare Hazara Neighbourhood Property Documents Invalid in Ghazni Province". *Hasht-e-Subh.* https://8am.media/eng/land-seizure-allegations-taliban-declare-hazara-neighborhood-property-documents-invalid-in-ghazni-province/

Mohammad. (July 9, 2024b). "Taliban Continue to Restrict Religious Freedoms: Muharram Mourners Protest New Restrictions". *Hasht-e-Subh.* https://8am.media/eng/taliban-continue-to-restrict-religious-freedoms-muharram-mourners-protest-new-restrictions/

Mohammad. (July 23, 2024c). "Three Years of Rule Rife with Discrimination: The Purge of Non-Pashtun Commanders in the Taliban Ranks Continues". *Hasht-e-Subh.* https://8am.media/eng/three-years-of-rule-rife-with-discrimination-the-purge-of-non-pashtun-commanders-in-the-taliban-ranks-continues/

Sawe, B. (September 10, 2019). "Ethnic Groups Of Afghanistan". *World Atlas.* https://www.worldatlas.com/articles/ethnic-groups-of-afghanistan.html

Schetter, C. (2005). "Ethnicity and the political reconstruction of Afghanistan", ZEF Working Paper Series, No. 3. Center for Development Research (ZEF), Bonn. https://www.econstor.eu/bitstream/10419/88366/1/578445514.pdf

Sinno, A. (October 25, 2021). "How ethnic and religious divides in Afghanistan are contributing to violence against minorities". *The Conversation.* https://theconversation.

com/how-ethnic-and-religious-divides-in-afghanistan-are-contributing-to-violence-against-minorities-168059

Wahlang, J. (June 28, 2023). "Islamic State Khorasan and Central Asia". Manohar Parrikar Institute for Defence Studies and Analyses. https://idsa.in/issuebrief/islamic-state-khorasan-and-central-asia-jwahlang-280623

World Health Organization (2023). "Appeal Afghanistan". https://www.who.int/emergencies/funding/health-emergency-appeals/2022/2023/2023-appeals/appeal-afghanistan

12 Consultative Democracy

An Embryonic Model for Afghanistan's Fragile and Fractured Geopolitical Matrix

Kondaraju Sandeep Royal

Introduction

The concept of Consultative Democracy (CD) presents a viable framework for addressing Afghanistan's geopolitical-strategic terrain. It examines the adaptation of the Chinese Consultative Democracy (CCD) model to Afghanistan's landscape, by integrating diverse stakeholders into the decision-making process and governance through increased stability, inclusivity, accountability, and socio-political cohesion for fostering sustainable governance and strategic unity in Afghanistan.

CD is a governance model that combines public consultation and deliberation in decision-making, ensuring inclusivity, transparency, and responsiveness (Zheng & Wang, 2014). It balances centralised leadership with grassroots input, reflecting diverse societal interests while supporting effective governance (Owen, 2020). Unlike electoral democracies that rely on majority vote decisions, CD engages all levels of formal and informal institutions in dialogue and consultation (Embassy of China, Republic of Bulgaria, 2005). Countries adopting CD have seen enhanced political, economic, and strategic landscapes through increased inclusion and representation (Heilmann, 2016).

CD emphasises inclusivity by creating a governance framework that stands for diverse societal interests (Martí, 2006) and engaging marginalised groups and various sectors. It enhances policy decisions with diverse perspectives (Cheek et al., 2021). Deliberation allows thorough discussion, enabling stakeholders to contribute effectively, fostering informed decision-making (Andrain, 1994). Transparency in government processes builds trust and accountability, empowering citizens to influence decisions. Responsiveness to public input ensures adaptive governance, while consensus-building promotes social cohesion and stability. These principles make CD a strong model for tackling complex governance challenges.

The process of CD involves community engagement, stakeholder meetings, policy formulation, implementation, checks and balances, evaluation, and retrospection.

The Sino-Afghan Nexus

The adaptation of CD in Afghanistan under Taliban rule requires understanding the historical and socio-cultural dynamics. Historically, Afghanistan and China have engaged in diplomatic and cultural exchanges dating back to the Ancient Silk Road. These interactions have fostered a shared understanding of governance practices, despite differing economic, cultural, and political contexts (Millward, 2007). Afghanistan's strategic location has made it a hub for all-weather simulation exchange with China. Chronological relations include Silk Road trade routes; people, ideas, and cultural exchanges; the diffusion of Buddhism in the medieval period; and diplomatic engagements along with economic cooperation in the modern era (Frankopan, 2015).

Socio-cultural elements, particularly Confucian principles of harmony and consensus-building, play a crucial role in Sino-Afghan relations, aligning with Afghan traditions and supporting the adaptation of CD by fostering mutual understanding, governance legitimacy, and community cohesion (Bell, 2015).

In contemporary times, Chinese investments in Afghan infrastructure and strategic economic initiatives through the Belt and Road Initiative (BRI) and the Global Security Initiative (GSI) (Xinhua, 2023) stabilise the region and support sustainable governance (Rolland, 2017). These linkages create opportunities for collaborative governance, involving local communities and civil society. Strategically, Sino-Afghan relations can mediate internal conflicts through efforts encompassing facilitating dialogue among Afghan factions, promoting transparency and inclusivity in governance, and developing infrastructure projects, such as roads, energy initiatives, trade corridors, and economic integration (Clarke, 2017). Diplomatic experiments and political-economic engineering efforts can facilitate dialogue and reconciliation, leveraging historical goodwill and economic incentives to promote inclusive governance. This collaboration can pave the way for effective CD implementation across national, provincial, and local levels.

Comparative Analysis of CD

The Chinese Experience of CD

CCD emphasises consolidation and consultation, operationalised through the Chinese People's Political Consultative Conference (CPPCC) since 1949. The CPPCC, including CPC members, other political parties, and social organisations, serves as a consultative assembly to deliberate on national policies and issues, ensuring alignment with central directives while incorporating diverse viewpoints (Zheng & Wang, 2014). Over its seven-decade-long history, the CPPCC has been crucial in promoting unity and democratic engagement, particularly during the reform period starting in 1978, when it supported economic modernisation and national rejuvenation.

The CPPCC's institutionalisation of CCD has achieved key milestones through distinct phases:

1. Founding and Early Development (1949-1978): Establishment of the PRC, provisional constitution, national economy restoration (Teiwes, 1990).
2. Reform and Opening-Up (1978-2012): Support for economic reforms, modernisation, and mobilisation of social forces.
3. The New Era (2012-Present): Advancement of five-sphere integrated plans, four-pronged comprehensive strategy, and promotion of national rejuvenation, contributing to political consultation, democratic oversight, and state administration (Jinping, 2020).

Benefits and Challenges of CD in China

The CCD model offers significant benefits and challenges. Its inclusivity promotes broad participation and national unity by standing for diverse groups and easing consensus on policies through extensive deliberation. This process supports long-term development goals and ensures policy relevance through collective input (Zheng & Wang, 2014).

Inclusive CD models provide effective and representative governance, fostering balanced and equitable economic development. These models enhance social stability by promoting cohesion and reducing conflict, resulting in an improved global image and strengthened international relations (Pan, 2003). Conversely, exclusive CD models often result in ineffective and biased governance, leading to skewed economic growth and increased inequality. This exclusivity heightens social conflict and instability, potentially straining international relations and inviting sanctions (Rolland, 2017). The analysis underscores the superiority of inclusive CD models in achieving sustainable development and geopolitical stability.

However, the model faces issues, such as CPC's consolidative control, which may limit political pluralism and dissent (Vogel, 2013). The complexity of the model requires advanced mechanisms for effective deliberation and consensus, which is crucial for policy coherence. Additionally, the CPPCC's broad scope struggles to address specific regional concerns, making it challenging to align national policies with local needs. Balancing these elements is essential for improving the model's governance effectiveness (Jinping, 2020).

Comparative Approaches to CD

China, Singapore, Norway, and Switzerland each apply CD uniquely. China's CPPCC facilitates policy development through dialogue with moderate inclusivity and limited transparency (He & Warren, 2011). Singapore integrates public and expert input, achieving high responsiveness and transparency but moderate inclusivity and deliberation (Tan, 2016). Norway emphasises broad stakeholder engagement, enhancing social harmony with high inclusivity and deliberation (Lægreid, 2017). Switzerland's direct democracy, featuring frequent referendums, offers high inclusivity, deliberation, and transparency, with moderate responsiveness and consensus-building (Kriesi & Trechsel, 2008). Each model highlights different strengths and limitations in consultative governance.

Advancing Inclusivity through CD in Afghanistan

Afghanistan, an Islamic state governed by Sharia law and Pashtunwali, operates under strict Taliban rule, which enforces its social and cultural policies rigorously (Matinuddin, 1999). Historically, Afghanistan has shifted through monarchy, republic, and theocracy, with its current autocratic structure centralising all power in the hands of the supreme leader and his clerical advisors, and as of 2023, it ranks as one of the least democratic countries globally (Lemm et al., 2022). The centralised presidential system includes three branches: executive, legislative, and judiciary, all headed by the president. Since the Taliban's takeover in August 2021, led by Mullah Hibatullah Akhundzada from Kandahar with the government based in Kabul, the country has been divided into 34 provinces. Each province is a key administrative unit, encompassing districts and numerous villages (Moir, 2020).

CD integrates diverse political, social, and ethnic groups into a collective decision-making framework (Dryzek, 2009). The Taliban and other major groups, as the governing authority, must embrace this model to help address Afghanistan's geopolitical-security challenges since their resurgence in 2021. They need to strengthen institutions and processes that facilitate broad-based participation. This includes reorganising consultative assemblies at all levels, integrating tribal and ethnic leaders, and ensuring policies reflect the needs and aspirations of all societal segments (Katzman & Thomas, 2017). Adapting CD could increase inclusivity and dialogue, potentially moderating extremist ideologies and addressing internal and external issues.

Levels of Consultative Assemblies

A National Consultative Assembly (NCA), modelled after the CPPCC, could foster consensus on key issues in a multi-tiered governance structure. National participants, ethnic representatives, tribal leaders, and scholars drive policy formulation and legislation (Sedra, 2016). This advisory body should extend to include multiple representatives from national institutions, ethnic groups, tribal leaders, political factions, and civil society, ensuring diverse voices in policy decisions (Starr, 2020). The potential of such assemblies was evident in the 2010-2011 Afghanistan Peace and Reintegration Program (United Nations Development Programme, 2017). Incorporating the Taliban and other stakeholders is crucial for national unity, stability (Katzman, 2010), and diverse Afghan voices in governance. The NCA should also integrate by bridging the gap between local communities, regional councils, and national interests (Schirch, 2010) to decentralise decision-making and empower communities. Since their takeover in August 2021, the Taliban control major urban and rural areas, imposing their governance (Moir, 2020).

Provincial Governors, appointed by the national government, manage administrative functions, while elected councils, such as those in Herat and Balkh, focus on local governance and development. Provincial leaders and community representatives implement these policies by region, while district and local grassroots leaders address local issues, ensuring effective governance and alignment with both national priorities and local needs (Sharan, 2011).

Community-level and local leaders are instrumental in mediating conflicts and supporting stability through negotiations with both Taliban and government officials (Moir, 2020). For instance, the Afghan Women's Network (AWN) advocates for women's rights and regional development (*Reports – AWN*, n.d.). The expansion of Shuras to include diverse groups can enhance their legitimacy and effectiveness (Barfield, 2010).

Tribal elders hold considerable influence, particularly in the Pashtun belt, where tribal loyalty often surpasses formal political affiliations (Dorronsoro, 2005). Shuras, such as the District Development Assemblies (DDAs) under the National Solidarity Program (NSP), facilitate local governance (Beath et al., 2013). Effective engagement with these stakeholders, community leaders, tribal elders, local councils, and citizens is essential for aligning policies with community needs and fostering social cohesion (Rashid, 2008). The local groups, in consultation with Taliban groups, can integrate traditional and modern governance systems, enhancing both legitimacy and effectiveness.

Application of CD

Afghanistan's historical trajectory, marked by conflict and instability, has been worsened by ethnic fragmentation, external interventions, and incapacitated governance structures (Barfield, 2010). The abrupt U.S. and NATO withdrawal in 2021 precipitated the collapse of the Afghan government and the resurgence of the Taliban (Gopal, 2014; Moir, 2020). The country's ethnic mixture, including the Pashtuns, Tajiks, Hazaras, and Uzbeks, intensifies sectarian friction, while economic sanctions, aid reductions, and a worsening humanitarian crisis compound the instability (Nojumi, 2002). The emergence of groups like the ISIS-Khorasan further threatens security. The Taliban's non-democratic governance model raises critical concerns about human rights and inclusivity, underscoring the necessity for alternative governance frameworks such as CD (European Union Agency for Asylum (EUAA), 2022; Minority Rights Group, 2023). Ministries, such as Education and Health, face challenges under Taliban rule (European Union Agency for Asylum (EUAA), 2022; Minority Rights Group, 2023), while National Security Forces, including remnants of the Afghan National Army (ANA) and police, continue to influence security dynamics despite Taliban control ("Afghanistan's Security Challenges under the Taliban", Crisis Group, 2022).

Inclusive and Shared Decision-making

Effective CD in Afghanistan will hinge on addressing entrenched socio-political, economic, and security challenges (Goodson, 2001). Inclusive representation is crucial for the success of CD, ensuring that all ethnic and social groups have a stake in governance and mitigating historical grievances. Collective decision-making, which engages multiple stakeholders, leads to more informed and effective policies that align with the population's needs and aspirations, enhancing socio-economic development and conflict resolution in Afghanistan. Ethnic inclusivity can reduce conflict and enhance national cohesion (UNAMA, 2021).

Policy Formulation, Institutional and Legal Framework Reforms

Involving women and minorities in local Shuras and Jirgas in policy discussions by ensuring local voices are incorporated into national strategies will improve policy effectiveness and increasing alignment with local needs (Fischer, 2012; Berman et al., 2018). Studies on decentralised governance highlight that such inclusive approaches uphold CD principles and foster socio-economic development, as evidenced by global socio-economic projects (O'Reilly, 2004; Vijayendra, 2012).

Establishment of the NCA could fortify local governance structures and integrate tribal and ethnic leaders. The NCA could conduct regular consultative meetings, formulate and implement policies and further check and evaluate their impact (Maley & Schmeidl, 2015; Aisha, 2004). The policy development process encompasses public consultation, stakeholder deliberation, drafting policies, review and feedback, finalisation, implementation, and ongoing monitoring and evaluation (Howlett & Ramesh, 2003). Ensuring these steps are systematically followed will enhance the legitimacy and effectiveness of the policies, addressing the complex socio-political landscape of Afghanistan.

Establishing and expanding fully functional institutions is critical for Afghanistan. Revising and adapting the 2004 Afghan Constitution to contemporary realities is essential, along with legal reforms that protect civil liberties, women's rights, and freedom of expression (United Nations, 2023). There are significant gaps in the enforcement of the legal framework. Strengthening judicial independence and combating corruption are vital, as effective judicial reforms can increase public trust (Eriksson, 2023).

Inclusiveness

Inclusiveness is vital for CD in Afghanistan, as it bridges ethnic and tribal divides and enhances socio-political cohesion (International Crisis Group, 2022). Mechanisms like community dialogues, policy forums, and participatory budgeting foster grassroots cooperation. Local councils with representatives from diverse groups can address grievances and build trust between the government and the populace. Historically, practices like shuras and jirgas have resolved disputes and supported social order. Integrating these into a broader democratic framework can enhance their legitimacy and effectiveness (Haidar, 2020).

Effective governance must integrate inclusiveness, promote education and awareness, uphold cultural sensitivity, focus on capacity building, ensure transparency, and establish rigorous feedback mechanisms (OECD, 2020).

Fostering Local Peace Through Culture

Empowering marginalised groups, including women and minorities, through reserved seats in consultative bodies ensures their participation in governance and protection of their interests (United Nations Development Programme

[UNDP], 2021). Community Development Councils (CDCs) under NSP have improved local infrastructure and could boost community engagement with expanded long-term objectives. In 2022, local dialogues in Helmand led to temporary ceasefires, indicating the potential for peace through consultative initiatives. Cultural sensitivity and education are essential, which underscores the transformative role of education in fostering sustainable peace and development (UNESCO, 2023).

Security and Stability

The Afghan Local Police (ALP) program demonstrates successful community engagement in security (United Nations Assistance Mission in Afghanistan, 2021). CD involving local leaders and communities in security planning can yield effective strategies. Expanding community-based initiatives within a consultative framework can bolster grassroots security, especially against threats like the ISIS-K (United Nations, 2023). Comprehensive security strategies, including community-based policing and intelligence-sharing, are essential.

Conflict Resolution

CD promotes conflict resolution through dialogue and negotiation, using traditional Afghan practices like jirgas and shuras. Local and national consultative forums address grievances and build consensus, as demonstrated by the Afghan High Peace Council (AHPC) (Afghanistan Research and Evaluation Unit [AREU], 2022). Engaging local communities in security through the ALP has reduced insurgent activities since 2022. Community-based policing and intelligence-sharing are recommended for stability (International Crisis Group, 2023). Platforms like the AHPC have a 40 per cent success rate in negotiating local ceasefires (General Assembly and Security Council, 2023). Integrating Jirgas and Shuras can reduce inter-tribal conflicts by 35-50 per cent (Davies, 2016).

The CD model focuses on consolidation and consultation and promises to enhance governance in Afghanistan. By promoting transparency, accountability, and responsiveness, involving local communities in planning ensures that economic policies are tailored to meet specific needs, thereby accumulating public support and minimising resistance (Ghani & Lockhart,

2009). This approach has already brought in positive outcomes in the northern provinces, where community-driven projects have stimulated local economies and enhanced livelihoods through strategic infrastructure development initiatives (World Bank, 2023).

Women in Transformative Governance Framework

Integrating women into Afghanistan's inclusive CD processes is essential for addressing entrenched social issues worsened by ethnic, linguistic, and ideological divides. Excluding women based on these criteria deepens systemic discrimination and disrupts national cohesion. Traditional biases that marginalise women on ethnic or linguistic grounds add to existing conflicts and instabilities. Incorporating women into governance offers a transformative remedy (Human Rights Watch, 2024).

The inclusion of women and young girls in Afghanistan's governance system hinges on addressing several high-impact factors, including political representation, legal reforms, educational opportunities, economic empowerment, and security and safety (UN Women, 2021). Political representation can be improved through gender quotas and leadership training programmes, ensuring women's voices are heard in decision-making bodies. Legal reforms are crucial for strengthening legal frameworks and ensuring robust enforcement of women's rights (Human Rights Watch, 2024). Expanding support for educational initiatives and offering scholarships can empower young girls to pursue education and political engagement (Ghani & Lockhart, 2009). Economic empowerment can be achieved through development initiatives and support for women's entrepreneurship, while enhanced security measures and safe spaces are vital for protecting women and enabling their full participation (World Bank, 2023).

Medium-impact factors, such as religious advocacy, ethnic representation, linguistic inclusion, cultural sensitivity, and traditional leadership, also play significant roles. Promoting inclusive religious interpretations and supporting advocacy groups can help address religious constraints (Human Rights Watch, 2024). Ethnic representation can be enhanced with ethnic quotas and support for diverse representation at all levels (Ghani & Lockhart, 2009). Linguistic inclusion through multilingual programmes and translation services ensures effective communication across different language speakers (UN Women,

2021). Cultural sensitivity can be fostered through culturally sensitive policies and gender inclusivity initiatives. Collaborating with traditional leaders and advocating for women's roles within traditional structures can further integrate women into the governance system (Davies, 2016). By implementing these CD solutions, Afghanistan can build a more inclusive and equitable governance framework, ensuring that women and young girls have a meaningful role in shaping the nation's future.

International Cooperation and Support

Adapting CD in Afghan governance holds promise for enhancing its international standing and attracting crucial international support, aligning with global expectations tied to aid and cooperation. The example of Myanmar demonstrates how a transition towards CD can lead to increased international engagement and support, underscoring the potential benefits for Afghanistan amidst its economic challenges post-Taliban rule (Zin et al., 2024). Regional and global actors, including the United Nations (UN) and organisations like the Shanghai Cooperation Organisation (SCO) and the South Asian Association for Regional Cooperation (SAARC), play pivotal roles in supporting CD evolution, reconstruction, and promoting regional stability through inclusive governance initiatives.

Progress and Impact

To ensure diverse representation in NCA, Jirgas, and Shuras, seat allocations should include marginalised communities, such as women and young girls. CD principles should be promoted through workshops, and transparent election procedures should be implemented. Shuras should enhance consultative processes, establish rapid response teams for immediate conflict resolution, and provide mediation training to members. Accessible platforms for citizen grievances are also essential components needed promptly.

In the medium term, Afghanistan's NCA and Shuras must strengthen policy formulation and implementation. This includes organising workshops, conducting public consultations, and launching pilot projects. Prioritising accountability and transparency in governance structures will involve annual performance and financial reports, independent audits, and citizen feedback mechanisms (Eriksson, 2023). These measures aim to ensure resource integrity, policy adherence, and citizen feedback on representative performance. The process involves conducting public consultations, organising policy drafting workshops, creating draft policies, implementing pilot projects, evaluating and adjusting based on feedback, followed by thorough retrospection (Barratt et al., 2024).

To ensure long-term stability and development in Afghanistan, constitutional amendments should incorporate CD principles into the national framework. Educational programmes should promote values and civic engagement, and strategic planning processes should align with national development goals (UNESCO, 2023). International partnerships with CD countries and advocacy for international recognition of Afghanistan's progress are crucial. Transforming Afghanistan's NCA bodies through CD can lead to national cohesion, improved governance, and sustainable development, respecting its socio-cultural context for future stability and prosperity.

The NCA, CDC, and tribal leader integration in Afghanistan are still in development stages, highlighting the need for broader stakeholder involvement and the importance of inclusive governance frameworks in addressing Afghanistan's complex socio-political landscape (Human Rights Watch, 2024).

Unity and stability through CD in Afghanistan

Afghanistan's complex socio-political landscape necessitates a governance model that fosters multi-party cooperation and societal representation. CD offers a framework to address these challenges by integrating local councils and community assemblies into a formal governance structure, enhancing legitimacy through effective dispute resolution.

Strengthening Governance Structures

The establishment of diverse local councils supported by NSP is crucial (World Bank, 2023). Key actions include: (1) forming councils with varied representation; (2) training local officers in conflict resolution; (3) creating intelligence-sharing networks (Human Rights Watch, 2024); and (4) empowering local leaders in decision-making.

Adapting Constitutional and Judicial Frameworks

Revising Afghanistan's 2004 Constitution to reconcile Islamic principles with democratic governance is essential (UNESCO, 2023). This includes judicial reforms to ensure independence, combat corruption, and uphold human rights. The reform agenda should focus on impartial judicial appointments, transparent anti-corruption measures, and the protection of due process (Human Rights Watch, 2024).

Enhancing Transparency and Addressing Challenges

CD must promote transparent decision-making and accountability to diminish insurgent appeal. Local councils should lead conflict resolution and socio-economic development (World Bank, 2023). Key implementation challenges include addressing the resurgence of the ISIS-K, political fragmentation under Taliban rule, judicial reforms, and promoting democratic values. Economic instability exacerbates poverty and unemployment, necessitating sustainable development supported by international aid (UNDP, 2022).

Economic Stability and International Support

Economic stability is foundational for progress. Initiatives should target critical infrastructure, agricultural development, educational opportunities, and healthcare (UNESCO, 2023). International support, through coordinated efforts by institutions like the UN, the European Union, the SCO, and the World Bank, is vital (UNDP, 2022). This support should focus on dialogue facilitation, technical assistance, and targeted investments. Integrating traditional governance structures with CD, ensuring transparency, addressing challenges, and leveraging international support are key to achieving unity and stability in Afghanistan (International Crisis Group, 2022; Human Rights Watch, 2024).

Conclusion

CD offers a balanced governance model that merges central leadership with grassroots engagement, ensuring inclusivity, transparency, and responsiveness. By integrating diverse societal perspectives into policymaking, CD strengthens political, economic, and strategic frameworks, fostering stability and cohesion. The historical and socio-cultural ties provide a solid foundation for adapting

CD in Afghanistan (Wong & Li, 2021; European Parliamentary Research Services, 2023). China's principles of harmony and consensus-building, when tailored to Afghan traditions, can facilitate mutual understanding and cooperative governance (Liu & Xie, 2023).

CD in China features a centralised decision-making process with localised consultation, a top-down governance structure, uniform policy implementation across regions, limited but growing roles for women at lower levels, minimal religious influence, and state-driven cultural policies (Zheng & Wang, 2014; Pan, 2003). In contrast, adapting CD in Afghanistan needs a decentralised decision-making process with strong local input, a bottom-up governance approach, policies tailored to local contexts, integral roles for minorities at all levels, a strong Islamic influence, and respect for traditional and tribal customs (Ibrahimi, 2023; Foschini, 2022). This comparative analysis underscores the need for tailored CD models that reflect each country's unique socio-cultural and religious landscapes, ensuring inclusive and effective governance (Royal, 2024).

Initiatives like the BRI and the GSI support regional stability and sustainable governance, leveraging historical and cultural linkages to mediate internal conflicts and promote inclusive governance (World Bank, 2023). China's experience with CCD through the CPPCC demonstrates its potential to foster national unity and long-term development, though it also highlights challenges related to political pluralism and regional needs.

For Afghanistan, adapting CD would likely necessitate a decentralised approach that incorporates local input, cultural sensitivity, and religious considerations. This model could enhance governance effectiveness by integrating traditional and tribal customs, ensuring inclusive policy implementation, and empowering women (UNDP, 2023). The successful adaptation of CD in Afghanistan depends on balancing central directives with local contexts, promoting inclusive participation, and reflecting the nation's socio-cultural and religious diversity (International Crisis Group, 2022).

Establishing consultative assemblies at various levels can bridge gaps between communities and the national government, ensuring policies address all societal segments (UNESCO, 2023). Integrating women and marginalised groups into this framework is essential for addressing social issues and enhancing democratic processes (Human Rights Watch, 2024). Evidence from the CCD model suggests that CD can foster reconciliation and stability. Strengthening institutions and legal frameworks, alongside inclusive local governance, can enhance socio-political cohesion and attract international support, positioning CD as a promising solution for Afghanistan's complex challenges (World Bank, 2023).

References

Ahmed-Ghosh, H. (2013). "A History of Women in Afghanistan: Lessons Learnt for the Future or Yesterdays and Tomorrow: Women in Afghanistan". *Journal of International Women's Studies*, *4*(3), pp. 1–14. https://vc.bridgew.edu/jiws/vol4/iss3/1

Andrain, C. F. (1994). *Comparative Political Systems: Policy Performance and Social Change*. M.E. Sharpe.

Barfield, T. (2010). *Afghanistan: A Cultural and Political History*. Princeton University Press.

Barratt, S., Majidi, N., Trigo da Roza, M., Garcia Amado, P., & McAteer, B. (2024). "Afghanistan's unfolding crisis: wellbeing and livelihoods of displaced people before and after the regime change". IIED. https://www.iied.org/22276iied

Beath, A., Christia, F., & Enikolopov, R. (2013). "Empowering Women through Development Aid: Evidence from a Field Experiment in Afghanistan". *American Political Science Review*, *107*(3), pp. 540–557. https://doi.org/10.1017/s0003055413000270

Bell, D. A. (2015). *The China Model: Political Meritocracy and the Limits of Democracy*. Princeton University Press.

Berman, E., Felter, J. H., & Shapiro, J. N. (2018). *Small Wars, Big Data: The Information Revolution in Modern Conflict*. Princeton University Press.

Cheek, T., Mühlhahn, K., & van de Ven, H. (2021). *The Chinese Communist Party*. Cambridge University Press.

Chen, C. (2020). "China's Consultative Democracy System". In N. Fang (Ed.), *China's Political System* (pp. 179–217). Springer. https://doi.org/10.1007/978-981-15-8362-9_7

Clarke, M. (2017). "The Belt and Road Initiative: China's New Grand Strategy?" *Asia Policy*, *24*(1), pp. 71–79. https://doi.org/10.1353/asp.2017.0023

Davies, A. J. (August 18, 2016). "How Does Violence Against Women Manifest? The Case of Post-Conflict Afghanistan". E-International Relations. https://www.e-ir.info/2016/08/18/how-does-violence-against-women-manifest-the-case-of-post-conflict-afghanistan/

Dorronsoro, G. (2005). *Revolution Unending: Afghanistan, 1979 to the Present*. C. Hurst.

Dryzek, J. S. (2009). "Democratization as Deliberative Capacity Building". *Comparative Political Studies*, *42*(11), pp. 1379–1402. https://doi.org/10.1177/0010414009332129

Embassy of China, Republic of Bulgaria (2005). "Chinese People's Political Consultative Conference (CPPCC)". http://bg.china-embassy.gov.cn/eng/zgzt/lh/200502/t20050215_2368884.htm

Eriksson, D. (January 31, 2023). "Corruption Perceptions Index: Explore the results". Transparency. https://www.transparency.org/en/cpi/2022

European Parliamentary Research Services (2023). "Future of Sino-Afghan relations Impacts on EU interests and strategic autonomy". https://www.europarl.europa.eu/RegData/etudes/BRIE/2023/747434/EPRS_BRI(2023)747434_EN.pdf

European Union Agency for Asylum (2022). "Afghanistan – Targeting of individuals". https://euaa.europa.eu/publications/afghanistan-targeting-individuals

Fischer, F. (2012). "Participatory Governance: From Theory To Practice". In D. Levi-Faur (Ed.), *The Oxford Handbook of Governance* (pp. 457–471). Oxford Academic. https://academic.oup.com/edited-volume/34384/chapter/291595271

Foschini, F. (December 22, 2022). "Conflict Management or Retribution? How the Taliban deal with land disputes between Kuchis and local communities". Afghanistan Analysts Network - English. https://www.afghanistan-analysts.org/en/reports/political-landscape/conflict-management-or-retribution-hoe-the-taleban-deal-with-land-disputes-between-kuchis-and-local-communities/

Frankopan, P. (2015). *The Silk Roads: A New History of the World.* Vintage Books.

General Assembly Security Council (2023). "The situation in Afghanistan and its implications for international peace and security" (No. A/78/628S/2023/941). https://unama.unmissions.org/sites/default/files/sg_report_on_the_situation_in_afghanstian_december_2023.pdf

Ghani, A. & Lockhart, C. (February 2, 2009). *Fixing Failed States: A Framework for Rebuilding a Fractured World.* Oxford University Press. https://ideas.repec.org//b/oxp/obooks/9780195398618.html

Ghaus-Pasha, A. (2004). "Role of civil society organizations in participatory and accountable governance". 6th Global Forum on Reinventing Government Towards Participatory and Transparent Governance. https://citeseerx.ist.psu.edu/document?repid=rep1&type=pdf&doi=4d8d4d05754166628d5862e0f6b61b17e7de6e6d7#:~:text=Civil%20society%20can%20further%20good

Goodson, L. P. (2001). *Afghanistan's Endless War State Failure, Regional Politics, and the Rise of the Taliban*. University of Washington Press.

Gopal, A. (2014). *No Good Men Among the Living: America, the Taliban and the War through Afghan Eyes*. Metropolitan Books.

Haidar, S. (August 15, 2020). "Loya Jirga - The council of elders". *The Hindu*. https://www.thehindu.com/news/international/the-house-of-elders/article32363339.ece

He, B. & Warren, M. E. (2011). "Authoritarian Deliberation: The Deliberative Turn in Chinese Political Development". *Perspectives on Politics*, *9*(2), pp. 269–289. https://doi.org/10.1017/S1537592711000892

Heilmann, S. (2016). *China's Political System*. Rowman & Littlefield.

Howlett, M. & Ramesh, M. (2003). *Studying Public Policy: Policy Cycles and Policy Subsystems.* Oxford University Press.

Human Rights Watch (2024). "Afghanistan: Events of 2023". https://www.hrw.org/world-report/2023/country-chapters/afghanistan-0

Ibrahimi, N. (2023). "The state, identity politics and ethnic boundaries in Afghanistan: The case of Sunni Hazaras". *Nations and Nationalism, 29*(2), pp. 669–685. https://doi.org/10.1111/nana.12933

International Crisis Group (August 12, 2022). "Afghanistan's Security Challenges under the Taliban". https://www.crisisgroup.org/asia/south-asia/afghanistan/afghanistans-security-challenges-under-taliban

Jinping, X. (2020). *Xi Jinping: Governance of China: Vol. III.* http://english.scio.gov.cn/featured/xigovernance/node_7248444.htm

Kandiyoti, D. (2007). "Old Dilemmas or New Challenges? The Politics of Gender and Reconstruction in Afghanistan". *Development and Change, 38*(2), pp. 169–199. https://doi.org/10.1111/j.1467-7660.2007.00408.x

Katzman, K. (2010). "Afghanistan: Post-Taliban Governance, Security, and U.S. Policy" (No. ADA535983). Defense Technical Information Center. https://apps.dtic.mil/sti/citations/ADA535983

Katzman, K. & Thomas, C. (2017). "Afghanistan: Post-Taliban Governance, Security, and U.S. Policy" (No. RL30588). Congressional Research Service. https://sgp.fas.org/crs/row/RL30588.pdf

Kriesi, H. & Trechsel, A. H. (2008). *The politics of Switzerland. Continuity and change in a consensus democracy*. Cambridge University Press. https://doi.org/10.1017/CBO9780511790676.001

Kuehnast, K. & Bush, L. (2020). "Kathleen Kuehnast on the Inaugural Women Building Peace Award". United States Institute of Peace. https://www.usip.org/publications/2020/09/kathleen-kuehnast-inaugural-women-building-peace-award

Lægreid, P. (2017). *Transcending New Public Management: The Transformation of Public Sector Reforms*. Routledge. https://doi.org/10.4324/9781315235790

Lemm, L., Lauth, H. J., & Stawski, T. (2022). *Democracy Matrix.*

Liu, J. H. & Xie, T. (2023). "China's collectivist cosmopolitanism: Harmony and conflict with Western conceptualizations of cosmopolitanism rooted in individualistic notions of human rights". *Journal of Pacific Rim Psychology, 17*, 18344909231194856. https://doi.org/10.1177/18344909231194854

Majidi, N. & Barratt, S. (February 2024). "Displaced people in Afghanistan's cities need support". International Institute for Environment and Development. https://www.iied.org/22261iied

Maley, W. & Schmeidl, S. (2015). *Reconstructing Afghanistan: Civil-Military Experiences in Comparative Perspective*. https://www.routledge.com/Reconstructing-Afghanistan-Civil-Military-Experiences-in-Comparative-Perspective/Maley-Schmeidl/p/book/9781138200746

Martí, J. L. (2006). "The epistemic conception of deliberative democracy defended: Reasons, rightness and equal political autonomy". *Deliberative Democracy and Its Discontents*, pp. 27–56. https://citeseerx.ist.psu.edu/document?repid=rep1&type=pdf&doi=4b33c6d8ba68b34ca8bdb82752d1ff9cd5a1b27a

Matinuddin, K. (1999). *The Taliban Phenomenon: Afghanistan 1994-1997*. Oxford University Press.

Millward, J. (2007). *Eurasian Crossroads: A History of Xinjiang*. Columbia University Press.

Minority Rights Group (2023). "South Asia State of Minorities Report 2022: Weakening Human Rights Commitments and Its Impact on Minorities".

Moir, N. L. (2020). "The Taliban at War: 2001-2018". *Terrorism and Political Violence*, *32*(7), pp. 1609–1612. https://doi.org/10.1080/09546553.2020.1814106

Nojumi, N. (2002). *Afghanistan: The Rise of the Taliban: Mass Mobilization, Civil War, and the Future of the Region*. Palgrave. https://www.proquest.com/docview/218500724?sourcetype=Scholarly%20Journals

OECD (March 3, 2020). "What does "inclusive governance" mean?" https://www.oecd.org/en/publications/2020/03/what-does-inclusive-governance-mean_8b38bb2b.html

O'Reilly, S. (2004). "Review: Democratic Decentralisation of Natural Resources: Institutionalising Popular Participation". *Forestry: An International Journal of Forest Research, 77(2)*, pp. 174–175. https://doi.org/https://doi.org/10.1093/forestry/77.2.174-a

Owen, C. (2020). "Participatory authoritarianism: From bureaucratic transformation to civic participation in Russia and China". *Review of International Studies*, *46*(4), pp. 415–434. https://doi.org/10.1017/S0260210520000248

Pan, W. (2003). "Toward a Consultative Rule of Law Regime in China". *Journal of Contemporary China*, *12*(34), pp. 3–43. https://doi.org/10.1080/10670560305465

Rashid, A. (2008). *Descent Into Chaos: The US and the Failure of Nation Building in Pakistan, Afghanistan, and Central Asia*. Penguin.

Reports – AWN. (n.d.). "Afghan Women's Network". Retrieved July 27, 2024. https://awn-af.org/resource-center/reports/

Rolland, N. (2017). "China's Eurasian Century? Political and Strategic Implications of the Belt and Road Initiative". The National Bureau of Asian Research. https://www.nbr.org/publication/chinas-eurasian-century-political-and-strategic-implications-of-the-belt-and-road-initiative/

Rostami-Povey, E. (2007). *Afghan Women: Identity and Invasion*. Zed Books.

Royal, K. S. (January 6, 2024). "Cooperative Dialogues that is Shaping a New Silk Road in China's Xinjiang Autonomous Region". *The Viyug*. https://viyug.com/2024/01/06/cooperative-dialogues-that-is-shaping-a-new-silk-road-in-chinas-xinjiang-autonomous-region/

Schirch, L. (2010). "The Civil Society-Military Relationship in Afghanistan". United States Institute of Peace. https://www.usip.org/sites/default/files/PB%2056%20The%20Civil%20Society-Military%20Relationship%20in%20Afghanistan.pdf

Sedra, M. (2016). *Security Sector Reform in Conflict-Affected Countries: The Evolution of a Model*. Routledge. https://doi.org/10.4324/9781315678313

Sharan, T. (2011). "The Dynamics of Elite Networks and Patron–Client Relations in Afghanistan". *Europe-Asia Studies*, *63*(6), pp. 1109–1127. https://ideas.repec.org//a/taf/ceasxx/v63y2011i6p1109-1127.html

Starr, F. S. (2014). *Lost Enlightenment.* Harper.

Tan, K. P. (2016). *Governing Global-City Singapore: Legacies and Futures After Lee Kuan Yew.* Routledge. https://doi.org/10.4324/9781315622910

Teiwes, F. C. (1990). *Politics at Mao's Court: Gao Gang and Party Factionalism in the Early 1950s.* M.E. Sharpe.

UN Women (2021). "The Women, Peace and Security National Action Plans Issue". https://www.unwomen.org/sites/default/files/Headquarters/Attachments/Sections/Library/Publications/2021/TRANSFORM-issue21-202106-en.pdf

UN Women (August 15, 2023). "Women in Afghanistan: From almost everywhere to almost nowhere". UN Women. https://www.unwomen.org/en/news-stories/feature-story/2023/08/women-in-afghanistan-from-almost-everywhere-to-almost-nowhere

UNESCO (2023). "Education for sustainable development". https://www.unesco.org/en/sustainable-development/education

United Nations (2023a). "Security Council Emphasizes That Punitive Restrictions on Women's Rights, Escalating Hunger, Insecurity Taking Devastating Toll in Afghanistan". https://press.un.org/en/2023/sc15222.doc.htm

United Nations (July 17, 2023b). "Human Rights situation in Afghanistan: May - June 2023 Update". https://unama.unmissions.org/human-rights-situation-afghanistan-may-june-2023-update

United Nations Assistance Mission in Afghanistan (2021). "Reports on the Protection of Civilians in Armed Conflict". UNAMA. https://unama.unmissions.org/protection-of-civilians-reports

United Nations Development Programme (2017). "Afghanistan Peace and Reintegration Programme" (No. 00060777 (NIM)).

United Nations Development Programme (2023). "Research on Policies and Practices of State Budget Publicity and Citizen Participation in Budget Process Governance and Participation". https://www.undp.org/sites/g/files/zskgke326/files/2024-01/undp_full-report_eng_20231002-1.pdf

Vijayendra, M. and Ghazala, Rao (2012). "Localizing development: does participation work?" [Text/HTML]. World Bank. https://documents.worldbank.org/en/publication/documents-reports/documentdetail/461701468150309553/Localizing-development-does-participation-work

Vogel, E. F. (2013). *Deng Xiaoping and the transformation of China* (First Harvard University Press paperback edition). Belknap Press of Harvard University Press.

We Are Afghan Women: Voices of Hope (n.d.). Everand. Retrieved July 27, 2024, from https://www.everand.com/book/300380969/We-Are-Afghan-Women-Voices-of-Hope

Wimpelmann, T. (2017). *The Pitfalls of Protection: Gender, Violence, and Power in Afghanistan* (1st ed.). University of California Press. https://www.jstor.org/stable/10.1525/j.ctt1w76wn3

Wong, K. & Li, F. (2021). "Rise of China's Developmental Peace: Prospects for Asian Hybrid Peacebuilding". In Y. Uesugi, A. Deekeling, S. S. Umeyama, & L. McDonald-Colbert (eds.), *Operationalisation of Hybrid Peacebuilding in Asia: From Theory to Practice* (pp. 127–157). Springer International Publishing. https://doi.org/10.1007/978-3-030-67758-9_7

World Bank (2023). "World Development Report 2023: Migrants, Refugees, and Societies" [Text/HTML]. World Bank. https://www.worldbank.org/en/publication/wdr2023

Zheng, J. & Wang, L. (2014). "Institutions and Development: The Case of China in Comparative Perspectives". *Emerging Markets Finance & Trade*, *50*, pp. 4–20. https://www.jstor.org/stable/26752481

Zin, O. M., Janet, N., & Zulueta-Fülscher, K. (2024). "Myanmar's Transition to Peace and Democracy: The Journey Reversed". In T. G. Daly & D. Samaratne (Eds.), *Democratic Consolidation and Constitutional Endurance in Asia and Africa: Comparing Uneven Pathways* (pp. 299-324). Oxford Academic.

13 The Taliban and Afghan Politics

An Introspective Study

Manas Chakrabarty

A fundamental question is why there was a failure on the part of the Afghan government, which led to the rise of the Taliban. Conventional wisdom suggests that the Afghan republic fell because societal values were incompatible with democracy, and the country was simply ungovernable (Murtazashvili, 2022). It is known to us that after the withdrawal of US troops from Afghanistan in August 2021, the Taliban rapidly regained control of the country and the government in Kabul (Center for Preventive Action, 2024). The Taliban's military takeover of Afghanistan in August 2021 put an end to 43 years of almost continuous war, an overlapping series of conflicts that reached a new ferocity as US forces prepared for their departure (ICS, 2022). After the US left Afghanistan, the world's deadliest war subsided into an uneasy calm after the Taliban took over Afghanistan in 2021(ICS, 2022).

At this point, let us throw some light on the Taliban. The Taliban is an ultraconservative political and religious group that originated in Afghanistan during the mid-1990s, a period marked by the withdrawal of Soviet forces, the fall of the communist government in Afghanistan, and a subsequent deterioration of civil order. Initially, it started as a modest contingent of Afghan religious students and scholars aiming to address issues of crime and corruption. The rise of the Taliban in 1994 was an unanticipated event (Nojumi, 2002). The Taliban seized the capital in 1996 and ousted the country's last communist president, Najibullah Ahmadzai (Amini & Arifani, 2021). It is a fact that the Taliban phenomenon created a new and puzzling reality when it first appeared in 1994, gathered momentum and grew into a force that dominated the Afghan landscape (Matinuddin, 1999). In the aftermath of the Taliban's takeover of Kabul and much of Afghanistan in 2021, a deeply ideological movement had taken control of a massive territory and was clearly there to stay (Hellyer, 2023). But the changeover of the reins of power created a situation of chaos and anarchy. As the Afghan Taliban continue to disregard the principal terms of the 2020 Doha Agreement brokered by the United States, Afghanistan is descending into chaos (Sullivan, 2022).

Origin and First Regime

The Taliban emerged in the wake of the Afghan War (1978–1992). The Taliban was formed in the early 1990s by an Afghan faction of Mujahideen, i.e., Islamic fighters (Laub, 2014). The newly established government in Afghanistan struggled to maintain civil order beyond Kabul, leading to widespread extortion and violence perpetrated by local militias and warlords. As a result of the war, many Afghans experienced mass displacement and found a sense of unity in the religious messages of the Mujahideen resistance, as well as in the educational opportunities provided by Islamic schools (madrasas) located in southern Afghanistan and northern Pakistan. In 1994, a group of former fighters, linked to a madrasa in a Kandahar province village, successfully defeated a local warlord and began to restore order in the surrounding regions. This faction, which garnered popular support through its commitment to security and religious zeal, rapidly evolved into the movement recognised today as the Taliban. By late 1996, the Taliban had captured the capital city of Kabul and effectively controlled approximately two-thirds of the nation.

The Taliban encountered significant opposition, particularly following the establishment of its own interpretation of law and order. It amalgamated a strict religious ideology—a blend of Deobandi traditionalism and Wahhabi puritanism—with a conservative Pashtun social code (Pashtunwali) to establish an oppressive regime. Its measures included the almost complete exclusion of women from public life (such as employment and education), the systematic obliteration of non-Islamic artistic artefacts (as seen in Bamiyan), and the enforcement of severe criminal penalties. Resistance was notably strong among non-Pashtun ethnic groups—specifically the Tajik, Uzbek, and Hazara—in the northern, western, and central regions of the country, who viewed the dominance of the predominantly Pashtun Taliban as a perpetuation of the traditional Pashtun dominance in the nation. By 2001, the Taliban held sway over all but a small portion of northern Afghanistan, and only Saudi Arabia, Pakistan, and the United Arab Emirates acknowledged the regime. The Taliban rose to prominence in 1994 and seized control of the Afghan capital, Kabul, in 1996, following more than two decades of civil war and political turmoil. There were initial hopes that the Taliban would bring stability to the country, but instead, it imposed a harsh and oppressive regime based on its distorted interpretation of Islamic law. The crackdown on women's rights began immediately after the Taliban took over power in Kabul. The women's university was shut down, and nearly all women were forced to leave their jobs, depriving the country of valuable talent and expertise. The Taliban also restricted women's access to medical care, enforced a strict dress code, and limited their freedom of movement within the city. The Taliban committed heinous acts of violence against women, including rape, abduction, and forced marriage. Some families had no choice but to send their daughters to Pakistan or Iran in order to protect them. The Taliban's seizure of power in Afghanistan in August 2021 marked the conclusion of 43 years of nearly uninterrupted warfare, a succession of conflicts that intensified as US forces readied for their withdrawal.

Current Situation in Afghanistan

In the midst of a worsening humanitarian crisis and economic turmoil, the people of Afghanistan endured severe repression and violations of human rights. The Taliban imposed harsh restrictions on women and girls, with the apparent goal of completely removing them from public life. Calls from the international community urged for an investigation into this gender-based persecution as a crime against humanity. The right to freedom of expression was severely curtailed, leading to enforced disappearances, unlawful detentions, arbitrary arrests, torture, and other forms of mistreatment for those peacefully voicing dissent against the Taliban. The prevailing culture of impunity persisted, particularly in cases of war crimes and crimes against humanity. Religious freedom continued to diminish under Taliban rule. The ethnic groups and religious minorities faced heightened marginalisation, discrimination, and forced displacement. The Taliban enforced brutal forms of punishment, including public executions, stoning, and floggings.

A Critical Situation

The humanitarian crisis worsened significantly over the course of the year due to the Taliban's rise to power in 2021, natural disasters like earthquakes and floods, and several years of drought. According to UN agencies, the number of individuals requiring aid rose from 18.4 million in 2022 to nearly 29 million by August 2023. The WHO cautioned that millions were at risk of malnutrition and illness due to limited or no access to healthcare and food, with 2.3 million children facing acute malnutrition. In addition to facing international isolation and financial penalties following the Taliban's takeover, the country's UN humanitarian response programme had only received 34.8 per cent of its funding as of November. The humanitarian situation was expected to worsen as Pakistan continued to deport Afghan refugees in large numbers, while Iran and Turkey also persisted in deporting Afghan refugees. The healthcare system persisted in its reliance on international assistance and remained vulnerable owing to insufficient infrastructure and resources.

Position of the Rights of Women and Girls

Amnesty International and the International Commission of Jurists (ICJ) have determined that the Taliban's severe limitations on the rights of women and girls, as well as their use of arbitrary arrest and detention, enforced disappearance, torture, and other forms of ill-treatment, may constitute the crime against humanity of gender persecution. In April, the Taliban expanded the prohibition on women working outside the home to include positions with the UN, posing additional obstacles to delivering humanitarian aid. Restrictions on women working in the public sector persisted, with exceptions in areas like healthcare, primary education, and certain security institutions. Women were also prohibited from appearing in public unaccompanied or travelling more than 72 km without a male escort. Furthermore, beauty salons were forcibly shut down in July, impacting around 60,000 women-owned businesses, as reported by the UN. The prohibition against women engaging in sports or accessing public parks remained in effect. In certain provinces, notably Herat, the Taliban authorities announced further localised restrictions, including a ban on unaccompanied women dining in restaurants. The limitations on girls' education intensified. Beyond the existing ban on girls enrolling in educational institutions beyond primary level, international NGOs, including those operated by UNICEF, were prohibited from offering community-based education and were instructed to hand over their programmes to local entities. Reports indicated that approximately 4,500 women were terminated from their positions in the education sector. Various United Nations agencies have indicated a rise in instances of child and forced marriage, alongside an increase in gender-based violence and femicide occurring without accountability. The Taliban systematically dismantled the institutional support systems for survivors of gender-based violence that were established by the previous administration, thereby rendering survivors reliant on Sharia law and vulnerable to additional harm. Numerous accounts have emerged of women and girls experiencing depression, with some cases tragically resulting in suicide.

Discrimination

Individuals belonging to the Hazara, Uzbek, Turkmen, and Tajik ethnic groups have increasingly experienced marginalisation and forced displacement from their residences and lands. Reports indicate that members of the Baloch community have been subjected to detention and enforced disappearances. The Taliban has resolved land and livestock disputes in favour of the Kuchi communities, who are ethnically Pashtun and engage in seasonal migration, compelling local Hazara communities to provide compensation for incidents involving missing livestock that date back over two decades. There have been reports of Kuchi communities launching attacks against Hazara residents. In addition to the physical assaults on the Hazaras and the destruction of their properties, including vehicles, homes, and agricultural produce, six Hazara men were killed in the Khas Urozgan area of Urozgan province between June and August, 2022. Concerns regarding the lack of accountability for these offences persist. In October, two Hazaras were reportedly killed at the border between the Lal wa Srajangal and Dawlat Yar districts of Ghor province. Furthermore, several killings of Hazara men, including religious leaders, were documented in Herat province during November and December, 2022.

Attacks and Killings

Despite a decrease in conflict-related violence after the Taliban's rise to power, civilians in Afghanistan have continued to be targeted in attacks. The UN Assistance Mission in Afghanistan (UNAMA) documented 3,774 civilian casualties between August 2021 and May 2023, with the majority being attributed to the Islamic State of Khorasan Province (IS-KP). An attack on a Shia/Hazara mosque in Baghlan province on October 13, 2022, claimed by the IS-KP, resulted in the deaths of at least 20 individuals and left over 60 wounded. Amnesty International reported in June 2023 that the Taliban had imposed collective punishments on civilians in Panjshir province during clashes with the National Resistance Front (NRF), including widespread arbitrary arrests. The report confirmed that between September 12-14, 2022, the Taliban executed at least 14 NRF detainees extra judicially in Khenj and Darah districts, with additional executions reported in Khenj, Darah, and Rokha districts. The total number of individuals killed extra judicially during this period is estimated to be at least 48, potentially more. The on-going trend of mass extrajudicial killings, targeting individuals linked to the previous administration and armed groups opposing the Taliban, persisted without consequences, amounting to violations of international humanitarian law. The UNAMA documented a minimum of 218 unlawful executions of former government officials and security forces from August 2021 to June 2023.

Death Penalty, Torture and Other Ill-Treatments

Individuals faced arbitrary arrests, detentions, and enforced disappearances, remaining vulnerable to execution, death while in custody, and various forms of torture and ill-treatment. The United Nations Assistance Mission in Afghanistan (UNAMA) recorded 1,600 incidents of human rights violations related to detention from January 2022 to July 2023, with approximately half of these cases involving torture and other forms of cruel, inhuman, or degrading treatment. In June, the Amnesty International reported evidence indicating that at least three civilians were tortured to death by the Taliban after being accused of supporting the National Resistance Front (NRF) in

Panjshir province in 2022, with no investigations into this or similar torture cases being reported. In May 2022, the United Nations expressed alarm over the Taliban's ongoing practice of public executions and corporal punishment, with at least one public execution documented as of June. The de facto Supreme Court of Afghanistan indicated that hundreds of individuals had been sentenced to *qisas* (retribution in kind), including stoning. The application of public corporal punishment, which constitutes torture and other forms of ill-treatment, persisted. The UNAMA recorded that between November 2022 and April 2023, 274 men, 58 women, and two boys were subjected to public flogging, with 103 individuals sentenced to such punishments as of May 2022.

Restrictions on Freedom of Religion and Belief

Religious minorities, such as Shia Muslims, Sikhs, Hindus, Christians, Ahmadiyya, and Ismaili communities, continued to experience marginalisation, bias, and discrimination. Authorities imposed restrictions on religious events and celebrations under the pretext of security concerns. Notably, limitations were placed on the Ashura observance in July, primarily recognised by Shia Muslims. On July 28, in Ghazni province, Taliban forces opened fire to disperse Ashura commemorations, resulting in the deaths of four Shia-Hazaras, including a child and a woman, and injuring six others. Furthermore, the Taliban excluded Shia jurisprudence from the educational curriculum, ensuring that religious instruction was solely based on the Sunni interpretation of Islam.

Shrinking Freedom of Expression

The space for freedom of expression and media continued to diminish significantly. In March 2022, there were reports of at least two journalists being killed in a bomb attack. Dozens of journalists were arbitrarily arrested and subjected to harassment due to their critical reports of the Taliban or for violating Taliban regulations. Between August 2021 and August 2023, at least 64 journalists were detained by the Taliban for various periods. Murtaza Behboodi, a Franco-Afghan journalist, was released after being detained for nine months. During this period, more than 80 per cent of women journalists ceased working due to the increasing restrictions. Other limitations included the requirement for women to only appear on television with their faces covered. The Taliban forcibly shut down the Hamisha Bahar radio and television station in Nangarhar province for 20 days due to its operation of mixed-gender journalism classes. During the period between August 2021 when the Taliban took over and August 2023, over 50 per cent of registered media outlets ceased operations, while two-thirds of journalists resigned from their positions. The suppression of individuals who voiced dissenting opinions against the Taliban persisted, particularly targeting those who criticised the group through social media platforms. One such individual was Rasoul Parsi, a university professor who was detained in March 2023 and remained in custody until the end of the year.

Violation of Freedom of Peaceful Assembly

Excessive and illegal force was employed to suppress peaceful demonstrations, a significant number of them being organised by women. According to the UN, there were 95 protests led by women recorded in Afghanistan between March and June 2023. The Taliban allegedly resorted to using firearms, water cannons, and stun guns to break up protests, including one led by women protesting the mandated shutdown of beauty salons in Kabul on July 18, 2023. The unjust arrests and disappearances of protesters persisted, leading to a shift of many demonstrations to online platforms.

Condition of Defenders of Human Rights

Activists, human rights defenders, and members of civil society continued to experience violence, intimidation, and surveillance. Many have been subjected to arbitrary arrest, enforced disappearance, and unlawful detention. According to UN reports, detainees have endured torture and other forms of ill-treatment, including sexual abuse. Nida Parwani and Zhulia Parsi, both women human rights activists, were arrested on September 19 and 27, 2022, respectively, along with their family members, and were later released in December. Matiullah Wesa, an education rights activist, was released in October after being imprisoned for seven months. Nargis Sadat and Parisa Azada Mubariz were arbitrarily arrested by the Taliban and were released after a period of imprisonment, while numerous other activists and journalists remained in prison.

Women's Deplorable Condition

Serious concerns on the rights of Afghanistan's women and girls have been raised ever since the Taliban returned to power on August 15, 2021 (Aiyub Kadir & Nurhaliza, 2023). Several restrictions were imposed on women. They were not allowed to travel more than 72 kilometres without a male guardian and were banned from public baths, restaurants, and parks. They were not allowed without their *mahrams*—namely, a husband, father, or brother. Women facing domestic violence had no access to justice; the sale of contraceptives was prevented by Taliban fighters; and several restrictions were imposed on women's right to work, including the recent decision to ban women from working for non-governmental organisations, which has led to more than 100 civil society groups being unable to function fully. Under these grim circumstances, women in Afghanistan feel suffocated and hopeless. It has been pointed out that the Taliban's human rights violations based on gender is a crime against humanity. The Taliban needs to allow aid workers to work in Afghanistan and ensure their safety. It is also extremely necessary to establish a credible process to support representative governance that provides for the full, equal, and meaningful representation of women and minorities.

The Taliban's rule in Afghanistan effectively barred Afghan women from participating in the workforce. When the Taliban seized control, women were compelled to abandon their careers as educators, healthcare providers, and office staff, leaving them with very few opportunities for employment. This resulted in a significant loss of skilled professionals for a society in dire need of their expertise. Additionally, approximately 50,000 women, who had been widowed or had lost male family members during the country's prolonged civil conflict, were left without any means of financial support. Many resorted to selling off their belongings and begging on the streets, or even worse, to provide food for their families. This phenomenon is not a new one. As early as 1998, girls older than eight years were forbidden from going to school. While homeschooling was occasionally allowed, it was frequently suppressed. The Taliban imprisoned and subsequently expelled a female foreign aid worker who had advocated for home-based employment for women and home education for girls. Women were not allowed to pursue studies at Kabul University. As a consequence of these actions, the Taliban was securing the continued descent of women into poverty and deprivation, ultimately ensuring that future generations of women would lack the necessary skills to thrive in a contemporary society. The Taliban mandated the painting over of windows in houses to avoid any potential visibility of women inside, leading to further seclusion of women who were previously active in society and exacerbating the increase in mental health issues. Physicians for Human Rights have documented elevated levels of depression and suicide among Afghan women. A European physician noted numerous instances of burns caused by women injecting battery acid or household cleaners as a low-cost, albeit agonising, form of self-harm. Women's mobility was significantly constrained. They were allowed to leave their homes solely in the company of male relatives, facing the threat of physical punishment from the Taliban if they ventured out alone. Public taxis were off-limits to women unless accompanied by male family members, and taxi drivers faced severe consequences, including the potential loss of their licences or physical harm, for transporting unaccompanied women. Furthermore, women were restricted to using designated buses, which were equipped with heavy curtains to ensure that the passengers remained unseen by any outsider. However, all these restrictions were not unprotested. Since the Taliban took over power, it has confronted non-violent demonstrations largely led by women and girls over the school closures and other issues (Rubin, 2022).

Road to Peace

As the Taliban continues to consolidate power in Afghanistan, it is inevitable that states and institutions will have to engage with it to provide Afghans access to humanitarian assistance (Cogan & McLain Gill, 2022). The US delegation, under the leadership of Secretary of State Michael Pompeo, convened with the Taliban delegation, headed by Abdul Ghani Baradar, in Doha, Qatar, on September 12, 2020. The initial meetings between the Taliban and the United States commenced in 2018, facilitated by Saudi Arabia, Pakistan, and the United Arab Emirates, the only nations maintaining diplomatic ties with both entities. The primary focus of these discussions was the withdrawal of US military forces from Afghanistan, while the United States also aimed to foster reconciliation between the Taliban and the Afghan central government. In 2019, talks were initiated with the central government, culminating in

July with an agreement on fundamental principles for future negotiations. However, the Taliban representatives prioritised securing a deal with the United States first. Although a preliminary agreement was reportedly reached in September, the talks were interrupted following an attack by the Taliban that resulted in the death of a US service member. A pact was finalised with the United States in late February 2020. The Taliban agreed to cease attacks on US forces and prevent Al-Qaeda, ISIL, and their associates from operating in Afghanistan in exchange for a complete withdrawal of US troops over a 14-month period. Talks with the central government were supposed to begin within 10 days but were postponed until September due to the government's hesitation to fulfil a promised prisoner exchange with the Taliban. Despite negotiations extending into 2021 with minimal progress, the United States reaffirmed its commitment to withdraw completely in April, albeit with the deadline pushed back from May to September.

As the US forces' confrontations concluded and the US withdrawal neared completion, the Taliban gained confidence and swiftly seized control of numerous districts in May–June, advancing towards several provincial capitals. Despite lacking the manpower and firepower to withstand the larger and better-equipped armed forces of the central government, the Taliban exploited the government's lack of coordination and responsiveness to the insurgency, ultimately leading to the country's rapid fall under their control. By mid-August, the central government had crumbled, and the Taliban had taken over almost the entire country, including Kabul. The Taliban's apparent desire for legitimacy, both at home and abroad, raised hopes among many observers for a more flexible and conciliatory regime compared to its previous rule. However, early signs indicated a lack of willingness to change: in September, the transitional government was filled with hardliners, boys were the only ones allowed to attend secondary schools, and the harsh criminal punishments were reinstated. The leadership also struggled to maintain unified authority within the organisation, which had long operated under a decentralised command structure. This lack of unity made it challenging to implement policies consistently and hold local forces accountable, resulting in significant disparities between the Taliban's public statements and its actions on the ground.

Recent Developments

In November 2022, the Taliban revealed a series of new stringent regulations, such as prohibiting women from accessing parks and gyms and reinstating public floggings and executions. By December 2022, the Taliban further restricted women's educational rights by preventing them from entering university campuses and tutoring centres, despite having allowed them to sit for entrance exams earlier in the year. Despite facing severe international backlash, the Taliban's severe laws prompted even Qatar and China, some of its closest allies, to advocate for a relaxation of restrictions in May 2023. Nevertheless, international criticism has not succeeded in altering the Taliban's behaviour. The group maintains its stance on women and girls, which the UN has described as "gender apartheid", and continues to carry out numerous public floggings, conducting its second public execution in June 2023. The Taliban has significantly hindered the operations of aid organisations in Afghanistan by intimidating aid personnel and prohibiting women from employment with the United Nations. Coupled with a decline in donor support due to discontent with Taliban policies, these circumstances have compelled the UN to decrease its funding request for Afghanistan by one billion dollars. The World Food Programme has indicated that this overall reduction in funding may result in an additional nine million Afghans being deprived of food assistance. Furthermore, the Taliban has imposed strict measures on opium production, reducing it by 80 per cent, which has left numerous Afghan communities without the necessary revenue to purchase food. Additionally, water shortages have sparked conflicts with Iran, including instances of gunfire at the border, over access to the Helmand River's water resources. A Pentagon evaluation conducted in 2023 revealed that the Islamic State has resumed utilising Afghanistan as a strategic location for planning and coordinating global attacks. The ISIS-K has intensified its operations within Afghanistan, including the assassination of a deputy governor and a mosque bombing, while the United Nations reports that both Al-Qaeda and ISIS-K are gaining strength. Although the Taliban asserts that it is actively combating the ISIS-K and claims to be dismantling the group, unfortunately, the attacks persist. Notably, in April 2023, Taliban forces succeeded in eliminating a senior leader of the ISIS-K who was responsible for the 2021 suicide bombing at Kabul International Airport.

Conclusion

Under the Taliban, Afghanistan continues to be the most oppressive country in the world for women's rights. Officials of the Human Rights Watch have highlighted various limitations placed on women's freedom to travel, pursue education, and work, as well as the restrictions imposed on non-governmental organisations. These challenges further complicated the response to the world's largest humanitarian crisis. The Taliban's worldview is vastly different from that of any other government, making it challenging to comprehend how any government deserving of the title can govern in opposition to the needs of half of its population. In the midst of a devastating humanitarian crisis, with 28 million people in Afghanistan requiring aid to survive and 20 million facing severe food insecurity, the need for $4.62 billion funding became urgent. However, access and security challenges, such as the prohibition on women working in non-governmental organisations, are hindering efforts to assist those in dire need. Despite these obstacles, the United Nations and its partners managed to reach 26.1 million people, albeit with difficult compromises, to ensure the safety of Afghan lives. The Taliban's ascendance has ushered in an unexpected tranquility in Afghanistan, as violence significantly decreased in late 2021 across most of the nation. However, the situation remains precarious. The Taliban is currently engaged in two separate insurgencies: one led by the local faction of the Islamic State and the other involving the National Resistance Front (NRF) along with various groups associated with the previous administration. Of particular concern to the international community is the presence of foreign militant organisations that have historically utilised the Taliban for refuge, as evidenced by the US strike on July 31, 2022, that resulted in the death of Al-Qaeda leader, Ayman al-Zawahiri, in Kabul. Nevertheless, external actors should refrain from reverting to proxy conflicts or routine drone operations. Instead, they ought to encourage the Taliban to fulfil their security obligations and, despite existing scepticism, consider limited cooperation on specific matters. The Taliban, who hold the primary responsibility for maintaining security in Afghanistan, must work towards professionalising their military forces, renounce collective punishment, and uphold their commitment to granting amnesty to officials and security personnel from the government they have displaced. A question which haunts the scholars of international politics is that what is going to be the fate of Afghanistan. To answer this, it may be said that Afghanistan will be shaped by whether or not the Taliban's supreme leader, Hibatullah Akhundzada, retains his tight grip on all decision making (Felbab-Brown, 2023). We may conclude by saying that time alone can tell what exactly is going to happen in Afghanistan and the role of the Taliban in the process.

References

Aiyub Kadir, M. Y. & Nurhaliza, S. (2023). "State Responsibility of Afghanistan Under Taliban Regime". *Jurnal Media Hukum*, 30(1), pp. 1–18. https://doi.org/10.18196/jmh.v30i1.16020

Amini, M. & Arifani, D. (2021). "The Taliban & Afghanistan: Conflict & Peace in International Law Perspective". *International Journal of Law Reconstruction*, *5*(2), p. 306. https://doi.org/10.26532/ijlr.v5i2.17704

Center for Preventive Action (2024). "Instability in Pakistan". https://www.cfr.org/global-conflict-tracker/conflict/islamist-militancy-pakistan

Cogan, M. & McLain Gill, D. (January 7, 2022). "Legitimacy and International Development in a Taliban-dominated Afghanistan". Air University (AU). https://www.airuniversity.af.edu/JIPA/Display/Article/2891270/

Felbab-Brown, V. (February 3, 2023). *Afghanistan in 2023: Taliban internal power struggles and militancy*. Brookings. https://www.brookings.edu/articles/afghanistan-in-2023-taliban-internal-power-struggles-and-militancy/

Hellyer, H. A. (2023). "Afghanistan Under the Taliban". *The RUSI Journal*, 168(6), pp. 76–83. https://doi.org/10.1080/03071847.2023.2278352

International Crisis Group (ICS) (August 12, 2022). "Afghanistan's Security Challenges under the Taliban". https://www.crisisgroup.org/asia/south-asia/afghanistan/afghanistans-security-challenges-under-taliban

Laub, Z. (July 2014). "The Taliban in Afghanistan". Council on Foreign Relations. https://www.files.ethz.ch/isn/177335/p10551.pdf

Matinuddin, K. (1999). *The Taliban Phenomenon: Afghanistan 1994–1997*. Oxford University Press.

Murtazashvili, J. B. (2022). "The Collapse of Afghanistan". *Journal of Democracy*, 33(1), pp. 40–54.

Nojumi, N. (2002). *The Rise of the Taliban in Afghanistan*. Palgrave.

Rubin, B. R. (October 20, 2022). "Afghanistan Under the Taliban: Findings on the Current Situation". Stimson Center. https://www.stimson.org/2022/afghanistan-under-the-taliban-findings-on-the-current-situation/

Sullivan, C. J. (2022). "Afghanistan in Anarchy: America's Withdrawal, Taliban Rule and Regional Implications for Central Asia". *Journal of Asian Security and International Affairs*, 9(3), 234779702211299. https://doi.org/10.1177/23477970221129908

14 Illusive Peace in Afghanistan
Ethnic Conflict and Possibilities of Peace

Ranjita Chakrabarty

Introduction

With the fall of the Afghan government and the Taliban's takeover in August 2021, the war between the United States (US)-backed Afghan National Security Forces and the Taliban insurgency effectively ended. The absence of this large-scale, organised conflict can give the impression that the country is more peaceful than it has been in decades. However, it was not so. Following the fall of democracy in Afghanistan in August 2021 when the Taliban regained control of the country after the US withdrawal, ethnic conflicts have intensified, especially between the Taliban (a largely Pashtun group) and other ethnic minorities, such as the Tajiks, Hazaras, and Uzbeks. Ethnic conflict in Afghanistan is a product of historical grievances, political marginalisation, and regional rivalries. The country's diverse ethnic groups have long competed for power, resources, and representation, leading to both civil war and periods of instability. The post-democratic era has seen ethnic tensions exacerbated due to political exclusion, sectarian violence, and the Taliban's perceived favouritism toward Pashtuns. This has been the usual way of looking at the deep ethnic divide in Afghanistan. After the prolonged period of Soviet presence and armed conflict, Afghanistan was faced with a complex challenge to develop institutions and set up political norms to regulate the public institutions and public life, in general. During the brief period of experimentation with democracy in Afghanistan, the socio-political dynamics underwent a major transformation (Sharma, 2016), and the use of the simplistic framework of domination and power exercised by the majority ethnic groups over the other minor ethnic groups leading to conflict wouldn't objectively explain the reasons behind the conflict. This concurs with the argument that the fall of the Najibullah government in 1992 with the help of Western powers also indicated the setback of political Islam and the rise of radical Islamic forces (Roy, 1995). The game that the external actors played with the ethnic groups for their own strategic interests led to the recasting of the mass mobilisation strategies and the conflicts between the ethnic groups. The political groups soon got tied to identity politics based on ethnicity (Sharma, 2016).

The paper attempts to understand the scenario post-2021, focusing on the twin questions: (a) How are ethnic issues instrumental in creating conflict in present Taliban-controlled Afghanistan? (b) Is there any possibility of peacebuilding in Afghanistan?

This chapter, in the following sections, attempts to chart out the political trajectory post- 2021 and the major ethnic groups in conflict. Further, it will try to explore the reasons behind the ethnic conflicts and the positions taken by various groups vis-à-vis the Taliban. It will further look into whether peace-building is possible in the country and the reasons behind the inferences that would emerge.

Political Trajectory of the Islamic Republic of Afghanistan

To begin, it would be apt to briefly review the formation of the Islamic Republic of Afghanistan in 2002, with the declaration of the former king, Zahir Shah, in the Loya Jirga (grand assembly) 2002 and the adoption of the new constitution in 2004. Karzai was elected president for two years in the jirga, in which the Afghan Interim Authority was also replaced with the Transitional Islamic State of Afghanistan (TISA). A constitutional loya jirga was held in December 2003, adopting the 2004 constitution, with a presidential form of government and a bicameral legislature (*BBC*, 2005). Karzai was elected in the 2004 presidential election, followed by his winning a second term in the 2009 presidential election. NATO and Afghan troops led many offensives against the Taliban in this period. By 2009, a Taliban-led shadow government began to form, complete with their own version of mediation court (Witte,

2009). Karzai, at the 2010 International Conference on Afghanistan in London, declared that he intended to reach out to the Taliban leadership to initiate peace talks. However, these steps were initially reciprocated with an intensification of bombings, assassinations, and ambushes (Trofimov, 2010).

In 2016, the government signed a peace deal with Hekmatyar's Hezb-e Islami, which was, at the time, the second- largest anti-government insurgent after the Taliban (*Al Jazeera*, 2016). As tensions between the U.S and Pakistan escalated with U.S President Donald Trump accusing the latter of supporting the Taliban, the country further experienced a series of crises. Meanwhile, President Ghani offered unconditional peace talks to the Taliban, which were rejected by the Taliban, who asked for talks with the U.S and demanded the withdrawal of U.S. forces from their country. On the occasion of Eid- ul-Fitr in 2018, a three-day ceasefire was declared, a step that was welcomed by the people who wanted it to be extended. This was, however, rejected by the Taliban who relaunched their military campaign against the government (Qazi, 2018).

After several years of back-and-forth negotiations, the US Trump administration struck a major deal with the Taliban in 2020, known as the Doha Agreement. The deal provided for a full but staggered US withdrawal from Afghanistan in exchange for a Taliban pledge not to allow Al-Qaeda, which was not a party to the agreement, to reestablish itself in the country and commit itself to talks with the Afghan government (Qazi, 2020). However, there emerged another crisis, with the Taliban demanding the release of Taliban prisoners to which the government did not agree, leading to relaunching of attacks by the Taliban. Subsequently, the government had to release all the prisoners, leading to the first Taliban-Afghan government talks in 2020. Meanwhile, the Biden government in the U.S. decided to withdraw the U.S forces. This decision had a major fallout. The elected government of Afghanistan was overthrown soon, and the Taliban assumed control. Following this, there was resistance from various regions, notable among them being the Panjshir valley-based resistance. However, it couldn't withstand for long, and soon, the Taliban were able to take control over the region.

Ethnic Groups and Conflicts in Afghanistan

Henry Bellew (1880), for the first time, talks about the races in Afghanistan wherein he divided the people into eight major groups, namely, the Pathans

(Pashtuns), Yusufzais, Afridis, Khattaks, Daticaes, Ghiljis, Tajiks, and Hazaras. The French anthropologist, Dollot (1937), used the term *groupe ethnique* for the first time for categorising the people of Afghanistan and categorised them into several ethnic units. It was Wilber (1956/1962) who, in the mid-1950s, introduced the ethnic taxonomy of the Afghan people into Anglophone literature.

Ethnic conflict in Afghanistan is rooted in its diverse population, with various ethnic groups, such as the Pashtuns, Tajiks, Hazaras, and Uzbeks, and the complex interplay between these groups has historically shaped Afghanistan's political and social landscape. However, the criteria, which have been established by anthropologists, do not match with the reality of social practices. As observed by Schetter (2003), it is interesting to note that it is erroneous to believe that the Pashtuns speak Pashto and are Sunni Muslims, since there are also Shiite Pashtuns in the Qandahar region and Pashtuns from Kabul who often do not speak a word of Pashto. A good example of the aforementioned is the former king, Zahir Shah. Moreover, it is observed, as Schetter points out, that those who were getting accultured by adopting the cultural practices of the dominant ethnic group would not disclose their real ethnic origins. As cited by Schetter, the case of former Afghan president Babrak Karmal is a pointer to this argument. Although Kamal used to highlight his Pashtun origin, many Afghans considered him to be a Tajik or a Kashmiri immigrant. Therefore, Schetter observes that it is extremely difficult to register exactly how many ethnic groups exist in Afghanistan and their size of population. Moreover, it is also a fact that different scientific approaches of researchers generated different ways of categorising ethnic groups. A German survey concluded that there are about 54 ethnic groups existing in Afghanistan (Orywal, 1986), whereas a Soviet study (Masson, 1964/65) has claimed the existence of 200 ethnic groups.

Despite the differences in most of the studies as well as in academic works, the following are listed as the major ethnic groups in Afghanistan. These are:

(i) **Pashtuns:** They are the largest ethnic group, traditionally dominant in Afghan politics and governance. The Pashtuns are primarily Sunni Muslims and have a strong tribal culture, predominantly located in the southern and eastern parts of the country. The Pashtun ethnic tribes are organised into four smaller groups of clans – Durrani, Ghilzais, Gurghust, and Karlanri. The Durrani are located in the south and southwest of Afghanistan. This group is broken into the major tribal components between the Zirak (Popalzai, Alikozai, Barkzai, and Achalzai) and the Panjpai (Nurzai, Alizai, and Ishaqzai). Additional claims of descent include the Yusefzai, Shinwari, and Mohamand, which are some of the most prominent Pashtun tribes in Peshawar. The second- largest Pashtun group is the Ghilzais, located throughout the east of Afghanistan. They are made up of tribes, including the Hotaki, Tokhi, Kharoti, Nasiri, Taraki, Suliman Khel, and Ahmadzi, among others. The Gurghust, the third group of Pashtuns, are made up of tribes of the Kakar and Musa Khel and Safi, from the Kunar region. The Karlanri are positioned along the Afghanistan-Pakistan border. This tribe is comprises the Wadak, Orakzai, Afridi, Wazir, Jaji, Tani, Khattak, Zadran, Mangal, Mahsud, and Khugiani (Barfield, 2010).

(ii) **Tajiks:** They are the second-largest group, concentrated in the northeast and parts of the capital, Kabul. The Tajiks are largely Sunni Muslims and have historically played prominent roles in trade, military, and politics. According to Schetter (2003), the term 'Tajik' meant an anti-ethnic notion. The term was used to denote, in social interactions, someone who did not belong to any other social category, for example, a Pashtun or a Hazara, and was used in a negative sense. The ethnic category, Tajiks, applied to the residual group of all Sunnite Persian-speaking villagers or urban dwellers who did not have a tribal background. It connoted those who were without genealogical knowledge and, therefore, without a shared history.

(iii) **Hazaras:** Predominantly Shia Muslims, the Hazaras are largely based in the central region of Afghanistan (Hazarajat). They have faced significant persecution and marginalisation throughout history. The Hazaras are historically backward and illiterate and, therefore, marginalised (Schetter, 2003).

(iv) **Uzbeks:** Primarily found in the northern regions, the Uzbeks are Sunni Muslims and have historically been involved in agriculture and trade.

(v) **Other Groups:** Smaller groups, like the Turkmens, Aimaqs, Balochs, and Nuristanis, also contribute to Afghanistan's ethnic diversity (The Asia Foundation, 2019).

Afghanistan's ethnic groups are, for the most part, separated into four distinct zones of the country. These zones are Herat, Kabul, Mazar-i-Sharif, and Kandahar. The mountainous terrain and topography distinctly divide the ethnic groups further (Hanley, 2011).

Afghanistan shares borders with Iran, a Shia-dominated region. However, it is the Sunnis who dominate Afghanistan despite its conquest by the Persian Shia Safavids in the 16th century. It was in the 18th century, when the Ghilzai and Durrani Pashtun tribes strived to establish empires as the Safavids gave way, that the Afghan kingdom was formed. In 1747, Ahmad Shah Durrani established the empire (Rubin, 2009). The question comes to mind as to why ethnic groups rose to political relevance in Afghanistan. To answer this question, one has to look back into history. The Afghan state was a creation of the rival colonial powers—British India and Russia—at the end of the 19th century. The ruling family of the Pashtuns were brought to power by British India. Therefore, it is natural that the ruling power in Afghanistan favoured Pashtun elements in their concept of the nation-state. As Schetter reasons, 'Afghan' is the Persian synonym for Pashtun, the Afghan national language was always Pashtu, and the history of Afghanistan was written from the Pashtun point of view. The Pashtuns were always the privileged ones in all areas and dominated the military. The economic sector and the educational institutions were dominated by the Tajiks. The Hazaras were the illiterates, poor and marginalised in general. This differential access to resources, as played by the ruling powers, led to the formation of ethnic stereotypes and created hierarchies within the Afghan polity. Ethnic stereotypes, like the Pashtuns as 'bellicose', the Tajiks as 'thrifty', the Uzbeks as 'brutal', and the Hazaras as 'illiterate' and 'poor', became permanently entrenched within the society and polity. Although this created an ethnic hierarchy, there were few ethnic conflicts. The main reason for this lack of conflict was rooted in the lack of interest of the rural people in the politics in Kabul. Therefore, the ordinary Afghans did not feel the urge to go for a collective political action to overthrow the ethnic hierarchy created by the state. Moreover, the Afghans recognised the nation-state as a hostile factor. For the ordinary rural dweller, the nation- state was an intruder in their social life and not looked at as an agent to facilitate access to resources and a good life. In fact, the contrast between urban and rural life was too prominent and glaring (Schetter, 2002).

Ethnicity became an important political-military variable within Afghan politics only in 1979 when the Afghan war broke out. Even though the war was dominated by the rivalry between communism and Islam following the ongoing Cold War, the warring parties, in order to increase their strength, ventured into ethnic politics and used it to increase their power within the conflict. Thus were created the ethnic militias (Roy, 1986). During the reign of Amir Abdur Rahman Khan (late 19th century), efforts were made to consolidate power through forced migration, repression, and marginalisation of non-Pashtun groups, particularly the Hazaras. Ethnic tensions intensified during the Soviet-Afghan War, as various ethnic groups joined different factions of the Mujahideen, the resistance movement against the Soviet forces. The Pashtuns, Tajiks, Uzbeks, and Hazaras aligned with different leaders, deepening divides. The collapse of the communist regime in the early 1990s led to civil war among various ethnic militias. The Pashtun-dominated Taliban emerged in the mid-1990s, taking control of much of the country and imposing strict religious laws, further marginalising non-Pashtun groups, especially the Shia Hazaras. The Taliban, largely Pashtun, were known for their repressive policies against non-Pashtuns, particularly the Hazaras. Massacres in Mazar-i-Sharif (1998) and Bamiyan province (2001) were part of the Taliban's ethnic and sectarian campaigns. After the fall of the Taliban in 2001, the US- backed Afghan government attempted to create an inclusive political structure. Ethnic power-sharing became a key part of the post-Taliban political order, with representation for the Pashtuns, Tajiks, Hazaras, and Uzbeks in both government and security forces. Despite these efforts, ethnic tensions persisted. Power struggles, especially in the security and political sectors, reflected deeper ethnic rivalries. Corruption, favouritism, and unequal resource distribution further exacerbated these tensions.

Despite efforts to include all ethnic groups in the political process, the Pashtuns have often been perceived as having undue influence, particularly in the Taliban's resurgence. The Taliban, largely seen as a Pashtun movement, further complicates efforts at ethnic unity. The Hazaras remain among the most marginalised ethnic groups, frequently targeted by extremist groups like the Taliban and the ISIS for their Shia faith. Sectarian violence against the Hazaras has been a persistent issue. In the north, the Tajiks and the

Uzbeks have often clashed for control of key cities and regions, particularly in the context of weakening central government control. Following the U.S. withdrawal and the Taliban's rapid takeover, ethnic groups like the Hazaras and the Tajiks expressed fears of renewed repression. The Taliban's rule has once again sparked concerns about Pashtun favouritism and marginalisation of minorities. Afghanistan's ethnic conflicts are often influenced by external powers, including Pakistan, Iran, Russia, and the U.S. These countries have historically supported different ethnic factions to advance their own strategic interests, further complicating internal dynamics.

Locating the Reasons behind the Tension

There are multiple reasons behind the ongoing ethnic conflict within Afghanistan. The most significant among them is the Pashtun dominance. The Taliban, primarily composed of Pashtuns, has been criticised for excluding other ethnic groups from meaningful participation in the government. Despite promises of forming an "inclusive" government, most key positions in the interim government have been filled by Pashtuns, sidelining Tajiks, Hazaras, and Uzbeks. This lack of representation has increased resentment, particularly among the Tajiks and the Uzbeks in the north and the Hazaras in central Afghanistan. Many non-Pashtun groups feel that their interests and security concerns are not being addressed by the Taliban. The Hazara ethnic group, primarily Shia Muslims, has faced heightened levels of violence and persecution under Taliban rule. The ISIS-K (the Islamic State's Afghanistan branch) and other extremist groups have also continued to target Hazara communities, especially in Kabul and the central region of Hazarajat. Schools, mosques, and gatherings of Hazaras have been bombed, leading to mass casualties.

The northern provinces, traditionally home to Tajiks, Uzbeks, and Turkmen, have seen increasing fragmentation and opposition to Taliban rule. These regions had long been a stronghold of anti-Taliban sentiment and were key areas of resistance during both the Soviet invasion and the Taliban's first reign in the 1990s. After the fall of the Afghan government, many regional leaders, including warlords like Abdul Rashid Dostum (Uzbek) and Atta Mohammad Noor (Tajik), fled the country, leaving a vacuum that the Taliban has struggled to fill. The Taliban vacillate between claims that they are a Pashtun nationalist force or a supra-ethnic Islamist group. They do not acknowledge any tribal or other ethnic differences and prefer to be known only as Muslims (Ruttig, 2010). The Pashtuns are one of the largest tribal societies in the world, and as in any tribal society, kinship is a significant factor. However, they prefer to point out, as opined by Ruttig (2010), that it is no longer the priority as it was in the past. The Taliban movement, as it stands today, is a 'complex consolidation of religious, tribal, and regional influence' (Ruttig, 2010). The destruction of the Afghan state over the past years has affected Pashtun tribal society to a large extent. Societal and political dynamics are questioned by younger generations (Sharma, 2016). The influence of Jirgas, which remained the most significant institution for the Pashtuns in the earlier days to resolve conflicts, over the Taliban has waned. Within the Taliban itself, there have been reported internal tensions between Pashtun and non-Pashtun Taliban fighters. These tensions arise from differing regional loyalties, tribal affiliations, and power struggles over control of territory and resources. The Taliban's centralisation of power has led to complaints about unequal distribution of resources. Non-Pashtun regions, particularly in the north and central highlands, have accused the Taliban of neglecting their economic development and infrastructure needs, worsening the disparities that existed even during the democratic era.

Resistance movements have emerged in the northern provinces, where ethnic Tajiks and Uzbeks have historically held power. Armed groups linked to these communities, including remnants of the Afghan National Army and local militias, have, at times, clashed with Taliban forces. Leaders like Ahmad Massoud, head of the National Resistance Front (NRF), based in the Panjshir Valley, have challenged the Taliban, though resistance has been largely limited due to the Taliban's military strength. In the northern provinces, some Uzbek militias have remained active, though their ability to mount significant resistance has been constrained by the Taliban's consolidation of power.

The Hazaras, who have long been persecuted for their Shia identity, have been displaced from their homes in regions like Daikundi, Bamiyan, and parts of Ghazni. There have been reports of land seizures, forced evictions, and property confiscation by the Taliban, especially in Hazara-majority areas, further fuelling ethnic grievances. The ISIS-K terrorist group, which views Shia Muslims as heretics, has escalated its attacks on the Hazaras. This sectarian violence, including bombings of Hazara mosques and schools, has heightened fears of ethnic cleansing.

Iran, which shares religious ties with the Hazara community, has expressed concern over the targeting of Hazaras by both the Taliban and ISIS-K. Tehran has attempted to provide diplomatic and humanitarian support to the Hazara population, while also engaging cautiously with the Taliban. Ethnic conflicts within Afghanistan have regional implications, with neighbouring countries like Pakistan, Iran, and Uzbekistan having vested interests in the stability of different ethnic regions and groups. Pakistan, in particular, has been accused of supporting the predominantly Pashtun Taliban, further complicating the ethnic balance within Afghanistan.

All four warring factions, which dominated the military and political actions in the last decade, were more or less supported by members of one of the four major ethnic groups. The political movements used ethnicity as the main argument for the legitimacy of their political existence, because all other ideologies—Islamic as well as communistic or royalist—lost ground as a basis for the mobilisation of the masses and as instruments of political demands. The leaders of the warring factions made their supporters aware of their social and economic deprivation on the basis of their ethnic belonging in the past and present. They claimed that the survival of their 'own ethnic group' was endangered through the aggressive behaviour of 'other ethnic groups'. Nevertheless, by means of the ethnic factor, the warring factions stirred up collective anxiety as well as hate and jealousy.

With the absence of a democratic system and the re-emergence of Taliban rule, the possibility of creating a unified Afghan national identity seems increasingly difficult. Ethnic rivalries, sectarian violence, and regionalism have deepened divisions in the country. Efforts to establish an inclusive government have failed, with minority groups feeling increasingly alienated. This lack of political inclusivity risks prolonging ethnic strife and violence. The fall of democracy in Afghanistan has reignited deep-seated ethnic conflicts, with the Taliban's Pashtun-centric governance exacerbating tensions between different ethnic and sectarian groups. While the Taliban seeks to establish control over the entire country, resistance movements, particularly in the north and among the Hazaras, continue to pose challenges. The marginalisation of non-Pashtun groups and the targeting of minorities, like the Hazaras, by extremist groups raise serious concerns about the future of ethnic and sectarian relations in Afghanistan. Without efforts toward genuine power-sharing and ethnic inclusivity, the country risks further fragmentation and violence.

Peacebuilding in Afghanistan: Possibilities and Challenges

Peacebuilding in Afghanistan has been a challenging and multifaceted process, especially given the decades of conflict, political instability, ethnic diversity, and external influence. After the fall of the Taliban in 2001, various international, regional, and national efforts focused on peacebuilding, but the return of the Taliban to power in 2021 has significantly altered the dynamics of these efforts. Despite these difficulties, several peacebuilding mechanisms have been proposed or implemented over the years, aimed at fostering reconciliation, stability, and sustainable peace in Afghanistan.

One of the primary mechanisms for peacebuilding is fostering inclusive political dialogue among all ethnic, sectarian, and political groups in Afghanistan. Without meaningful participation from groups like the Tajiks, Hazaras, Uzbeks, and other minorities, the peace process risks deepening ethnic divisions. The traditional Afghan method of resolving national issues through a Loya Jirga, a grand assembly of tribal elders and community leaders, has often been used to build national consensus. The Loya Jirga is a culturally rooted conflict resolution mechanism that has been applied during various periods of Afghan history, including the Bonn Agreement after the fall of the Taliban in 2001. Given the multi-ethnic nature of Afghanistan, peacebuilding requires both inter-ethnic (between Pashtuns, Tajiks, Hazaras, Uzbeks, etc.) and intra-ethnic (within each ethnic group) dialogue. Fostering trust among these groups through dialogue and cooperation is crucial for long-term peace.

A key element of peacebuilding is ensuring that the government structure reflects the country's diverse ethnic makeup. Historically, efforts have been made to include all major ethnic groups in power-sharing arrangements, whether in government ministries or the military. These arrangements are vital to address grievances related to political exclusion and marginalisation. Decentralising political power to allow greater autonomy for provinces and local governments could help address the centralisation issues that have historically fuelled conflict in Afghanistan. This would allow ethnic groups to have more control over local affairs, reducing the sense of exclusion from national governance. Peacebuilding has often involved negotiations with non-state armed groups. The Doha Agreement (2020) between the U.S. and the Taliban was an attempt to incorporate the Taliban into the political process, although its ultimate implementation was controversial. Continued dialogue between the Taliban and other political factions, especially those from non-Pashtun backgrounds, is essential for lasting peace.

A key peacebuilding mechanism is the Disarmament, Demobilization, and Reintegration (DDR) process, which aims to disarm combatants, disband militias, and reintegrate former fighters into civilian life. After the fall of the Taliban in 2001, several DDR initiatives were launched, but their effectiveness was often limited by local power dynamics and the ongoing insurgency. Post-2001, international efforts focused on building a national security force that included members from all ethnic groups. The idea was to create a professional, multi-ethnic military and police force that could provide security across the country. However, ethnic favouritism, corruption, and factionalism within the military and police undermined these efforts. Strengthening local policing through community-based approaches can help build trust between citizens and the state, especially in rural areas. Locally trained police forces, with the involvement of tribal elders and community leaders, can play a role in maintaining peace and security at the local level.

Addressing war crimes and human rights abuses committed during decades of conflict is essential for long-term peace. Transitional justice mechanisms, such as truth commissions, reparations, and trials for war criminals, have been proposed but rarely implemented effectively in Afghanistan. Building a fair and effective justice system is critical for peacebuilding. Corruption, impunity, and the lack of judicial infrastructure have undermined faith in Afghanistan's legal system. Ensuring justice for ordinary citizens, as well as for ethnic and religious minorities, is crucial to prevent future conflicts.

Afghan civil society organisations, including women's groups, youth organisations, and local NGOs, have played a significant role in advocating for peace, reconciliation, and human rights. These groups often work in areas that the government cannot reach and can mediate local disputes, promote dialogue, and provide services to marginalised communities. Women have been particularly active in peacebuilding efforts in Afghanistan. Although their inclusion in official peace negotiations has often been limited, women's groups have been at the forefront of advocating for peace, education, and community development. Women's participation is seen as critical for sustainable peace, particularly in challenging traditional power structures that exclude women from decision-making. Locally established peace committees, often led by tribal elders and community leaders, have been a traditional mechanism for resolving conflicts at the village or district level. These grassroots mechanisms can help resolve disputes over land, water, and other resources, which often fuel local conflicts in Afghanistan.

Economic development and the fair distribution of resources are key to addressing the underlying grievances that fuel conflict. Job creation, infrastructure development, and access to education and healthcare are vital for reducing poverty and inequality, which are often drivers of violence. Since the majority of Afghanistan's population lives in rural areas, rural development programmes that improve agriculture, irrigation, and infrastructure can help build peace by addressing economic hardships that contribute to conflict.

Afghanistan's peace and stability are heavily influenced by its neighbours, including Pakistan, Iran, India, China, and Russia. Regional cooperation is essential for peacebuilding, as neighbouring countries have often supported different factions within Afghanistan for their own strategic purposes. Regional dialogue, confidence-building measures, and economic cooperation could help reduce external interference and promote stability. The UN and other international organisations have played a vital role in peacebuilding, providing diplomatic, humanitarian, and technical support. The UN Assistance Mission in Afghanistan (UNAMA) has been involved in monitoring human rights, supporting electoral processes, and facilitating dialogue among conflicting parties. After the fall of the Taliban in 2001, international donors played a key role in Afghanistan's reconstruction. However, corruption, inefficiency, and lack of coordination often reduced the impact of this aid. Going forward, international assistance focused on local needs and involving local communities in decision-making can support peacebuilding.

Peacebuilding Concerns and Illusory Peace in Afghanistan

Peacebuilding in Afghanistan requires a multi-layered approach that addresses both the immediate security concerns and the deeper structural issues that have fuelled decades of conflict. Efforts to create inclusive political dialogue, reform the security sector, ensure justice and accountability, empower civil society, promote economic development, and engage with regional and international actors are all essential for long-term peace. But the question today is whether peacebuilding is at all possible in Afghanistan with the return of the Taliban in 2021. It is often pointed out that there has been a shift in the way the Taliban dealt with affairs in 2001 and now, post- 2021. But the problem is one of degree, to understand whether it is a superficial shift or a radical shift in their position.

While the Taliban may control most of the country, they face growing opposition, particularly from the National Resistance Front (NRF) and groups like the ISIS-K (Islamic State Khorasan Province). The NRF operates in pockets, especially in Panjshir Valley, while the ISIS-K has carried out deadly terrorist attacks, particularly targeting Shia Hazaras, Sufi shrines, and even Taliban forces. This violence, while not as widespread as during the US occupation, undermines the notion of genuine peace.

The Taliban are predominantly Pashtun, and their return to power has led to fears of ethnic marginalisation among other groups, such as the Tajiks, Hazaras, Uzbeks, and Turkmen. While the Taliban claim to represent all Afghans, there are clear signs of ethnic favouritism and marginalisation of non-Pashtun communities, which fuels resentment and potential for future conflict.

Afghanistan's Shia Hazara minority has long been a target of discrimination and violence, both under the previous Taliban rule in the 1990s and today. They continue to suffer attacks by the ISIS-K, which sees them as heretics, and face restrictions from the Taliban, who have not offered sufficient protection. This creates a dangerous sectarian divide that threatens to escalate into more targeted violence.

One of the most glaring issues under the Taliban regime is the severe rollback of women's rights. Women and girls have been banned from secondary education, many workplaces, and public life. The Taliban's strict interpretation of Sharia law has effectively excluded women from participating in the economy and society, leading to both domestic and international outrage. While the Taliban frame these actions as part of their governance, they contribute to a sense of underlying social unrest and inequality.

Journalists, civil society members, and activists face intimidation, harassment, and detention under Taliban rule. Independent media have been severely restricted, with many journalists fleeing the country. This suppression of dissent creates a surface calm, as opposition is silenced, but it also builds up frustration and anger within the population.

Since the Taliban took over, Afghanistan's economy has been in freefall. The cessation of international aid, which previously accounted for around 75 per cent of government spending, has led to a liquidity crisis, loss of jobs, and economic collapse. The Taliban have been unable to replace this lost aid or implement effective governance structures to stabilise the economy.

Afghanistan faces one of the world's worst humanitarian crises today, with millions of people suffering from extreme poverty, hunger, and malnutrition. According to international aid organisations, nearly 23 million Afghans face acute food insecurity, and the situation is exacerbated by droughts, internal displacement, and the inability of the Taliban to engage with international financial institutions. This humanitarian catastrophe undercuts any notion of peace or stability, as desperation leads to social discontent and potential unrest.

The Taliban have promised to crack down on opium production, but Afghanistan remains the world's largest producer of opium, which is central to the livelihoods of many farmers in rural areas. Any attempt to curb the opium trade without providing alternative economic opportunities could lead to increased poverty and rebellion.

The Taliban government has not been officially recognised by any major international power. This lack of recognition severely limits Afghanistan's access to international funding, diplomatic engagement, and economic partnerships. It also makes it difficult for the Taliban to build legitimacy, both domestically and internationally. Afghanistan's assets, worth billions of dollars, remain frozen in foreign banks, and international sanctions continue to isolate the Taliban. This economic strangulation contributes to the country's ongoing economic crisis and hampers efforts at rebuilding, even as the absence of international aid and engagement leads to greater suffering among the population. While some regional powers (such as Pakistan, China, Russia, and Iran) have engaged with the Taliban to some extent, this has been limited to strategic interests rather than full diplomatic support. This fragmented approach leaves Afghanistan in a precarious position on the global stage, with limited avenues for international cooperation or development assistance.

The Taliban are not a monolithic entity; they are composed of various factions with differing views on governance, particularly regarding how to engage with the international community and how to handle domestic issues, like women's rights and education. Some factions are more hardline, while others advocate for pragmatic engagement with the world. These internal divisions create instability within the ruling structure and may lead to future conflict or fragmentation of Taliban control. While the Taliban seek to consolidate power, their conflict with the ISIS-K continues. The ISIS-K views the Taliban as too moderate in their version of Islamic governance, and the group has carried out attacks against Taliban fighters, government offices, and civilians. The rivalry between these Islamist factions could evolve into larger-scale violence, threatening the Taliban's hold on power and further destabilising the country. The current state of Afghanistan lacks a broad-based political settlement. The Taliban came to power through military means, not through negotiations that involved the diverse political, ethnic, and social groups in the country. This has created a lack of legitimacy for the Taliban's rule in the eyes of many Afghans, particularly among minority groups and former political elites, and also a backsliding of ethnic conflicts. Therefore, even if there is calm, it is not peace but an illusory peace. The notion of "illusory peace" in Afghanistan today refers to the perception that while there may be an absence of large-scale conventional conflict following the Taliban's return to power in 2021, the underlying issues that have long fuelled instability remain unresolved. This creates a fragile and deceptive calm, where the appearance of peace hides deeper tensions, violence, and structural weaknesses.

The exclusion of political opposition and the reliance on force to maintain order creates a superficial peace. While there may be no immediate large-scale uprising, the lack of inclusive governance and political dialogue means that long-term stability remains elusive. Potential future negotiations involving broader Afghan society may be required to build a more sustainable peace.

Concluding Observations

The Taliban's governance model, based on their interpretation of Sharia law, contrasts with the aspirations of many Afghans, especially urban populations who experienced more liberal policies under the previous US-backed government. The disconnect between the Taliban's ideology and the diverse needs of Afghanistan's population creates conditions for social unrest, as large segments of the population feel disenfranchised. The Taliban's ability to build credible institutions that can govern effectively remains in doubt. Afghanistan has long struggled with weak institutions, corruption, and a lack of infrastructure. The Taliban's focus on religious governance, rather than institution-building, may leave the state ill-prepared to handle the complex challenges of modern governance, further weakening their control over the country.

While Afghanistan may not be engulfed in the large-scale warfare seen during the US occupation or the civil wars of the 1990s, the current situation represents a fragile, illusory peace. The Taliban's control has not brought about true reconciliation or addressed the root causes of conflict, including ethnic divisions, economic collapse, and political exclusion. Moreover, insurgent groups like the ISIS-K, internal Taliban divisions, and widespread human rights abuses continue to threaten Afghanistan's stability. This "peace" is more of a pause in overt conflict rather than the achievement of a lasting, just, and inclusive settlement. The humanitarian crisis, suppression of dissent, and lack of international legitimacy further undermine the prospects for long-term stability, making the current calm precarious and unsustainable. As long as these underlying issues persist, the illusion of peace may be shattered by renewed violence and instability in the future. Any future peace and stability in Afghanistan will likely depend on efforts to balance power among its various ethnic groups, respect minority rights, and create an inclusive political system.

References

Al Jazeera (September 22, 2016). "Afghanistan: Hezb-i-Islami armed group signs peace deal". https://www.aljazeera.com/news/2016/9/22/afghanistan-hezb-i-islami-armed-group-signs-peace-deal

Barfield, T. (2010). *Afghanistan: A Cultural and Political History*. Princeton University Press.

BBC (December 19, 2005). "Afghan MPs hold landmark session". http://news.bbc.co.uk/2/hi/south_asia/4540756.stm

Bellew, H. (1880). *The Races of Afghanistan: Being a Brief Account of the Principal Nations Inhabiting that Country*. Thacker, Spink, and Company.

Dollot, R. (1937). *L'Afghanistan Histoire, Description, Moeurs Et Coutumes, Folklore, Fouilles*. Payot.

Hanley, R. (2011). "Ethnic Violence, Impact on Afghanistan". U.S. Army War College.

Masson, V. M. (1965). *Istorija Afganistana-2 Volumes*. Nauka.

Orywal, E. (1986). *Die ethnischen Gruppen Afghanistans: Fallstudien zu Gruppenidentität und Intergruppenbeziehungen*. Reichert.

Qazi, S. (June 18, 2018). "Afghanistan: Taliban resume fighting as Eid ceasefire ends". *Al Jazeera*. https://www.aljazeera.com/news/2018/6/18/afghanistan-taliban-resume-fighting-as-eid-ceasefire-ends

Qazi, S. (February 29, 2020). "Afghanistan's Taliban, US sign agreement aimed at ending war". *Al Jazeera*. https://www.aljazeera.com/news/2020/2/29/afghanistans-taliban-us-sign-agreement-aimed-at-ending-war

Roy, O. (1986). *Islam and Resistance in Afghanistan*. Cambridge University Press.

Roy, O. (1995). *Afghanistan: From Holy War to Civil War*. Darwin Press.

Rubin, B. (2009). "The Transformation of the Afghan State". In J. A. Thier (Ed.), *The Future of Afghanistan*. United States Institute of Peace.

Ruttig, T. (June 4, 2010). "How Tribal Are the Taliban?" Afghanistan Analysts Network. https://www.afghanistan-analysts.org/wp-content/uploads/downloads/2012/10/20100624TR-HowTribalAretheTaleban-FINAL.pdf

Schetter, C. (2002). "Der Afghanistankrieg - Die Ethnisierung eines Konflikts". *Internationales Asienforum*, 33(1), pp. 15–29.

Schetter, C. (2003). "Ethnicity and the Political Reconstruction in Afghanistan". London School of Economics. https://eprints.lse.ac.uk/28376/1/Schetter_LSERO_version.pdf

Sharma, R. (2016). *Nation, Ethnicity and the Conflict in Afghanistan Political Islam and the rise of ethno-politics 1992–1996*. Routledge.

The Asia Foundation (2019). "Survey of the Afghan People (2004-2019)". https://dataverse.ada.edu.au/dataset.xhtml?persistentId=doi:10.26193/VDDO0X

Trofimov, Y. (September 10, 2010). "Karzai Divides Afghanistan in Reaching Out to Taliban". *Wall Street Journal*. https://www.wsj.com/articles/SB10001424052748703720004575476913015061 57

Witte, G. (December 8, 2009). "Taliban establishes elaborate shadow government in Afghanistan". *Washington Post*. https://www.washingtonpost.com/wp-dyn/content/article/2009/12/07/AR2009120704127.html

Contributors

Saman Ayesha Kidwai is Research Analyst (Counter Terrorism) at Manohar Parrikar Institute for Defence Studies and Analyses. She holds a master's degree in Conflict Analysis and Peacebuilding from the Nelson Mandela Centre for Conflict and Peace Resolution, Jamia Millia Islamia. Her areas of interest include political violence, counter-terrorism and geopolitics, primarily within South Asia, West Asia, and the Horn of Africa.

Shirish Waghmare is a performance-driven professional with 9 years of experience in research, academics, and project implementation in sustainability, gender, sexual and reproductive health rights, education, and the healthcare ecosystem. Currently a research associate at Dr. Vishwanath Karad MIT World Peace University, Pune, he teaches Master of Social Work and MBA students while coordinating research activities and rural immersion programmes. Previously, Shirish served as Assistant General Manager – Operations at Sevasadan Life Line Superspeciality Hospital, where he optimised operations and improved patient satisfaction. As Project Manager at SAMYAK, he led advocacy initiatives for safe abortion access in Maharashtra and Rajasthan. Shirish holds a Master's degree in Social Work (MSW) in Rural Community Development and an MBA in Healthcare Administration and Hospital Management, alongside various diplomas in journalism, human rights, labour laws, and women's studies. He is currently pursuing a Ph.D. in interdisciplinary studies, underscoring his commitment to continuous learning and excellence in both academic and healthcare sectors.

Vaasu Sharma serves as a foreign policy analyst in India, presently engaged in his doctoral studies at the University of Haifa (Israel) within the International Relations Department. He was formerly employed as Research Consultant at WION International (Zee Media Network) in New Delhi. Vaasu holds a Master's degree in International Relations, specialising in Diplomacy Studies, from the University of Haifa. He exhibits a profound understanding of Middle Eastern affairs and has made significant contributions to chapters concerning Indian foreign policy and India-Israel relations in various scholarly publications. Furthermore, he was affiliated with the BRICS International Youth Forum in India during the period from 2016 to 2017.

Rushita Shetty is an independent researcher based in India. She completed her MA in Geopolitics and International Relations from Manipal Academy of Higher Education (MAHE), India. Her area of research interest covers identity, gender, and minority issues, focusing on Afghanistan and the Middle East.

Dr Kshipra Vasudeo is Assistant Professor of Political Science at the Centre for Distance and Online Education (CDOE) at the University of Mumbai. She is also a Visiting Faculty at Rajiv Gandhi Centre for Contemporary Studies, teaching Ph.D. research scholars for their coursework. The focus of her academic and research career has been on Africa's evolving geopolitical dynamics, security architecture, and the role of major powers, like India and China, in the region. Her M.Phil. dissertation, "South Africa in BRICS: Issues and Challenges", explored South Africa's role within the BRICS bloc, providing insights into the internal dynamics and economic challenges faced by the nation. Her Ph.D. thesis, "India-China Competition in the Indian Ocean: Implications for Coastal Countries of Africa (2000-2019)", examined the strategic competition between India and China, offering policy recommendations for African coastal states. She was awarded ICSSR Full-Time Doctoral Fellowship for her Ph.D. research work from the Indian Council for Social Sciences Research (ICSSR), Government of India.

Aditi Bhaduri is a journalist and political analyst, specialising in West Asian and Eurasian geopolitics. She has contributed to many books on geopolitics and is a columnist with a number of publications. She is the founder-editor of International Affairs Review, a bilingual portal on Eurasian geopolitics. Fluent in Russian, she has translated numerous archival and literary works from Russian to English. She was the 2011 recipient of the Sarojini Naidu Prize awarded by The Hunger Project.

Ziba Akbari is a Ph.D. candidate in Political Science at Deakin University and a research assistant at the Alfred Deakin Institute. Her research focuses on the Kurdish issue, ethno-political minorities in the Middle East, and human security in fragile states. She has published three papers and has contributed to several conferences, including the MESF Conference 2024, The Middle East After the War on Gaza, and the Australian Political Studies Association's (APSA) Annual Conference.

Dr Sanchita Bhattacharya is a research fellow in New Delhi- based Institute for Conflict Management. She has co-authored the book, *The Taliban Misrule in Afghanistan: Suicide Brigades, the IS-K Military Strength and its Suicide Vehicle Industry*, along with Musa Khan Jalalzai. She works on terrorism and socio-political issues of Pakistan. She also has an avid interest in the Af-Pak region. Her articles and commentaries have been published in *East Asia Forum, Australian Outlook, The Kabul Times, The Friday Times, The Quint*, etc. She has written research papers in national and international journals and has also contributed chapters in various edited volumes.

Puspa Kumari is an esteemed Pashto language expert and researcher specialising in South Asia, with a particular focus on Afghanistan and its neighbourhood. She earned her bachelor's degree in Pashto Language, Literature, and Culture Studies from Jawaharlal Nehru University in New Delhi, where she later completed dual master's degrees in Pashto Language and Linguistics. Puspa's research interests encompass Indo-Afghan relations, international relations, and the internal politics and developments of Afghanistan and its neighbourhood. She has contributed significantly to the field through numerous published articles that explore the complexities of Afghanistan's socio-political landscape.

Kondaraju Sandeep Royal is a research scholar pursuing an MBA from IGNOU. He holds a master's degree in Politics and International Relations from Pondicherry University and a bachelor's in History, Economics and Political Science from CHRIST (Deemed to be University). His research spans International Relations, Geo-security, Cooperation and Inter-Civilisational dynamics, with a particular focus on Sino-Indian foreign policies, the Indo-Pacific region, and the broader Global South. He explores neighbourhood affairs, security dilemmas, and (De)Securitization frameworks, offering nuanced insights into geopolitics and diplomacy. He has gained research experience at institutions like the Foreign Policy Research Centre, The Viyug, Chennai Centre for China Studies, and the Nepal Institute for International Cooperation and Engagement. His work bridges scholarly research with real-world applications, aiming to make complex geopolitical issues more accessible and foster informed public discourse on critical global challenges.

Dr Manas Chakrabarty is currently Senior Fellow at ICSSR, attached to the Department of Political Science, University of North Bengal, Darjeeling, in West Bengal. He was also Emeritus Professor of the UGC. Dr Chakrabarty, with his 33 years of post- graduate teaching experience, has carried out extensive research, and he has to his credit 236 research articles in leading professional national and international journals, 5 books and 27 chapters in different books. He has delivered more than 200 keynote addresses in different national and international seminars and chaired about 150 national and international seminar sessions. He has also delivered a huge number of lectures at the Academic Staff Colleges of the UGC across the country. So far, 27 scholars have been awarded Ph.D. degrees under his supervision, and he has also supervised several M.Phil. dissertations. He is the recipient of the Indian Political Science Association National Award (Life Time Achievement), 2017.

Dr Ranjita Chakrabarty is a Professor at the Department of Political Science, University of North Bengal, Darjeeling, West Bengal. She specialises in gender and politics, environment and politics and development studies. She has worked on projects on trafficking of women, Human Development Report of Dakshin Dinajpur District, West Bengal, and as advisor to projects on coastal security and community policing. She has edited a book on Gendered Insecurities in South Asia and contributed articles to various journals and edited books. Her recent articles in edited books on Sardar Patel (accepted and to be published by Routledge, UK) are in the process. She is also the associate editor of *Journal of Asian Security and International Affairs*, a Scopus Indexed Sage journal. She has recently joined as the Associate Editor of the Sage journal, *South Asian Survey*. She is also actively engaged with various civil society organisations within the region and is a member of research bodies of different universities. She has also organised multiple seminars, both national and international, within the university. Presently, she additionally holds the administrative post of Director, Internal Quality Assurance Cell of the University, and the Presiding Officer of the Internal Complaints Committee of the University.

Index